Helen Keller

History Maker Bios

Jane Sutcliffe

ﾠLERNER PUBLICATIONS COMPANY • MINNEAPOLIS

For Eileen

Illustrations by Tad Butler

Text copyright © 2009 by Jane Sutcliffe
Illustrations copyright © 2009 by Lerner Publishing Group, Inc.

Lerner Publications Company
A division of Lerner Publishing Group, Inc.
241 First Avenue North
Minneapolis, MN 55401 U.S.A.

Website address: www.lernerbooks.com

Library of Congress Cataloging-in-Publication Data

Sutcliffe, Jane.
    Helen Keller / by Jane Sutcliffe.
        p.   cm. — (History maker biographies)
    Includes bibliographical references and index.
    ISBN 978–0–7613–4223–6 (lib. bdg. : alk. paper)
    1. Keller, Helen, 1880–1968—Juvenile literature. 2. Deaf-blind women—United States—Biography—Juvenile literature. I. Title.
    HV1624.K4S87 2009
    362.4'1092—dc22 [B]   2008048905

Manufactured in the United States of America
1 2 3 4 5 6 – PA – 14 13 12 11 10 09

Table of Contents

INTRODUCTION

Helen Keller could do almost anything. She was a brilliant thinker. She understood several languages. She wrote books and gave speeches all over the world.

There were only two things that Helen could not do. She couldn't see. And she couldn't hear. She never let that stop her. She did what she set out to do just the same.

People were amazed when they saw all that Helen could do, despite all she could not. She showed the world that anyone can have big dreams.

This is her story.

1 THE NO-WORLD

Helen Keller discovered words early. She was born on June 27, 1880, in Tuscumbia, a little town in Alabama. Helen was a bright, beautiful child. When she was only six months old, she began to talk. She delighted her parents by saying "tea, tea, tea." She said "wah-wah" for "water."

Helen's father
(LEFT) and mother
(RIGHT)

Then, when Helen was not yet two, she became very sick. For days, she had a fever. The family doctor told Kate and Arthur Keller that their little girl might die.

One morning, though, the fever suddenly left. At first, the Kellers were overjoyed. Then they realized that something was wrong. When Kate waved her hand before Helen's eyes, she didn't blink. When she rang a dinner bell, Helen didn't seem to hear it.

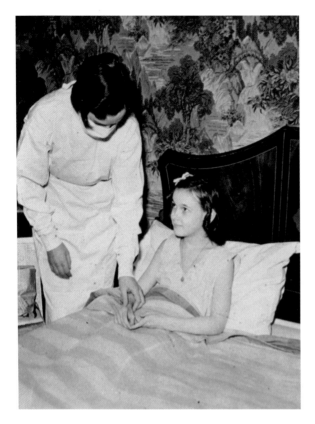

The illness had left Helen blind and deaf. She could no longer see her mother's face or hear her father's voice. Suddenly, she lived in a lonely world of darkness and silence. Later, she called it her "no-world."

Helen could no longer hear words, so she could not learn words. She forgot the few words she had learned as a baby. She remembered only "wah-wah" for "water."

For everything else, she made motions. When she wanted bread, she made the motion of slicing and buttering bread. For her father, she pretended to put on glasses. For her baby sister, she sucked her thumb.

Still, Helen's motions weren't enough. There was so much more that she wanted to say! But without words, she couldn't always make herself understood. Often she exploded in anger. She kicked and screamed and cried until she was worn out. Sometimes her tantrums went on all day.

Deaf children are taught sign language so they can speak through motions. Young Helen used her own signs.

Her parents didn't have the heart to punish her. Instead, Helen was allowed to do pretty much as she pleased. At meals, she grabbed food from other people's plates. She threw dishes and lamps. Once she locked her mother in the pantry. Another time, she pinched her grandmother.

Helen was becoming wild. Her parents knew they had to find a way to help her. They took her to one doctor after another. The answer was always the same. No one could help Helen see or hear again.

Doctors treated many patients with ear and eye problems in the late 1800s. But they could not help Helen.

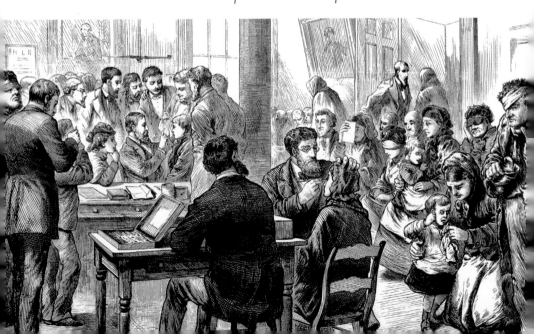

When Helen was six, her parents took her to a doctor in Baltimore, Maryland. The man agreed that Helen could not be cured. But he had an idea. She could be taught, he said. He gave them the name of a man in Washington, D.C., who might help.

The man's name was Dr. Alexander Graham Bell. Dr. Bell was famous for inventing the telephone. But he was also a well-known teacher of deaf people. The Kellers went to Washington at once.

Alexander Graham Bell helped deaf children learn to speak. Helen's parents hoped he could help her too.

Right away, Helen loved Dr. Bell. He seemed to understand all her signs. She sat on his lap and played with his watch.

Dr. Bell's words gave the Kellers hope at last. He told them to write to the Perkins Institution for the Blind in Boston, Massachusetts. That's where they would find someone to teach Helen, he said.

Mr. Keller wrote immediately. Before long, an answer came back. The school would send a teacher. Her name was Annie Sullivan. She would help Helen find a way out of her no-world.

"I AM GLAD TO WRITE YOU A LETTER"

Helen did not forget Dr. Bell's kindness. When she learned to write, she wrote many letters to her new friend. The first one began, "I am glad to write you a letter." And Dr. Bell was pleased to write to Helen. Their letters continued back and forth for thirty-five years, until Dr. Bell's death in 1922.

2 TEACHER

March 3, 1887, would turn out to be the most important day in Helen's life. But six-year-old Helen didn't know that. She knew only that something special was happening in the Keller house.

Annie Sullivan had been a student at the Perkins Institution for the Blind. She was only twenty when she came to teach Helen.

She could feel people hurrying here and there. She stood on the porch steps and waited. Suddenly, she felt footsteps approaching. Her teacher, Annie Sullivan, had arrived.

Helen wasn't so sure she wanted Annie there. She was used to having her own way. She fought Annie. Once she struck Annie and knocked out a tooth.

But Annie was just as tough as Helen. When Helen tried to snatch food from Annie's plate, Annie stopped her. When Helen threw her spoon to the floor, Annie took Helen's hand and made her pick it up. Slowly, Helen began to obey her new teacher.

While Annie taught Helen about manners, she was also teaching her about words. She used a special finger alphabet for deaf people. Her fingers formed a different shape for each letter. Helen felt each letter shape with her hand. Annie gave Helen a doll and spelled *D-O-L-L* with her fingers. She gave her some cake and spelled *C-A-K-E*.

DOLL *was the first word Helen learned to spell.*

Helen around the age of seven

For weeks, Annie spelled words for Helen. Helen was quick to imitate Annie's finger movements. But she didn't know she was spelling words. To her, it was all a game. She even tried to teach Belle, her dog, to spell with her paw. Belle wasn't interested.

Then one day, Annie took Helen outside. She started pumping water from the well. Helen felt Annie place her hand under the spout. She felt cool water pouring over one hand. In the other hand, she felt Annie's fingers spell *W-A-T-E-R*—slowly, at first, then faster and faster.

The water pump outside Helen's childhood home

Suddenly Helen understood. *W-A-T-E-R* was the cool, wet something spilling into her hand. It had a name!

Everything had a name! Helen was in a hurry to know them all. Annie's fingers spelled word after word for Helen. Then Helen pointed to Annie. *T-E-A-C-H-E-R*, Annie spelled. From then on, that was Helen's name for Annie.

Teacher called Helen "all fingers and curiosity."

After that, Teacher "talked" into Helen's hand nearly all the time. She described everything she saw and heard. Helen didn't understand all the words at first. But she learned quickly. Each new word made her happy. Her wild behavior stopped.

Best of all, words gave her a way to learn about the world. Teacher made maps of clay and told her about great mountains and rivers. She gave her a fossil to feel and told her about dinosaurs. She took her for walks in the woods and taught her about nature.

Soon Helen learned to read. Her fingers felt raised letters. Later, she read special books with patterns of raised dots. That kind of writing is called Braille. Her fingers flew as she read.

She learned to write too. She loved to write cheery letters to her friends and family. She signed them, "From your little friend, Helen A. Keller." (The *A* was for "Adams.") Everyone who read her letters was astonished. Helen had learned so much so fast! The director of the Perkins Institution for the Blind was amazed. He wrote an article about Helen.

Suddenly, little Helen was big news. Reporters began to write about her. Word spread quickly. Soon, people all over the world were talking about her.

Helen used a special board with grooves to write. This kind of writing is called squarehand.

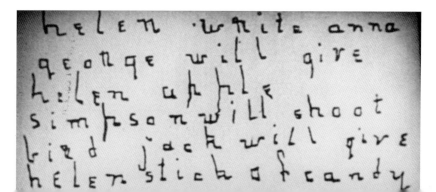

Ten-year-old Helen (LEFT) and Teacher use the finger alphabet to talk.

In May 1888, Helen took a trip. Annie and Mrs. Keller went too. They visited Dr. Bell in Washington, D.C. They met President Grover Cleveland at the White House.

Then they went to Boston to the Perkins Institution. Helen made friends with the students there. She was delighted to find that deaf and blind children there knew the finger alphabet too. At last, she could talk to other children in her own language.

Helen stayed at the school that spring and fall. While she was there, she started learning French. She learned some Latin and some Greek words too. Soon, she was using the foreign words in her letters. She made almost no mistakes.

Still Helen pleaded to be taught more. "I do want to learn much about everything," she wrote. But that wasn't quite true. Helen wanted to learn *everything* about everything.

WELCOME TO THE CIRCUS, HELEN!

One day, the circus came to town. Helen couldn't see the circus, so she was allowed to feel it instead. She rode an elephant and petted the lion cubs. When a monkey did tricks for the audience, she was allowed to keep her hand on him to "watch."

3 CLASS OF 1904

Helen's hands were always in motion. She used her hands even when she was talking to herself. When Helen was nine, she made a big decision. She wanted to speak with her mouth instead of her hands. She began taking lessons to learn to talk like other people.

It wasn't an easy job. Helen couldn't hear what words were supposed to sound like. She couldn't hear the sounds she made either. She never knew if she was getting the words right. Mostly, she got them wrong.

She did learn to read lips with her fingers. She placed her hand lightly over a speaker's mouth and throat. Then she "listened" to what the person said. But she still had to spell her reply with her fingers.

Helen uses her hand to "hear" what Teacher is saying.

Then Helen and Teacher met two men who were opening a school for deaf children in New York City. The two men felt certain they could help Helen speak clearly. Perhaps she could even learn to sing!

For Helen, this sounded like a dream come true. In October 1894, she became a student at the school. Teacher went with her.

Helen liked New York. She liked her studies too, especially her classes in German. The only subject she didn't like was math. She had a bad habit of guessing at the answer instead of working it out. Still, she worked hard.

Helen poses in her class picture at the school for deaf children. Helen sits in the front row, FAR LEFT, holding Teacher's hand.

She worked hardest at her speaking lessons. "Oh . . . how I should like to speak like other people," she wrote to a friend. She was willing to work day and night, she said. But her hard work wasn't enough. Her words still were not clear.

Once, when she was little, Helen told friends she wanted to go to college. It was a surprising dream. At that time, few girls went to college. For Helen, it seemed impossible. But Helen was used to doing what everyone else thought impossible.

A Good Memory and a Sad Tale

When Helen was eleven, she wrote a story called "The Frost King." The story was printed in a magazine. Then came terrible news. Her story had really been written by someone else. A friend had read the story to Helen years before. Helen did not recall the story. But somehow she had remembered it clearly. Helen was embarrassed by her mistake. She wrote in her journal, "My heart was full of tears."

A person reads a Braille book. When Helen was in school, many of her books were not in Braille.

In 1896, sixteen-year-old Helen entered the Cambridge School for Young Ladies. Her studies there would help her get ready for college. For the first time, she was in classes with students who could see and hear. Teacher went to all her classes with her. She sat by Helen's side and spelled the lessons into her hand. Most of Helen's books were not printed in Braille. Teacher spelled those too.

It was a lot of work for both Helen and Teacher. Even so, Helen made amazing progress. She passed all her exams, many with honors.

In September 1900, Helen entered Radcliffe College. She was already famous. But this time, she was making history. She was the first deaf-blind person ever to go to college. To welcome Helen, her classmates gave her a Boston terrier as a present. She named the dog Phiz.

Helen plunged right into her studies. She took classes in French, German, history, English, and more. Her best subject was

writing. And her best stories were the ones she wrote about her own life. Her stories were beautiful, funny, and full of joy.

Teacher reads to Helen by spelling words into her hand. Phiz lies by Helen's feet in this photo.

Other people heard about Helen's stories. They urged her to turn them into a book. In 1903, Helen's book, *The Story of My Life*, was published. She dedicated it to her good friend, Alexander Graham Bell.

At last, on a June day in 1904, Helen sat with ninety-six other women. Ninety-five of them were her classmates. The other was

Annie Sullivan. With her teacher by her side, Helen received her college degree, with honors. At twenty-four, Helen Keller was a college graduate.

Helen wore a cap and gown for her graduation from Radcliffe College.

4 INTRODUCING HELEN KELLER

Helen had spent nearly her whole life learning. It was time to do something with what she'd learned. She had told Dr. Bell once that she wanted to be a writer. She had already written one book. She decided she would keep writing.

Helen (SEATED)
with John Macy
and Annie

Helen and Annie moved into a big farmhouse in Massachusetts. Soon Annie's husband, John Macy, joined them. (They married in 1905). John helped Helen with her writing.

In 1908, Helen's second book, *The World I Live In*, was published. Helen knew that most people could not even imagine what it was like to be blind and deaf. So she told them. She described how she experienced the world, especially through touch. "My hand is to me what your hearing and sight together are to you," she wrote.

Readers loved the book. They were curious about Helen's dark, silent world. They would never tire of reading about her life.

Helen wanted to write about more than just her life, though. She wanted to write about her ideas.

Helen had strong opinions about how the country should be run. She believed that owning private property was a bad idea. Instead, she believed, everything should be shared equally by all. (That idea is called socialism.)

In Helen's day, women were not allowed to vote. She thought that was wrong too. She marched in parades to show her support for women's rights.

Helen marched in this 1913 parade in Washington, D.C. The parade was in support of women's right to vote.

Books that Helen read helped her form her opinions and ideas.

Many people frowned at Helen's ideas. Some even said that because she was blind and deaf, she didn't know any better. That made Helen angry. Attack my ideas, she invited. But she felt it wasn't "fair fighting" to remind people that she couldn't see or hear. After all, she could still think and read.

Helen also had opinions about how to help blind people. The government should do more, she argued. The blind needed more education and more jobs. They needed more Braille books. Helen wrote articles and visited schools to help.

She wanted to do more. She wanted to speak at meetings and in lectures. To do that, she would have to improve her speech. Once more Helen worked hard to learn to talk. She took lessons from a singing teacher. Slowly her voice grew stronger. Her words became clearer.

Helen spoke out about the need for Braille books. Here, volunteers for the Red Cross help create Braille versions of printed books.

Helen and Teacher began giving lectures. They spoke all over North America. Teacher told the audience how she had taught Helen about words. Then it was Helen's turn. How proud she was that she could make herself understood at last! Wherever they went, they were greeted with cheers and applause.

Helen (LEFT) gets ready to board a plane. Helen and Teacher traveled across the United States giving lectures.

Helen met President Calvin Coolidge at the White House in 1926. She had become so famous that she met nearly every U.S. president of her time.

Helen's words always gave hope to blind people. But Helen knew the blind needed more than hope. They needed help. In 1924, she began speaking to raise money for the American Foundation for the Blind. She spoke in homes, in churches, and at meetings. People flocked to see the famous Helen Keller. When she asked them to donate money, they did. "Purses Fly Open to Helen Keller," read one headline.

I'm Just Here for the Seals

For a while, Helen and Teacher spoke in theaters. Their "act" was sandwiched in among all kinds of others. They might follow a famous singer, a man on stilts, or a pack of trained seals.

With Teacher, Helen spoke to thousands of people in hundreds of cities across the country. In 1930, at the age of forty-nine, she spoke before the U.S. Congress. She wanted the government to help provide more Braille books for the blind. Soon after, the idea became law.

Helen was busier than ever. She was excited about her work for the blind. But Annie was tired. She was often sick. On October 20, 1936, at the age of seventy, she died. Helen held her hand as Teacher took her last breath. It was the same hand that had first spelled words to her as a little girl.

Nearly all her life, Teacher had been by her side. At fifty-six, Helen would have to go on without her.

5 AFTER TEACHER

Polly Thompson had been Helen's assistant for many years. She lived and traveled with Helen after Teacher's death. But no one could really take Teacher's place.

Helen missed Teacher. But there was work to do. She had already done so much to help blind people in the United States. She wanted to do the same for the blind in other countries.

In 1937, Helen and Polly traveled to Japan. Helen was to raise money for blind and deaf people there. People must have been very eager to hear what Helen had to say. She gave ninety-seven speeches in thirty-nine cities.

The Japanese people greeted Helen like a star. Children lined the streets to see her. They waved flags and shouted her name. Her trip was a tremendous success.

THE DOG LOVER

Helen had always loved dogs. On her trip to Japan, she was given a puppy as a gift. The dog was an Akita, a favorite breed in Japan. When Helen took her puppy home with her, it became the first Akita dog in the United States.

Then, just a few years later, on December 7, 1941, there was startling news. Japanese planes attacked U.S. ships at Pearl Harbor, Hawaii.

Suddenly, the United States was at war. Soldiers were being wounded on battlefields. Many had become blind or deaf. Helen visited hospitals. She held soldiers' hands and gave them words of encouragement. Most of all, she showed them that living without sight or hearing did not mean living without hope.

Helen (CENTER) and Polly (RIGHT) visit a wounded soldier during World War II.

By the end of the war, Helen was sixty-five years old. Many people began to slow down at that age. Not Helen. "Life is either a daring adventure or nothing," she said. And she was ready for adventure.

With Polly by her side, Helen traveled the world. She took her fight for the blind to thirty-five other countries. She spoke at universities and hospitals. She met with presidents, kings, and queens. She received honors and awards wherever she went.

Polly (LEFT) helps Helen (CENTER) put on a sari, an Indian dress, for an event in India.

First Lady Eleanor Roosevelt (LEFT) speaks with Helen. Mrs. Roosevelt praised Helen's work overseas.

Over and over, Helen spoke to cheering crowds. Over and over, she urged people to find ways to help the blind help themselves. Over and over, her words brought hope to the blind.

Helen had not forgotten about writing. In 1954, at the age of seventy-four, she completed a new book. *Teacher* was written to honor her teacher, Annie Sullivan. Helen had never stopped missing Teacher. She gave credit to Teacher for all she had accomplished in her life. "People think Teacher has left me," she told a friend, "but she is with me all the time."

These were busy years for Helen. She appeared in a movie about her life. The movie later went on to win an Academy Award. And in 1955, she left for a lengthy tour through Asia. She traveled forty thousand miles in five months. She was seventy-five.

It was time for Helen to slow down at last. She was happy to stay at her home in Connecticut. (She had moved there many years before.) She surrounded herself with books. She read and studied. She told friends she wanted to learn new languages. "I shall devote my old age to study," she said. She still had not lost her hunger for learning.

In 1964, Helen was awarded the Presidential Medal of Freedom. It is the nation's highest honor for civilians. But Helen was too ill and frail to receive the medal in person.

On June 1, 1968, Helen died. It was just weeks before her eighty-eighth birthday. She was one of the most famous women in the world. People everywhere knew the story of Helen's life.

Many people had felt sorry for Helen. They thought she must have lived a life filled with silence and darkness. But those people were wrong. Helen had lived a life filled with friends and adventure. She had lived a life filled with joy.

TIMELINE

In the year . . .

1882   Helen became blind and deaf after an illness.

1886   she met Dr. Alexander Graham Bell.

1887   Annie Sullivan came to Tuscumbia and began teaching Helen.   Age 6

1894   she attended a school for the deaf in New York.

1896   she attended the Cambridge School for Young Ladies.   Age 16

1890   she entered Radcliffe College.

1903   her first book, *The Story of My Life*, was published.

1904   she received a degree from Radcliffe and became the first deaf-blind person to graduate from college.   Age 24

1908   *The World I Live In* was published.

1913   she began giving lectures with Annie Sullivan.

1924   she began her work for the American Foundation for the Blind.   Age 44

1936   Annie Sullivan died.

1937   Helen traveled to Japan.

1946   she made her first world tour to speak on behalf of the blind.   Age 66

1955   *Teacher*, her book about Annie Sullivan, was published.

1964   she was awarded the Presidential Medal of Freedom from President Lyndon Johnson.   Age 84

1968   she died on June 1.   Age 87

A Visit to Ivy Green

The house where Helen grew up was called Ivy Green. In 1954, it became a memorial to Helen Keller.

Every year, people visit Ivy Green. They come to see the cottage where Helen was born. They see the porch where she first met Annie Sullivan. They touch the black well pump in the garden.

Each summer, a famous play is performed there. *The Miracle Worker* tells the story of Annie's struggle to teach the wild young Helen. And it shows the "miracle" that happened at that pump. People come to watch Helen's story. They see that miracle happen right where it happened for Helen—Ivy Green.

Helen was born in this cottage, across from the main house at Ivy Green.

FURTHER READING

Donaldson, Madeline. *Louis Braille.* **Minneapolis: Lerner Publications Company, 2007.** Read about the young Frenchman who, at the age of fifteen, invented an alphabet of raised dots for the blind.

Keller, Helen. *To Love This Life: Quotations by Helen Keller.* **New York: AFB Press, 2000.** This book has wise and funny sayings from Helen Keller. It is for older readers.

McPherson, Stephanie Sammartino. *Alexander Graham Bell.* **Minneapolis: Lerner Publications Company, 2007.** Learn about the famous inventor of the telephone, teacher of the deaf, and Helen's friend.

WEBSITES AND FILMS

American Manual Alphabet: Chart
http://www.iidc.indiana.edu/cedir/kidsweb/amachart.html
Learn to use the finger alphabet that Teacher taught to Helen.

Anne Sullivan Macy
http://www.afb.org/annesullivan This website features photos and a timeline of Annie's life.

Helen Keller Kids Museum Online
http://www.afb.org/braillebug/hkmuseum.asp
Click through a timeline of Helen's life, with photos and interesting facts.

The Miracle Worker. **DVD. Directed by Arthur Penn. Santa Monica, CA: MGM Home Entertainment, 2001.** Based on the famous play, this 1962 movie is the story of young Helen Keller and Teacher and what happened that day at the well pump.

What is Braille?
http://www.afb.org/braillebug/Braille.asp Read all about the code of dots used to print books for the blind.

SELECT BIBLIOGRAPHY

Herrmann, Dorothy. *Helen Keller: A Life*. New York: Alfred A. Knopf, 1998.

Keller, Helen. *The Story of My Life*. Garden City, NY: Doubleday, 1954.

Keller, Helen. *Teacher: Anne Sullivan Macy*. Westport, CT: Greenwood Press, 1985. First published 1955 by Doubleday.

Keller, Helen. *To Love This Life: Quotations by Helen Keller*. New York: AFB Press, 2000.

Keller, Helen. *The World I Live In*. New York: Century Co., 1908.

Lash, Joseph P. *Helen and Teacher: The Story of Helen Keller and Anne Sullivan Macy*. New York: Delacorte Press, 1980.

Nielsen, Kim. *The Radical Lives of Helen Keller*. New York: NYU Press, 2004.

INDEX

Acknowledgments

For photographs: The images in this book are used with the permission of: ©Bettmann/CORBIS, pp. 4, 26, 27, 40, 41, 43; © Time Life Pictures/Getty Images, pp. 7, 19; Courtesy of the National Library of Medicine, p. 8; © CAROLING LEE/ZUMA Press, p. 9; The Granger Collection, New York, p. 10; © SSPL/The Image Works, p. 11; Courtesy of Perkins School for the Blind, Watertown, MA, pp. 14, 20, 38, 39; Thaxter Parks Spencer Papers, R. Stanton Avery Special Collections Department, New England Historic Genealogical Society, Boston, MA., p. 15; © The Toronto Star/ZUMA Press, p. 16; Courtesy of the American Foundation for the Blind, Helen Keller Archives, pp. 17, 24, 27, 28, 30, 35, 42; Everett Collection, pp. 18, 23; Library of Congress (LC-DIG-ggbain-11365), p. 31; (LC-USZ62-68305), p. 32; Library of Congress (HABS ALA,17-TUSM, 4-4), p. 45; © CORBIS, p. 33; © Roger-Viollet/The Image Works, p. 34. Front cover: © Library of Congress (LC-USZ62-112513); back cover: © Todd Strand/Independent Picture Service.

For quoted material: p. 12, Helen Keller, *The Story of My Life* (Garden City, NY: Doubleday, 1954), 288; p. 18, Dorothy Herrmann, *Helen Keller: A Life* (New York: Alfred A. Knopf, 1998), 56; p. 21, Joseph P. Lash, *Helen and Teacher: The Story of Helen Keller and Anne Sullivan Macy* (New York: Delacorte Press, 1980), 93; p. 25, Keller, *The Story of My Life*, 344; p. 25, Lash, 134; p. 30, Helen Keller, *The World I Live In* (New York: Century Co., 1908), 5; p. 32, Kim Nielsen, *The Radical Lives of Helen Keller* (New York: NYU Press, 2004), 49; p. 35, Lash, 530; p. 40, Helen Keller, *To Love This Life* (New York: AFB Press, 2000), 35; p. 41, Helen Keller, *Teacher: Anne Sullivan Macy* (Westport, CT: Greenwood Press, 1985, originally published 1955 by Doubleday), 23; p. 42, Herrmann, 308.

A TREASURY OF
American
Scrimshaw

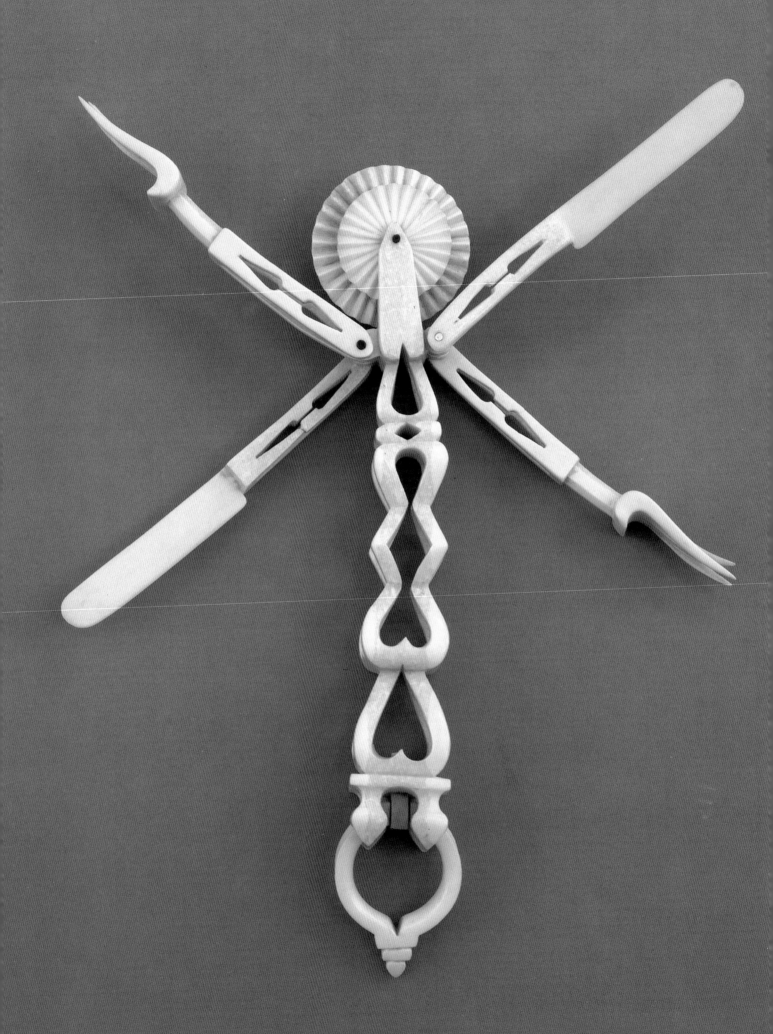

A TREASURY OF
American
Scrimshaw

A COLLECTION OF THE
USEFUL AND DECORATIVE

MICHAEL McMANUS

PENGUIN
STUDIO

(Frontispiece) JAGGING WHEEL *in walrus ivory.* (The
Kendall Whaling Museum)

PENGUIN STUDIO
Published by the Penguin Group
Penguin Books USA Inc., 375 Hudson Street,
New York, New York, 10014, U.S.A.

Penguin Books Ltd, 27 Wrights Lane,
London W8 5TZ, England

Penguin Books Australia Ltd, Ringwood,
Victoria, Australia

Penguin Books Canada Ltd, 10 Alcorn Avenue, Suite 300,
Toronto, Ontario, Canada M4 V3 B2

Penguin Books (N.Z.) Ltd, 182-90 Wairau Road,
Auckland 10, New Zealand

Penguin Books Ltd, Registered Offices:
Harmondsworth, Middlesex, England

First published by Penguin Studio, an imprint of Penguin Books USA Inc.

First printing, January 1997
10 9 8 7 6 5 4 3 2 1

Library of Congress Catalog Card Number: 95-71878

Book designed by Marilyn Rey
Printed and bound by Dai Nippon Printing Co., Hong Kong, Ltd.

ISBN: 0-670-86234-7

For Fran and Hon

Acknowledgments

From the beginning of this project to the final book I have received enormous help, support, and encouragement. All of it has been greatly appreciated. The late Dale McConathy, my professor at New York University, initiated the project by guiding me to the very first collection of scrimshaw, which was located at the then–Peabody Museum in Salem, Massachusetts. Next, the Early American Industries Association awarded me a grant to research tools made of scrimshaw. Charles Hummel's encouragement meant a lot to me. The late Robert Bishop, friend, mentor, and boss, continually encouraged my research.

At The Kendall Whaling Museum in Sharon, Massachusetts, Stuart Frank, the director, could not have been more helpful. His scholarship, organized mind, and willingness to share made my work easier and much more enjoyable. Also, I wish to thank Joost Schokkenbrock, Ellen Hazen, Gare Reid, and Michael Dwyer for their help and cooperation at the various times when I did research at The Kendall Whaling Museum.

Support at the Mystic Seaport Museum was always forthcoming from Revell Carr, the director, Philip Budlong, Rodi York, Nancy Seager, Peggy Tate Smith, and the photographer Mary Ann Stets, whose fine work contributes so much to this publication.

My contact at the New Bedford Whaling Museum has been my friend and fellow scrimshaw enthusiast Judith Lund. Time and again her help and friendliness made my work easier and more fulfilling. Thanks also go to Anne Brengle, the director, and to Kenneth Okolski.

Peter Fetchko at the Peabody Essex Museum in Salem, Massachusetts, some fifteen years ago arranged for me to see the entire scrimshaw collection, thus starting my interest in the utilitarian aspects of this field. Daniel Finamore and Paul Winfisky, along with volunteers Robert Eaton and Mitchell Comins, also receive my thanks. And then there is Mark Sexton, who did such an exquisite job photographing the pieces from the Peabody Essex Museum, The Kendall Whaling Museum, and the New Bedford Whaling Museum. What a singular pleasure to have his work represented here. Thanks also to his cohorts Kathy Flynn and Jeffrey Dykes.

The help and knowledge of three librarians need to be acknowledged most gratefully. They are Neville Thompson at The Henry Francis DuPont Winterthur Museum, Peg Zebrowski at the South Shore Branch of the Miami Dade Public Library, and Burton Abelson at the Donnell Reference Services of the New York Public Library. Their work was an extraordinary help to me.

Three scholars in the field of scrimshaw also receive my gratitude. They are Norman Flayderman, Margaret L. Vose, and Ed Stecewicz.

Eva Van Hees deserves a very warm and special thank you for tackling the task of transferring a handwritten manuscript to the word processor. Betsy Rowe did the initial typing, which I am gratefully acknowledging.

Long-time friends were never short on support and hospitality. Special thanks go to Anne and Butch Bessette, Bill Blass, and Susan and Shell Evans. Ann Carmel, Ned and Carol Farman, Cheryl Hoenemeyer and Harriett Stanley, Looey and Tod Johnstone, Dermot Meagher, Dawn and Joe Sharp, and Dory and Charlie Wilson were all kind enough to open their hearts, homes, and refrigerators to the meandering researcher. Oh, how I enjoyed that hospitality.

My editor, Cyril I. Nelson, receives kudos from me on too many levels to mention. Suffice it to say he never stinted on his encouragement, advice, and support, all of which I was most pleased to receive. Thank you, Cyril.

Over the years the following institutions have allowed me to snoop and pry into their scrimshaw collections. Each one in its own way added to my knowledge in the field and I wish to acknowledge them here: Philadelphia Maritime Museum, Philadelphia, Pennsylvania; Falmouth Historical Society, Falmouth, Massachusetts; East Hampton Town Marine Museum, Amagansett, New York; Old Lighthouse Museum, Stonington, Connecticut; Newport Historical Society, Newport, Rhode Island; Heritage Plantation, Sandwich, Massachusetts; Mariner's Museum, Newport News, Virginia; National Maritime Museum, San Francisco, California; Shelburne Museum, Shelburne, Vermont; Sag Harbor Whaling and Historical Museum, Sag Harbor, New York; The South Street Seaport Museum, New York, New York; The Whaling Museum, Cold Spring Harbor, New York; Duke's County Historical Society, Edgartown, Massachusetts; Cape Cod National Seashore, Marconi Station, South Wellfleet, Massachusetts; and Nantucket Historical Association in Nantucket, Massachusetts.

In ending, let me state that any errors or shortcomings are all my own.

NOTE TO THE READER

In going through this book, it is important to keep in mind that the great majority of the pieces illustrated were made anonymously during the nineteenth century. Because the objects were created on board whaling ships, there is no way of determining exactly where they were made. For these reasons it has not been possible to include in the majority of the captions for the illustrations names of the artists, specific dates when the pieces were made, or the places where they were made.

Contents

Introduction

Scrimshaw first came to my attention back in the early 1960s. The President's wife, Jacqueline Kennedy, had given John F. Kennedy several pieces of this American folk art that he quite prominently displayed on his desk in the Oval Office. From then on, whenever I found myself in a New England coastal town, I would keep an eye out for scrimshaw. Unfortunately no purchases were ever made, for the necessary cash always seemed in short supply. Years passed before this near-passive delight moved on to the next stage.

In 1981, while I was pursuing a master's degree in American folk-art studies at New York University, the late Professor Dale McConathy in his course "Structure and Function of Museums" assigned me the task of exploring the art and function of scrimshaw at the Peabody Essex Museum in Salem, Massachusetts. After suitable arrangements had been made, I eventually found myself at a table in the registrar's office perusing the large, handwritten account books dating from 1799, when the East India Marine Society was founded (that being the beginning of what is now the Peabody Essex Museum).

The word scrimshaw had not come to the fore in 1799, however. The earliest written reference to one of the many forms of the word "scrimshaw" is found in the log of the brig *By Chance* out of Dartmouth, Massachusetts, dated May 20, 1826, when the following entry appeared: "All these 24 hours of small breezes and thick foggy weather, made no sail. So ends this day, all hands employed Scrimshonting." It wasn't until 1841 that the word was first printed. Francis A. Olmsted wrote in *Incidents of a Whaling Voyage*, "There are found aboard a whaler, a great variety of small tools expressly intended for 'scrimshawing' or nice mechanical contrivances for fabricating various articles out of teeth and jawbone of the sperm whale." Herman Melville uses the word "skrimshander" in *Moby Dick* (1851).

Salem's East India Marine Society was the first museum to collect scrimshaw. The twelfth entry in their earliest accession book lists a whale's tooth that was given to the Society about 1821. In 1907, another accession book states that three utilitarian pieces were purchased. More buying and further donations followed. By 1921, there were enough examples of this art form to display them in the newly opened Marine Room. These swifts, bodkins, pickwicks, boxes, and teeth all dated from 1820 to 1840. At the time, it must be remembered, scrimshaw was not sought after as it is today, for it was considered everyday stock in trade.

The more I dug into the background of scrimshaw the more interested I became. Because of a very active schedule as the Director of Exhibitions at the Museum of American Folk Art in New York City under my mentor Robert Bishop, the Director of the Museum, I could not actively pursue my research into scrimshaw. Of course, I read *Scrimshaw and Scrimshanders* by Norman Flayderman and *Graven by the Fishermen Themselves* by Richard Malley. And in December, 1982, I managed to view again and again The Barbara Johnson Whaling Collection that Sotheby's was putting up for auction in four sales in New York. By that time I had become aware of the fact that it was the utilitarian pieces of scrimshaw that held my fascination.

About that time a notice in the *Newtown Bee* about the Early American Industries Association caught my eye. E.A.I.A. is "a collector's organization, international in scope, devoted to encourage study and better understanding of early American industries in the home, in the shop, on the farm, and on the sea; and also to discover, identify, classify, preserve, and exhibit obsolete tools, implements, and mechanical devices in early America." The utilitarian scrimshaw I had been viewing included many types of tools—tools for use on board the whaling vessels and tools for use at home in the kitchen or for sewing. An application was requested and sent in. Recommendations from those in the scrimshaw world were given with great enthusiasm and encouragement. All felt that here was a gap that needed to be filled. Most research in the field had been devoted to the decorative whale's teeth. A study involving tools that were also scrimshaw would broaden the canvas.

I was awarded a grant in April 1988. My stated purpose was fivefold: 1) Define the extent and scale of such tools. 2) Indicate the reasons the scrimshanders selected bone and ivory to create these instruments. 3) List the particular skills needed to fabricate tools of bone and ivory. 4) Give an explanation of the scrimshander's tradition of decoration in tools. 5) Identify the makers and users of bone and ivory tools.

It became apparent very soon that little or no background information had been kept about scrimshaw tools. This lack can be advantageous because first research has few or no parameters or definite guidelines, meaning that unexpected finds are possible.

For the next several months any spare time found me nosing about scrimshaw collections in various museums. Encouragement never ceased. Directors made sure all doors were open to me; curators and registrars were extremely cooperative. Fourteen institutions were visited, including The Kendall Whaling Museum in Sharon, Massachusetts, New Bedford Whaling Museum (Massachusetts), Nantucket Historical Association on Nantucket Island, Mystic Seaport, Mystic, Connecticut, Peabody Essex Museum of Salem, Massachusetts, The South Street Seaport in New York City, and Sag Harbor Whaling and Historical Museum in Sag Harbor, New York, to name just a few. Correspondence was held with thirteen more collections. The final outcome?

Some 3,294 tools were considered, and of these there were 191 different types. Only eighty-seven of these types had decoration of any sort on them, but there were over 100 kinds of patterns used. Another interesting point: only fifty-nine of the 3,294 objects had identified makers, and only twenty-eight different men made these fifty-nine tools. One word was sufficient to explain why the scrimshanders selected bone and ivory to create these objects: accessibility. No formal training was ever given to these men. They learned through peer example, trial and error, and their natural inclination.

After all this work I still did not feel that enough was known, but a beginning had been made into this part of America's heritage. I realized this was a cumulative process, where bit by bit the story gets told. My filing cabinets began to burst as more and more information was amassed. I hurried off to yearly Whaling Symposiums held at The Kendall Whaling Museum. Here among experts of the scrimshaw world I picked brains, and sometimes I was able to help others with information I had culled. I grabbed any chance to visit small, local museums and historical societies on the eastern seaboard, where I could try to find another cogent tidbit.

One of my original goals continued to go unanswered. What were the meaning and the sources of the many decorative patterns? Although some decorative patterns were repeated, they were not done in such quantities that would suggest a known tradition. The answers, I felt, might be found at The Henry Francis DuPont Winterthur Museum, in Winterthur, Delaware. Their library with its decorative-arts book collection might provide the meaning and sources for the decorative patterns used on the handmade scrimshawed tools and add to my understanding of the role of decorative arts in utilitarian objects.

My stay at Winterthur meant long hours in the library ferreting out the needed information. There were plenty of blind alleys because this was an interdisciplinary study, one that involved the sea, the whaling industry, the world of tools, the home, and the field of art. Connections needed to be drawn between pastime work and utilitarian work. There were tomes on patterns, on symbols, on utensils, on marine antiques, on tools, on toys, on ornamentation, and on kitchenware. It was clear that ornamental embellishments joined line, proportion, and harmony of parts in making what was useful also beautiful. By the completion of my stay at Winterthur, I knew a large part of the picture had unfolded.

An added advantage to doing scholarly research at Winterthur was its proximity to The Hagley Museum and Library, Wilmington, Delaware, which houses trade catalogues, including those of tools dating from the eighteenth century.

I then began to consider taking this project an additional step: to write a book based on the utilitarian aspect of scrimshaw. So I began by posing the question, "What purpose would this book serve?" There is an increasing generic interest in the field of scrimshaw, and because of this more questions are being asked and consequently there is a need to know more about the field. A book about useful and decorative scrimshaw could very well attract more attention to the subject. It would be addressed to the layman in a manner that would be inviting but hopefully would also interest the scholar. Such a book would then add to the existing literature on the folk art of scrimshaw.

The book would constitute a different approach from the few other pictorial books on scrimshaw. It would not concentrate on one collection, and it would not concentrate on the carved or engraved whale's teeth.. In addition, sharing my information might entice others to visit the various public collections.

These objects, so painstakingly made by nineteenth-century whalemen, would help cast a different light on the whaling industry by telling a specific social history that contains an American aesthetic tradition. Here would be one step more in preserving this part of America's folk-art history, an aspect that has been neglected. It would not present a romantic tale of high adventure at sea as it sometimes has been depicted, but instead the difficulties and hardships would be revealed.

Finally, so many of these objects crossed over into fields other than just scrimshaw. The book would appeal to those in the tool world, the needlework world, the kitchen world, and the decorative-arts world.

When a book contract was completed, I selected objects from four major museums: The Kendall Whaling Museum in Sharon, Massachusetts; Mystic Seaport Museum in Mystic, Connecticut; New Bedford Whaling Museum in New Bedford, Massachusetts; and the Peabody Essex Museum in Salem, Massachusetts. The pieces chosen were divided into the following categories: the background of whaling and scrimshaw; for use on board; for use at home; decorative but still useful; known and supposed makers; ornamentation; and things that were not what they seemed.

When discussing the objects, it was necessary for me to explain that it is quite difficult to distinguish teeth ivory from whalebone, and to know the difference between sperm-whale ivory and walrus ivory. Terminology can be confusing because many refer to baleen as being bone. I chose to use baleen. Jagging wheels are also commonly known as crimpers. I basically stuck with the former term.

Although most scrimshaw is American and thought of as being made by Yankees, whalers of other nationalities made it also. These men served on American-owned ships as well as vessels from their homelands. Yankee captains often had to hire foreigners to replace the many deserters from whaling ships. In addition, other nations hired Yankee whalers so that they could learn whaling from them. The art of scrimshaw came along at no extra cost. And, although scrimshaw was primarily associated with whaling, it was also made on navy and merchant-marine vessels. Yankee utilitarian scrimshaw has up to now been so neglected that there are very few fakes being passed around. This cannot be said of scrimshawed whales' teeth.

From its inception until now, this is the story of my chosen field—one that has provided me with many, many hours of joy and satisfaction.

CHAPTER ONE

A Background of Whaling and Scrimshaw

It was the Basques and Gascoynes who first began systematic commercial whaling in Europe's Bay of Biscay during the twelfth, thirteenth, and fourteenth centuries. In North America, colonists in Massachusetts sought whales along the shores of New England, but it was the Long Islanders who in 1640 established the first regular American whaling business. Their prey was the right whale, so named because the hunters believed it was the "right" whale to catch. This whale, which swam close to shore and had no teeth but baleen in its mouth, continued to be hunted even at Nantucket Island, Massachusetts, where by 1700 whaling was a thriving industry. Sperm whales did not appear on the scene until Nantucket whaler Christopher Hussey captured one in 1712. It became immediately evident that this type of whale produced a very high quality of oil, particularly the spermaceti oil found in its head cavity. Because the sperm whale lived farther out in the ocean, it meant whalers needed to travel farther from their coastlines, and by 1732, Nantucket ships were plying the Davis Strait near Greenland.

Sperm-oil candles were being manufactured in 1749 to supply the growing demand. This and the significant increase in the use of oil lamps meant that more whaling was necessary. By the time of the American Revolution whaling was an important industry centered in Nantucket, which already had 150 whaling vessels. Although the vessel *Beaver* out of Nantucket rounded Cape Horn in 1791 or 1795, depending on one's source of information, the period from the Revolutionary War to the end of the War of 1812 was obviously an unstable time for whaling. Following the wars, a period of prosperity ensued and whaling was revitalized, which meant the commissioning of the additional vessels and opening of new ports.

The sperm whale with its singular blow hole and the right whale with two blow holes were still the species that were most often hunted. The sperm, also called *cachalot* in French, was the largest whale with teeth and the only toothed one

sought for its oil. The sperm whale, certainly the epitome of what most people think that whales look like, inhabited all the oceans and migrated from area to area. Males could attain a length of sixty feet, but females rarely grew over forty feet; both could dive to the incredible depth of two miles. Their name, however, is a misnomer. Originally it was thought that the substance found in its head cavity was sperm, and thus the reason for the name. The substance was oil, not sperm, but the label remained.

Knowing the value of the sperm-whale's oil and realizing that their whaling grounds or points of congregation were far flung, whalers traveled to the far corners of the world even before covered wagons settled the American West. The sperm whale, whose oil produced the best illumination and the best lubricants, became the mainstay of the industry, for it supplied needs both at home and abroad. The bright clean light of this product burned everywhere from lighthouses to private homes.

Americans did not have a monopoly on the whaling industry, but they did send out over three times as many vessels as those from foreign lands. Whaling, therefore, was significant to the American economy and absolutely vital to New England.

Accompanying all this industry was something new. In the log book of the brig *By Chance* out of Dartmouth, Massachusetts, we first learn about the practice of scrimshaw. This first mention is found in the entry of May 20, 1826. Because of fog and lack of wind the brig was virtually becalmed, and the crew occupied their time scrimshawing. Such long periods of inactivity led to boredom, and this combined with terrible food and wretched living conditions caused a significant number of desertions. Whaling at best was a hardship, and at worst it suffered from the most abysmal working conditions in America, except for slavery. Deductions from the sailors' pay were made for every possible reason and purchases from the slop chest, which is where supplies were kept, were done at exorbitant rates.

But the quest went on, and by 1835 there were almost thirty whaling ports. In that year, also, the ship *Ganges* out of Nantucket killed the first right whale on America's northwest coast. So a new fishery was established and even more vessels were needed. The Golden Era of whaling was in full swing. Now, however, the leading whaling port was New Bedford, not Nantucket. This occurred because longer distances meant larger ships, and the Nantucket harbor was not deep enough to handle them. Difficulties began to appear, even as the fleet increased in size and reached its apogee in 1846 with 729 vessels. Sperm whales were becoming scarce, which resulted in longer voyages to search for them and, consequently, more expensive outfitting for the ships.

In 1848, a whaleship the *Superior* out of Sag Harbor, Long Island, began hunting in the Arctic. The whales were not sperms but bowheads, found only in these waters. Although their oil could not match the quality of the sperm whale, there was plenty of it. In addition, the bowhead had the longest baleen plates of all whales, some measuring up to fourteen feet. This was to be that mammal's undoing, for the right and its larger relative the bowhead were the only whales that had baleen of commercial length and quality.

The California Gold Rush in 1849 led to desertions from whaling, but not enough to curtail growth of the industry. New Bedford did not reach its peak until 1857, at which time 329 vessels were using the port. But these vessels took months to reach the whaling grounds, and because it was not profitable to return home without a full load, captains remained at sea for three and four years at a time searching for the oil of the twenty-five to thirty whales it would take to fill their holds. Greed, however, led to a glut of oil on the market and, consequently, the lowering of prices. The ordinary seaman now earned about as much as a low-level textile hand in a New England mill. A different and undesirable type of whaleman was employed as a result. The depression of 1857 took its toll, but the major decline of whaling was caused by the discovery of petroleum in Pennsylvania in 1859. A much less expensive means of lighting had been discovered.

By now, few Yankee men were shipping out a second time. In addition to the danger, the horrid food and living condi-

LOWER JAW OF A SPERM WHALE,
ivory, bone,
H. 4', W. 7', L. 15". This photograph and all other illustrations of objects in the collection of the Peabody Essex Museum, Salem, Massachusetts, were made for this book by Mark Sexton. (Peabody Essex Museum)

Of whales that were hunted, only the lower jaw of the sperm whale had teeth. Ranging from four to ten inches in length, there could be as many as fifty teeth in a large whale. The teeth were not used to chew the giant squid that they ate, but only to cut up the squid into large chunks. Although the lower jaw illustrated is only fifteen feet long, many sperm-whale jaws measured between forty and fifty feet. The lower jaw was the first part of the animal that was hoisted on board the ship, but it was not until all the money-making work was completed that the teeth were distributed to the crew. Custom and tradition dictated that the ivory should be given to the whalers, for although considered worthless by the industry, they were the perfect material for scrimshawing. The teeth, the odor of which was vile, were extracted from the jaw with cutting spades and small tackles. Hollow for a good portion of their length, these teeth were soaked in brine to soften them for engraving. The jaw also produced panbone, seen here at the top of the photograph, which measured from two to eighteen feet in length. Also considered of no value, this close-grained bone was cut, sawn, and sliced to be used mostly by the carver for utilitarian objects. Jawbone was softer than a tooth and therefore more easily worked. Bones from other types of whales were seldom scrimshawed because of their oily and porous quality.

PIECE OF BALEEN,
H. ¼", W. 5½", L. 52". This photograph and all other illustrations of objects in the collection of the Mystic Seaport Museum, Mystic, Connecticut, were made for this book by Mary Ann Stets. (Mystic Seaport Museum)

Whales that do not have teeth use baleen for the feeding process. This black or brown material hangs from the upper portion of the animal's mouth like a vertical venetian blind. When the whale's jaw opens it fills both with water and with whatever else the water contains. When the jaw closes, the whale's tongue forces the water out through the baleen, which acts like a food strainer, trapping plankton that is then swallowed. Baleen, which is similar in texture to the hoofs and horns of cattle, has a lengthwise grain. After the baleen is taken from the whale, the one-to-fifteen-foot-long pieces are scraped, steamed, cut, and split into usable sizes. Until about 1844, baleen, which is also known as whalebone, had very little value and was not actively sought. Then it began to be utilized in the production of corsets, whips, fishing rods, umbrellas, cushions on billiard tables, or other items that needed stiffening yet would also bend. With the advent of this new value, only the trimmings were given to scrimshanders. By the last part of the nineteenth century, baleen became more valued than sperm oil. The whales most hunted for baleen were the right whale and the Arctic bowhead. It was baleen alone that kept the whaling industry afloat until the 1900s. With the invention of spring steel in 1906 baleen became outmoded and whaling all but ceased.

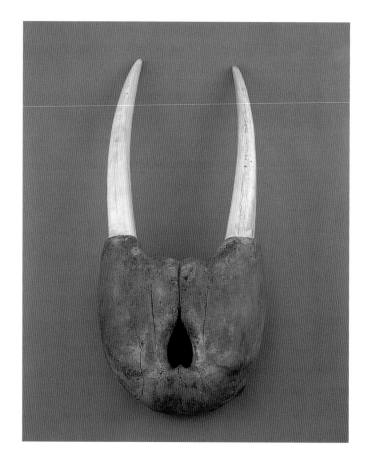

WALRUS TUSKS IN SKULL (Anatomical Specimen),
walrus ivory and bone,
H. 5⅝", W. 8⅞", L. 20⁵⁄₁₆". This photograph and all other illustrations of objects in the collection of The Kendall Whaling Museum, Sharon, Massachusetts, were made for this book by Mark Sexton. (The Kendall Whaling Museum)

Yankee whalers began serious whale hunting in Arctic waters in the 1840s. Scrimshanders had to deal with the fact that the whales found there had no teeth, so they used the ivory tusks of the walrus. Ranging in size from eighteen to thirty-two inches, the tusks were used by the walrus for digging shellfish to eat, for climbing steep ice banks, and for defending itself. Frequently, the whalers traded goods with Eskimos to obtain the tusks, which were also known as "morse" ivory. Although second in popularity to whale teeth for making scrimshaw, they still only comprised ten percent of the field. Scrimshanders found that carving the tusks was almost the same as working whale's teeth, and that their length and straightness were ideal for use whenever long pieces of ivory were desired. It is very difficult to distinguish between walrus ivory and whale ivory.

tions, the low pay, and the cruel punishments meted out by the captains, there was the unbearable boredom of life on board a whaling ship.

Then the Civil War began and it, too, took its toll on the whalers. The Confederates sank as many whaling ships as possible, but it was the Union that did the most damage. It commandeered forty whaling vessels so that they could be sunk in southern harbors. The idea was to load these ships with stone and then capsize them so that they would block the channels and prevent Confederate ships from leaving their home ports. The Stone Fleet, as it was known, was a war-time failure and a major loss to whaling.

By 1870, baleen had become significantly more important. It supplied the need for stays, corsets, riding and carriage whips, umbrellas, or anything else needing both strength and flexibility. The Arctic became a favorite hunting ground because of its bowhead whales. But nature proved an adversary, and in 1871 over thirty ships were crushed by ice. Twelve more met the same fate the following year. This was yet one more blow to whaling. In 1877, only 163 American whaling vessels were active. By the time Thomas Edison made the incandescent lamp in 1879 whale oil was destined for use just as a lubricant and not as a source of light. The slide continued, however, with some diehards holding on until 1920, when whaling was entirely over in the United States. It had played a major role from about 1795 to 1865. Meanwhile, the whale population had been decimated; right whales were on the verge of extinction.

Scrimshaw, which had always been an adjunct to the whaling industry, came to be recognized as a separate art form only after whaling ended. Whalers were certainly not the first to work ivory, for it is an ancient craft dating as far back as the Stone Age. Whalemen were quite different from other ivory carvers because they belonged to a specific group, one that had no connection with an artistic milieu. Scrimshaw had enormous variety, and for the most part it was not fashioned for monetary gain. It was simply an appealing and harmless pastime used to ward off the boredom of a whaling voyage. Because of its difficulty scrimshaw consumed hours of time and provided a means to combat homesickness and the desire for women. Both the derivation of the word scrimshaw and the date of its origin are unknown. Its many variations— scrimshone, scrimshorn, scrimson, scrinshon, and squinshon—are probably just due to poor spelling.

In dealing with scrimshaw it helps to place it in its context

and social history. Doing so enhances the appreciation of the object. Many whalemen were Jacks-of-all-Trades when it came to manual labor, and they knew the satisfaction of working with their hands. One theory explains that when the whalemen reached the Pacific at the end of the eighteenth century and saw the natives of the South Sea islands carving wood and shell, they made a mental connection to the ivory teeth of the whales. In whatever way scrimshaw began, some time between 1821 and 1831 an engraved whale's tooth made its way into the collection of what now is the Peabody Essex Museum. Its insignificance at that time is made apparent by the vague information about it in the museum's accessions book.

It has been estimated that about 200,000 whalers from New England and New York created scrimshaw. Although these scrimshanders were not artists per se, their work has a compelling beauty that holds one's interest through its display of craftsmanship. This pastime, distinctive to American whaling, produced objects that range from the splendid to the obviously unsuccessful, but ninety percent of the work lies somewhere in between. The carvers did what they wanted and how they wanted with whatever skill and patience they possessed. Because scrimshaw was not meant for sale, there were no quality standards to be met. Unlimited time produced unique pieces, even within a type, that were meant for friends, relatives, and lady loves. Most crews were encouraged to scrimshaw so as to obviate the possibility of troublemaking. Baleen, composed of keratin, the same substance as human fingernails, became less available to carvers as it became a more valuable cash commodity. The teeth and jawbones of the whale were always distributed when they were available. Holding true to form, a Yankee never wasted a thing, not even a whale's tooth.

For a period of roughly one hundred years whalers produced a wide variety of scrimshaw, but it is the engraved and/or carved teeth that have received the most attention and admiration. The teeth, which are found only in the lower part of the whale's mouth and cannot bite or chew due to the lack of corresponding upper teeth, have held their attraction because of their decoration, including whaling scenes, family members, religion, love, women, and patriotism.

This first chapter discusses the basic composition of scrimshaw and how it developed, and illustrates fine examples of scrimshawed teeth, which are generally considered classic scrimshaw.

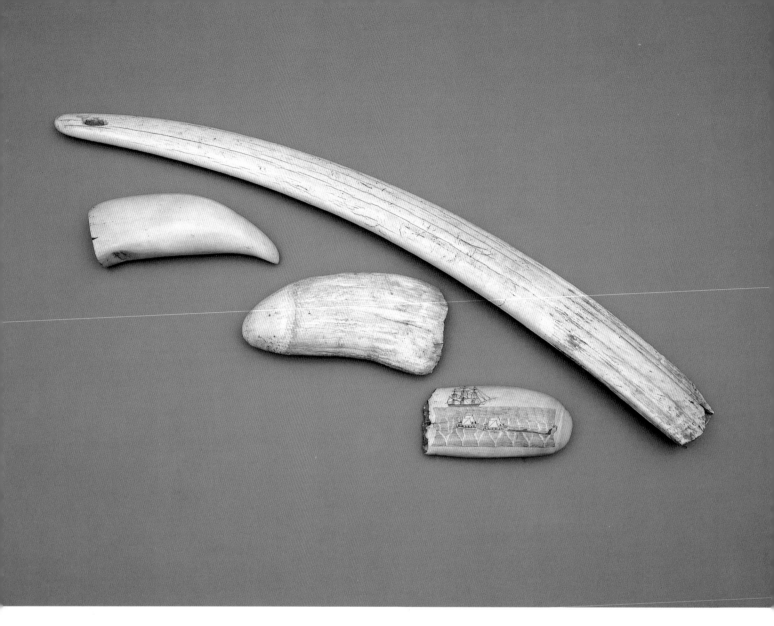

PANBONE,
H. 2⅜", W. 3", L. 32".

POLISHED SPERM-WHALE TOOTH,
H. 2⅛", W. 2¾", L. 8".

UNPOLISHED SPERM-WHALE TOOTH,
H. 2¼", W. 4⅛", L. 9½".

ENGRAVED SPERM-WHALE TOOTH,
ivory, ink,
H. 1⅞", W. 3", L. 6¾". This photograph and all other illustrations of objects in the collection of the New Bedford Whaling Museum, New Bedford, Massachusetts, were made for this book by Mark Sexton. (All pieces are in the collection of the New Bedford Whaling Museum)

Here we have three teeth and a piece of panbone in various stages of being turned into scrimshaw. The center tooth has been sawn from the jaw of the sperm whale, and it is still in its rough stage. Hollow halfway up the center, teeth used for scrimshaw come only from the lower jaw of the sperm whale. These teeth average from four to ten inches in length, with the smaller ones being in the very front or back of the jaw. The larger teeth exist in the middle at either side of the mouth. Their shape can be very different, some being curved, some cone-shaped, and still others rounded. After the distribution of the teeth, usually by the second mate, work would begin on removing the ribs and ridges on the outer surface. A tooth could become brittle in the air, so work was usually completed while it was fresh from the whale. Otherwise it would have to be soaked in brine to keep it soft. The upper tooth was filed and sanded with an abrasive, probably sharkskin or pumice, to prepare it for carving or engraving. Its shape plays a major role in the design to be used. The third tooth was engraved with a whaling scene, the lines of which are emphasized with ink, which covered the engraving and then was quickly rubbed off, leaving only the incised lines highlighted with color. Ivory takes color easily and that includes unwanted stains. The subsequent polishing and buffing give the tooth a glow that is unattainable in bone. Teeth were also cut into pieces to be used in an assortment of objects. Much scrimshaw was made of ivory rather than bone, which was more brittle and lighter in weight. Panbone, an example of which is the long scimitar-shape piece above the teeth, is part of the sperm-whale jaw and is harder than the other bone. Consequently, it was also desirable for carving. Bone can be detected by its telltale gray lines or pit marks, depending on whether it has been used lengthwise or has been crosscut.

6

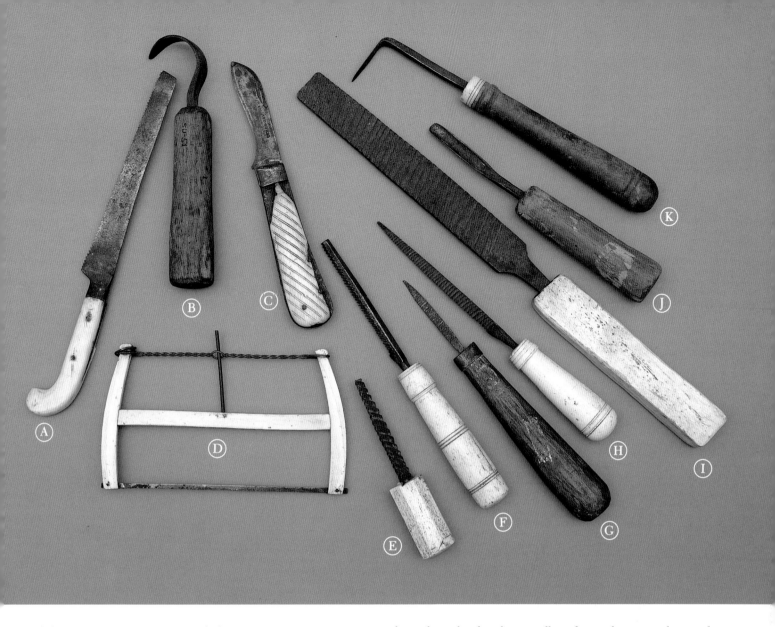

(A) SAW,
bone, metal,
H. 3⁷/₁₆", W. 1⅛", L. 8¼".

(B) SCRAPER,
wood, metal,
H. 1", W. 1⁷/₁₆", L. 5¾".

(C) KNIFE,
bone, metal,
H. ⅝", W. 1", L. 6⅜".

(D) SAW,
bone, metal,
H. 3¼", W. 1¼", L. 5½".

(E) TRIANGULAR FILE,
bone, metal,
H. ¹³/₁₆", W. ¹³/₁₆", L. 4¼".

(F) TRIANGULAR FILE,
bone, metal,
L. 7", Diam. ¾".

(G) FLAT FILE,
wood, metal,
H. ¾", W. 1", L. 6⅞".

(H) TRIANGULAR FILE,
bone, metal,
L. 7", Diam. ⅞".

(I) FLAT FILE,
bone, metal,
H. ¾", W. 1", L. 12¼".

(J) GOUGE,
wood, metal,
L. 6¼", Diam. 1".

(K) SCRAPER,
wood, ivory, metal,
H. 7", W. 1¼", L. 7⅜".

(All pieces are in the collection of the New Bedford Whaling Museum)

These eleven hand tools were all used in making scrimshaw, and eight of the eleven implements have scrimshaw as part of their construction. All relatively small, the tools combine both what was readily available and what could be handmade or gerry-rigged. First, the surface of the tooth or bone had to be prepared. The saw would cut with the aid of a chisel or a jackknife, the latter being the most essential instrument of all. It was also employed in carving and engraving. The chisel doubled as a scraper, and with the knife it was also involved in inlay work. A gimlet—made perhaps from a nail—bored any desired holes. Awls and sail needles with their sharp points were taken in hand for fine engraving and for pierced and filigree work. Files of different grades were employed for a variety of reasons. Print or script was usually scratched in the surface with either a jackknife or a sail needle. Generally, no lathes were used, as most turning was done by hand with a file or chisel. Having dexterous hands was an enormous asset because one miscalculation or slip of an instrument could mean having to start all over again. It is known that ship's carpenters and coopers had access to more tools than the normal seaman and scrimshanders of great experience would probably have accumulated a better grade of tool. Worn and dull tools often needed sharpening, which resulted in the altering of their size.

WILLIAM TELL · OF NEW-YORK · HOMEWARD BOUND · IN THE

WILLIAM TELL,
*Edward Burdett, c. 1833, whale panbone, polychrome, mahogany
frame, bronze,
H. ⁹⁄₁₆", W. 6¼", L. 12⁹⁄₁₆".* (The Kendall Whaling Museum)

Panbone, the large flat slabs of white bone taken from a sperm-whale's jaw, provided a good surface on which to engrave whaling or whaling-related scenes. Except for the teeth, it was the favorite part of the whale to scrimshand. In the United States, ship portraiture began about 1800, and many thin slabs of panbone were the basis for such portraits. Although the scrimshander might produce some crude pictures on a panbone, his portrayal of a ship and its gear was nearly always accurate, for who else but the sailor would know

better? Edward Burdett was one of the earliest scrimshanders to produce ships' portraits, and he was the first-known Yankee scrimshander to sign his name. This is the last and the largest of six pieces that have come to light, and it is the only one done on pan-bone, the others having been executed on teeth. Both of the ships shown on the panbone are the *William Tell*. The version at the left illustrates the vessel in all its full-rigged glory. On the right side we see the damaged ship with most of its sails down and an upside-down American flag, which was a recognized distress signal. As noted on the panbone, the *William Tell* had lost its rudder and research later determined that it went to Valparaiso, Chile, for repairs. Burdett died in 1833 when he became entangled in a flying line and was tossed overboard and drowned.

9

SUSAN'S TOOTH,
attributed to Frederick Myrick, c. 1826–1830, ivory, black coloring,
H. 1½", W. 2½", L. 5¾". (New Bedford Whaling Museum)

Perhaps the most famous scrimshaw known are the *Susan's* teeth.
These are some of the earliest identified teeth. The carver of this
example was Frederick Myrick, a Nantucket man, who is considered
in the first rank of scrimshanders, although he took part in only two
whaling expeditions. It was on the second trip aboard the maiden
voyage of the *Susan* that Myrick did his fine work. The voyage, lasting from 1826 to 1830, sailed out of Nantucket, rounded Cape Horn,
and thence into the Pacific Ocean. This tooth reflects the *Susan's*
stay off the coast of Japan, as is inscribed above the ship. Whaleboats
are shown in action, and the cutting-in platform is seen amidships. A
serpentine vine encircles an eagle that grasps an E Pluribus Unum
banner in its beak while its talons clutch five arrows. This vignette is
completed with two crossed American flags. The beauty of the
engraved scene on this tooth makes it obvious why Myrick's work is
so highly valued.

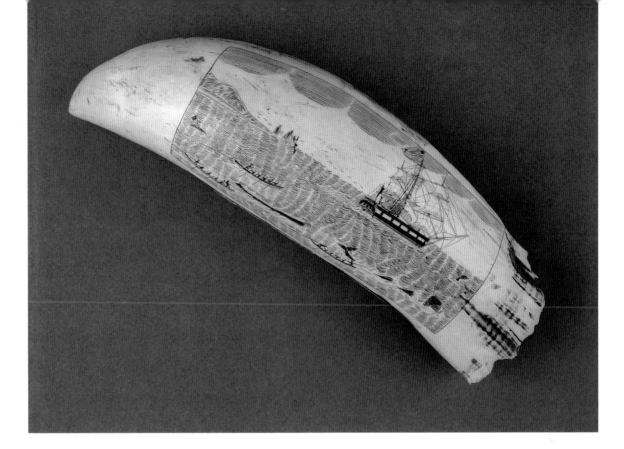

TOOTH, WITH WHALING SCENE,
ivory, coloring,
H. 2¼", W. 3", L. 8½". (Peabody Essex Museum)

Whaling scenes were, understandably, one of the most popular sub-
jects for the carved teeth, of which the piece illustrated here is a particularly fine example. The mother ship was usually depicted in the
background (as seen here), while the whaleboats pursued the prey—
sometimes being smashed to smithereens by the whale. Sperm whales
in groups called pods were the whales depicted most often, whether
surfacing, diving (called sounding), harpooned, on a "Nantucket
sleigh ride," or being flensed (cut into). It is both suitable and ironic
that the whale hunt should be portrayed on a tooth. This eight-and-
one-half-inch tooth with a sperm whale engraved on its reverse side
was made on board the ship *Averick*. The waif flag at the far left
marks the position and ownership of a captured whale carcass.

TOOTH, FANNY CAMPBELL,
after 1845, ivory, coloring,
H. 1½", W. 2½", L. 5". (Peabody Essex Museum)

This elegantly costumed figure with a plumed hat illustrates a well-
known sailor's tale. Transferred by the pin-prick method from the
frontispiece of a book published in 1845, the engraving shows us
Fanny Campbell, the female pirate. Fanny, called Captain
Channing, dressed as a man and sailed to Cuba to free an impris-
oned lover. Accomplishing this, she then captured an armed British
vessel, all the while keeping her crew from discovering that she was
a woman. Writing under the pen name of Lieutenant Murray,
Murray Ballou Maturius published his account of Fanny Campbell
in 1845, which helps date this piece, for the book's frontispiece was
the source of the engraved image. As in this case, it is generally true
that the best examples of figural scrimshaw are copied from picture
sources.

TOOTH, ANGELS HELPING A MAN,
ivory, coloring,
H. 2", W. 2½", L. 7". (Peabody Essex Museum)

When looking at scrimshawed teeth, one must be aware that the subject matter is quite important, for it usually reflects social history—in this case, Christianity in the nineteenth century. On this seven-inch ivory tooth a man is being led across a river under the watchful eyes of two angels, a fairly common religious theme. Church groups and charitable organizations such as the Sailor's Aid Societies often put Bibles and related reading matter on departing ships, especially if a captain's wife was accompanying her husband. The bark *Sunbeam* received one hundred books in 1904 from the New Bedford Port Society. It has been recorded that some whalers rested on the Sabbath, but generally when whales were spotted, it meant business and money—Sunday or not.

Historically, engraved teeth have been considered the most important form of scrimshaw. Obviously, there are large differences in quality. Some have simple outline drawing, while others, such as this one, have intricate shading. There are some examples that are engraved on both sides. The use of color is rare, so most engraving is highlighted with diluted lamp black, soot from try pots, tar, or, if lucky, India ink. Tobacco juice, leaving a sepia tone, was occasionally applied. After excess coloring was wiped away, the tooth was given a high sheen by rubbing it vigorously with a cloth dabbed with oil, wax, or ashes. Oils from the palm of the sailor's hands were also often effective as a polishing agent.

TOOTH, WIFE AND CHILDREN,
c. 1850, ivory, coloring,
H. 2", W. 3", L. 7". (Peabody Essex Museum)

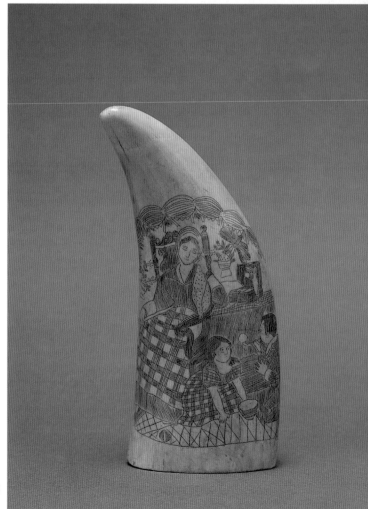

This ivory whale's tooth, decorated on only one side, depicts a faithful wife and her two children, who are blowing soap bubbles. Museum records at the time of its purchase in 1909 state that the tooth was the work of a sailor on a whaling voyage about 1850. As with most incised teeth, this scrimshaw is strictly ornamental and reflects the whaleman's longing for his home life. Multiple portraits on scrimshaw are rare, thus giving this piece added interest. Sometimes the scrimshander drew freehand, but usually he borrowed an image from a magazine and transferred it onto the tooth by the pin-prick method. The picture would be securely attached to the tooth by the whaleman, and with a sail needle or similar device he would puncture the image through the paper onto the ivory. To avoid the dots being seen, the transfer process had to be done lightly. An alternative method of transferring a picture was to prick only the paper, and then use pencil dots to transfer it to the tooth. *The New York Weekly, Fireside Companion, Harper's Weekly,* and *Godey's Lady's Book* all had printed illustrations and were frequently seen on board whaling vessels. Proof of this is found in a letter to the editor in *Godey's* from a seaman telling of an 1844 whaling voyage on the *N. P. Talmage.* Somewhere near the Aleutian Islands they met the ship *Alert* of New London, Connecticut, and reading material was exchanged. When looking through the new batch of magazines, the seaman found a copy of *Godey's* that duplicated one he had just traded.

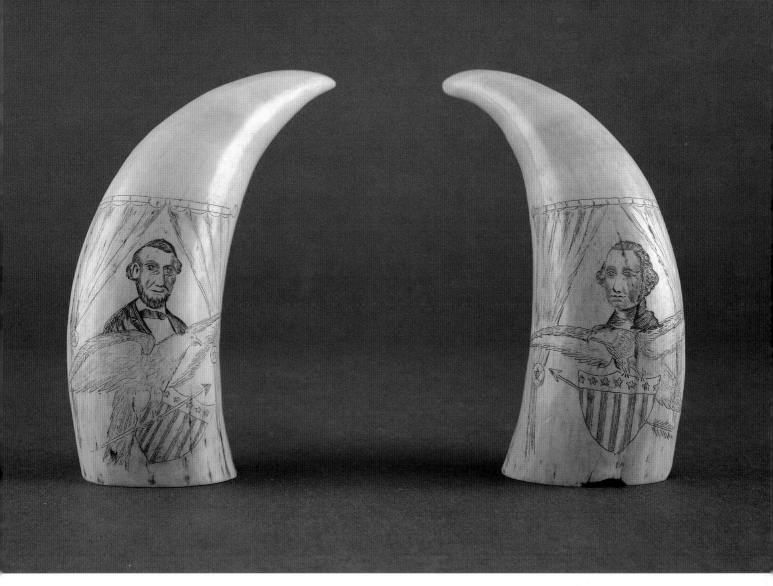

TOOTH, LINCOLN,
ivory, black coloring,
H. 5⅝", W. 2½", L. 6¼". (New Bedford Whaling Museum)

TOOTH, WASHINGTON,
ivory, black coloring,
H. 5⅝", W. 2½", L. 6¼". (New Bedford Whaling Museum)

Scrimshaw abounds with the human figure—historic, symbolic, or simply generic. Such portraits were engraved on teeth either freehand or by some method of transferring the image. George Washington and Abraham Lincoln were exceedingly popular motifs in all the folk, commercial, and fine arts. National pride surged at the time of Washington's death in 1799 and again following the War of 1812. Washington's popularity as a patriotic symbol was exceeded only by that of the eagle. Portraits of Lincoln surged after his assassination in 1865 because the public now thought of him as a martyr who deserved both compassion and dignity. This pair of teeth, with their crude freehand portraits, are obviously by the same scrimshander, both having the divided curtain backdrop, the spread-winged American eagle, and a patriotic shield. The eagle accompanying Lincoln is perched on an arrow, while the one with Washington sits atop the shield. Scrimshawed portraits of both these presidents were in the collection of yet another United States president, John F. Kennedy.

13

CHAPTER TWO

For Use on Board

There was no mistaking a whaling vessel. Their square lines and work-blackened sails, the men on lookout atop the masts, the three to six boats dangling from davits, the tryworks on deck, and cutting-in accouterments all gave it a very distinctive appearance. The two main types, the "bark" and the larger and sturdier "ship," were both three-masted, but had different rigging. At deck level they ranged from 95 to 120 feet in length and were designed wide in the beam to accommodate the storage of barrels. This width also gave the ship equilibrium during the time of "cutting in," the label given to the process of getting the fat off of the whale's body. The hanging boats, when lowered, were the craft that actually pursued the prey. Headed by one of the mates, they measured from twenty-eight to thirty feet long and were six feet wide—large enough to hold the oarsmen, a harpooner, lancer, and all the accompanying equipment.

Life on board a whaler was not pleasant. The captain had it best, of course. The mates or officers, along with those hired to perform special tasks, such as the cooper or carpenter, had separate or shared quarters less commodious than the captain's. The foremast hands or seamen, either with experience or greenhands with no experience, were condemned to the forecastle or fo'c'sle, where twelve to twenty men slept on crude double-decker bunks in a very small space with minimal light or ventilation, which came from the single hatch that also provided the fo'c'sle's only method of entrance or exit. Outfitting the ship for a three- or four-year sojourn was comparable to providing minimal housing, except that all the needs of the fishery had also to be included. In remote waters replacement of equipment vital to the success of the voyage was nearly impossible.

However, whalemen were innately resourceful. They had to wear many hats, depending on the needs of the day, and as a result of necessity scrimshaw played an important role on the ship. In fact, the objects comprising utilitarian scrimshaw are larger in both number and variety than the more famous engraved teeth.

Scrimshanders made almost every type of tool or item needed on board the whaling ship. The sailmaker's fids, thimbles, awls, and grease cups, and a vast array of carpenter's tools could all be scrimshawed, and they are now considered important talismans of the past.

It is necessary to look at extant pieces to try to determine their function. Disuse has already meant loss of identity and purpose for some objects, but initial research and what can be built upon it can lead to proper identification and classification.

What steps can be taken toward identification? First determine what the object had to do with the history of whaling. Is it complete, or is it broken or only half-made? Who used it and for what purpose? Eliminate unlikely possibilities. Check for patents and patent numbers. Most pieces will not be dated or signed because the makers felt that was totally unnecessary. This information may lead to an educated guess that allows the researcher then to evaluate the success of its design, balance of parts, function, and even adaptation from the norm. The patina of the object indicates the degree of its use.

Tools, as Henry Ward Beecher said, are an extension of the user's hands. They are the conversion of raw material into useful items that supplement human energy and reduce the time factor. They help to accomplish something and are an indispensable ingredient of progress.

The first tools, dating some two-and-one-half million years ago, were made of bone and antler, which is analogous to the creation of scrimshaw tools. They were hand tools requiring muscle power for use. Then came stone and wood implements, followed by metal hand tools, some of which required animal power. Workers designed their own tools to fill their needs, whether it was chopping, sawing, slicing, drilling, boring, scraping, holding, or measuring. These tools were personal items, even when the time came that the metal parts were purchased. Great care was given to the handle and the assemblage of the parts. Individualism was maintained. This factor remained as specialization appeared. Early on, all people working in wood, regardless of the final product, used the same tools, but when specific items for specialized tasks came into being, the creator still customized the handle to the fit of his hand. Because the tool was meant to produce only one thing at a time there was pride in both the tool and the work. By the mid-nineteenth century, mass production began creeping in and all was soon to change. In 1850, productive energy came from three sources: manpower supplied 23%; animal power 51%; and mechanical power 26%.

On the whaler, however, manpower remained supreme, for many things were still handmade, many of them out of necessity. Scrimshawed objects were being produced by the whalemen specifically for outfitting the ship, for pursuit of the whale, and for use of the men while on board. These utilitarian pieces were all devised without the advantage of having on hand all the necessary materials and tools. As the scrimshan-

der's skills and dexterity improved, he learned to deal with the materials available on board and thus create mostly unornamented tools for a variety of purposes ranging from repairs to needlework.

Ivory and bone were by-products of the whale and were what was available for use. These materials cost nothing, were plentiful, and had the strength and durability necessary for many tools and ship paraphernalia. This was particularly true when the material was freshly fashioned. Utilitarian objects like handles and blocks were cut and formed from both ivory and panbone, whether combined with metal and wood or by itself. Bone from the sperm whale was the only whalebone used as other types of bone were oily and porous.

Ivory and bone were also used to create personal things that sailors used on board. In fact, they were often the very tools needed to make scrimshaw. These men appreciated the "feel" or "heft" of the material. The clean, honest lines of these simple well-proportioned tools make these objects a form of marine folk art that is much valued today.

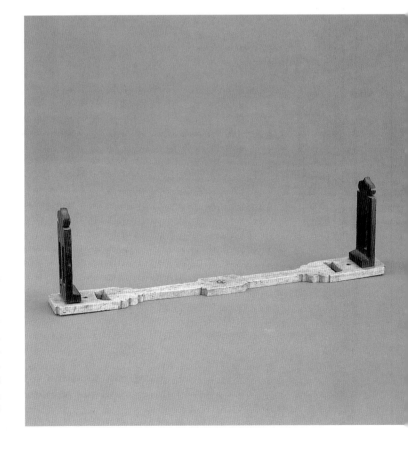

PELORUS,
whale skeletal bone, wood, non-ferrous metal, pins,
H. 4⁹/₁₆", W. 1⁵/₈", L. 15¹/₁₆". (The Kendall Whaling Museum)

Another name for the pelorus was the dumb compass. This was a tool that could be purchased, but it was also easily homemade. Intended to measure the direction of objects from the ship, the pelorus was used when sightings across the compass were impossible because of some sort of obstruction. This instrument, which could be rotated to a desired position and clamped into place, had sight vanes and a compass card, both of which could also be clamped into a fixed position. The pelorus would be set so that 0 degrees was dead ahead either over or parallel to the center of the ship. When these directions were measured they were called relative bearings and could thus be converted to compass directions or bearings.

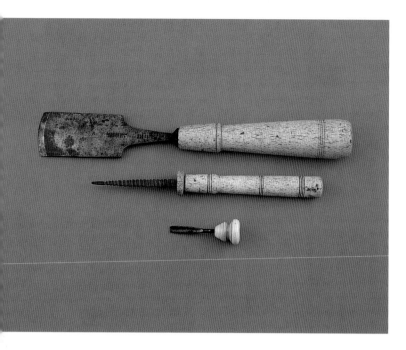

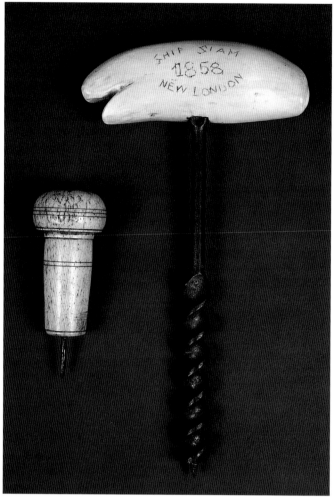

CHISEL,
whale skeletal bone, steel,
H. 1¹/₁₆", W. 2", L. 14¹/₁₆". (The Kendall Whaling Museum)

FILE,
whale skeletal bone, steel,
H. 1¹/₁₆", W. 1¹/₁₆", L. 10¹/₄". (The Kendall Whaling Museum)

GOUGE,
sperm-whale ivory, steel,
H. 1¹/₁₆", W. 1¹/₁₆", L. 3¹/₈". (The Kendall Whaling Museum)

A tool that was basically used for wood carving, the chisel was often employed to smooth the initial rough shaping done by a gouge. The mostly rectangular blade had a sharp, straight cutting edge that came in many widths. Wood was cut, pared, or separated by hitting the top or by applying hand pressure to the top. This meant that handles were frequently damaged and needed replacements, which could either be bought or handmade, as is the case here. Again, those that were handmade were to a specific size and contour of the owner's dimensions. Like the file, the steel for the chisel was imported, this one having been made by Barton Bros. Sheffield Extra Carbonized Steel in England.

The file is an abrasive tool designed to reduce rough surfaces. The teeth were indented by a chisel before the metal was hardened. Those with ridges in only one direction, such as this example, were known as singlecut files, while those with double criss-crossed ridges were called doublecuts. There were five grades of cuts ranging from dead smooth to rough. An exterior with no cuts was called the safe side. Before 1862, this tool was either handmade or imported; after that they were manufactured in the United States.

The gouge, a member of the chisel family, is a carving tool with a curved cutting edge, called the sweep, at the end of the blade. The blades were usually short and had widths from 1/4" to 2". Shipwrights and wood turners used this instrument to cut or pare hollow and round surfaces that were usually ornamental. They were often sold without a handle in order that the owner could custom make one designed for his own grip.

AWL,
bone, metal,
L. 4", Diam. 1½". (Mystic Seaport Museum)

AUGER,
dated 1858, whale ivory, steel,
H. 1½", W. 5", L. 9¼". (Mystic Seaport Museum)

The awl was a tool used by the Vikings. The first white settlers in the New World found the American Indians using awls. Although it seems no more than a sharp point attached to a handle, the awl had specific uses. The primary one was to enter wood by spreading the fibers apart as opposed to cutting it, as an auger would. Secondly, it could mark a surface with guide lines, and it could be used for carving scrimshaw. Awls were also known as prickers. Its haft, for economic and convenient purposes, was easily replaceable because the metal prong, which incidentally was often known to be a pitchfork tine, was easily broken.

First used by the Romans and the Vikings, augers were carpenter's tools made to bore holes. The metal bit determined the size of the hole. The handle was known as the haft and with the bit formed a "T" to insure rotational leverage. Early augers were plain, but around 1800 the spiral or twist was invented in Connecticut. A third name for the spiral or twist was the screw. On board, this tool had many uses. The whale-shaped haft of this auger lets us know that it was used in 1858 on the ship *Siam* out of New London, Connecticut.

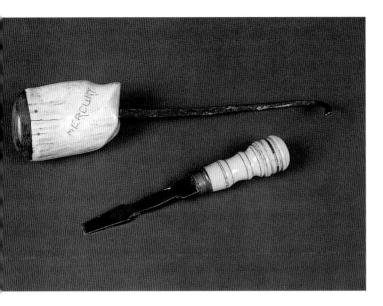

REEFING HOOK,
whale ivory, wood, metal,
H. 2⅛", W. 3¼", L. 9¼". (Mystic Seaport Museum)

SCREWDRIVER,
ivory, brass, steel, wax,
L. 6⅛", Diam. 1". (Mystic Seaport Museum)

Seams on wooden ships often needed recaulking. The first step in accomplishing this was to rake out the old caulking, a substance composed of oakum or old rope that had been picked apart and used as the sealer. The tool used for this cleaning was called a reefing hook, a rake, or a hoe. The reefing hook was usually handmade from an iron bar measuring 1/4" to 3/8" in diameter. The *Mercury*—the name inscribed on the haft—was probably one of two vessels so named that sailed in 1839 out of Stonington, Connecticut, or New Bedford, Massachusetts.

Until about 1812, a screwdriver was known as a turnscrew. This tool was, of course, primarily used to tighten or loosen a screw, but it was also used as a lever for other purposes. Round handles were the norm. This screwdriver may originally have been longer and was broken in use. When this happened the tool was shortened and a new handle was added; thus the reason for the scrimshaw addition.

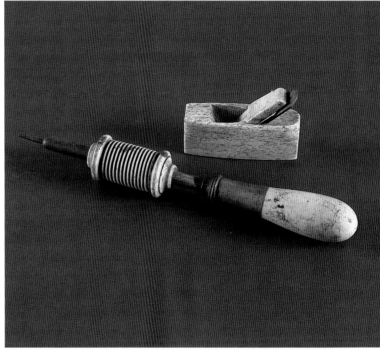

PLANE,
whalebone, metal,
H. 2¾", W. 1¼", L. 4¼". (Peabody Essex Museum)

BOW DRILL,
ivory, metal,
H. 1¾", W. 1¾", L. 12¼". (Peabody Essex Museum)

Invented by the Romans, the plane is a hand tool intended to smooth a surface by shaving it, or to reduce it in size, and also shape, fit, and finish an object. Specialized planes were also used for specific purposes by various trades, including shipwrights. This coffin-shaped bone instrument was known as a spar plane. Specifically designed for rounding and trimming masts, spars, and oars, it measured from 3 to 7 inches in length and could be guided with one hand. Commonly handmade, this scrimshawed tool helped replace many a whale-smashed oar.

The now obsolete bow drill dates back to the Bronze Age and is the oldest form of mechanical-drilling device. Also called a fiddle drill, this example has ivory replacement pieces, the original parts being either worn down or broken. To use this, one would also need a bow and bow string, with the string being wound around the cylindrical stock, which joined a steel rod that held the bit. While one hand held onto the head of the drill and pressed it down upon the work, the stock rotated the bit by means of the back and forth movement of the bow.

BOW SAW,
bone, metal,
H. 13½", W. 1¼", L. 23¼". (New Bedford Whaling Museum)

Bow saws, known in some quarters as turning or coping saws, are a
form of the frame saw. Commercial steel saws were not produced in
the United States until 1806, so until that time, and even after, bow
saws were ordinarily homemade. Coopers and carpenters knew that
with a bow saw you could always see what you were cutting, and that
it could saw both straight or round edges. The name for the bone
sides of this tool was "cheeks," and these cheeks held the blade, the
central bar, and the stretcher. The thin blade, also known as the web,
could be turned in other directions by moving the side handles. If
the blade needed to be tightened, the wing nut on the stretcher was
adjusted. When this nut was tightened, the lower end of the saw, the
part with the blade, was spread, forcing the blade to become inflex-
ible.

ADJUSTABLE THREAD DIE,
bone, bronze,
H. 4", W. ⅞", L. 12¼". (New Bedford Whaling Museum)

The adjustable thread die was a factory-made tool used to form threads on nuts and bolts. Originally, it was constructed by a blacksmith. The bronze mechanism of this example was geared to produce twelve threads to the inch on wire. The simple, well-balanced bone housing was undoubtedly a replacement for the original wooden one. The carver kept his decoration to a minimum with only minor symmetrical line scribing on each of the handles.

TRY SQUARE,
bone, black ink, copper,
H. ⅝", W. 8⅛", L. 12⅜". (New Bedford Whaling Museum)

This simple but aesthetically pleasing try square was intended for marking or checking lines or surfaces that had to be at right angles to each other. This happened when the end of a board, an edge, or a surface needed to be squared, or when the squareness of a planed or sanded piece needed checking. The try square has two legs set at a 90-degree angle to each other. The shorter of the two parts is called the stock or handle. The other, labeled the tongue or blade, was inserted into the stock. Most tongues have perforations or a rule to allow for marking or measuring. To allow for accurate measurements the tongue is left about half an inch out of the handle before the markings. Three well-placed diamond-shaped copper inlays cover rivets that hold the two scrimshaw parts firmly together. Try squares were made in various sizes.

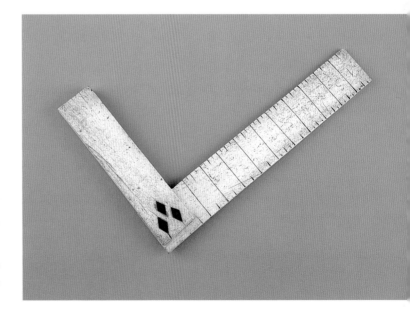

BEVEL GAUGE,
panbone, metal,
H. ¾", W. 1¼", L. 15¼". (Peabody Essex Museum)

Bevel gauges, such as this panbone example, are a type of square and range in size from seven inches to fifteen inches or longer. Shipwrights made use of the simple and often homemade tool to set a constant angle anywhere from 0 to 180 degrees; the exception was a 90-degree angle. The bevel gauge could transfer an angle in or on ships, which were renowned for their various unusual shapes and angles, especially in interior partitions. The wing nut at one end allows for a quick adjustment of the moveable blade, which, when tightened, keeps a locked position. The blade, or tongue, sets into the stock in a manner similar to that of a pen knife. Various sizes and forms of the bevel gauge would have been found in the shipwright's tool box.

MARKING WHEEL,
ivory, metal,
H. ½", W. ⅞", L. 5". (New Bedford Whaling Museum)

Dressmakers, who work with patterns, will recognize this tool right away. Sailmakers also used a marking wheel in preparing canvas to be made into sails. The scoring gauge or wheel marks the outline of the piece to be cut by leaving small nicks on the fabric. The scrimshawed handle has simple but effective turning and scribing that does not interfere with the strong hand grip. The ogee-shaped finial at the end is evidence of the scrimshander's expertise. This is an excellent example of decorative work enhancing the look of a utilitarian object.

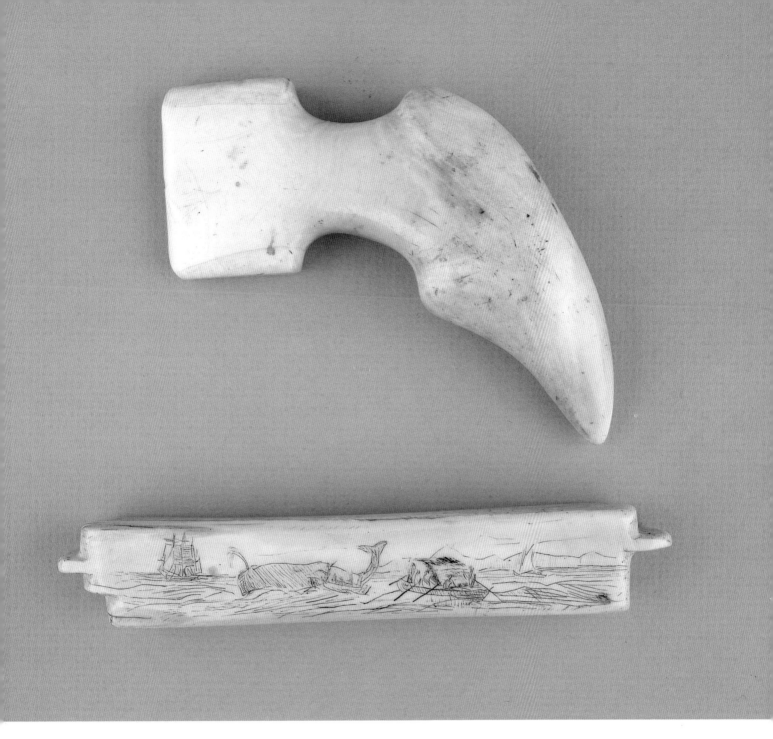

SEAM RUBBER,
ivory,
H. 1¼", W. 5", L. 4". (Peabody Essex Museum)

GAUGED SEAM RUBBER,
ivory, coloring,
H. 1", W. 1", L. 6½". (Peabody Essex Museum)

A sailmaker's tool, the seam rubber was usually handmade and was always made in one piece, whether it was made of ivory, like this one, or of a dense hardwood. The natural shape of the tooth's tip makes an efficient handle for the spade-shaped blade. Additional names for this instrument are sail smoother, creaser, press, liner, and marker. Thrifty captains, who did not want the cost of new sails taken out of their lay, insisted on patching worn-out or torn canvas sails. When two pieces of canvas were joined the seams were about one inch wide, which explains the two-inch width of the rubber's blade. Even before the sewing took place, the seaman would rub down the canvas with this implement to give a sharp fold. The seams were generally sewn twice, with the selvage of one piece sewn to the edge of the other. It would then be folded to the desired width and pressed once more. Turned over, the seam would be sewn on the second side and pressed yet again. The mender would press and rub away from himself the waxed twin stitches to attain the desired flatness and smoothness. The two notches on the ivory gauged rubber with the engraved whaling scene are intended for different widths in the canvas folds. Judging by the number of seam rubbers that have survived, it seems evident that the whale's-tooth seam rubber was the more popular type of the two shown.

NEEDLE CASE,
bone, cork,
H. 1", W. 1", L. 5". (Peabody Essex Museum)

GREASE CUP,
ivory, wax, metal, string, leather,
H. 6", W. 2½", L. 2½". (Peabody Essex Museum)

Needle cases, such as this one with its cork stopper, were ideal for storing sewing needles when not in use. Most were cylindrical with a simple design similar to the ring turning seen here. The cork ensured a tight closure to prevent the salt air from intruding. This style remained common throughout the nineteenth century. Needles for both personal and professional use would be kept in this scrimshaw container. Larger versions held pencils or knitting needles.

The horn grease cup held and protected needles while the sails were being made or repaired. Holding square or triangular pointed needles for sailmaking or larger ones for sewing a rope to the edge of a sail, this container was attached to the seaman's belt for easy access. Its inner bottom contained either a dollop of wax or oil-soaked wadding to keep the needles in place and to prevent the ends from rusting.

ROPE WINDER,
wood, panbone, rope,
H. 25", W. 13", L. 10". (Peabody Essex Museum)

The most important gear on a whaleboat was the manila-hemp rope. This three-stranded line, which had a thickness of up to three quarters of an inch, was half again as strong as ordinary rope of the same size. Although it was light in weight it had to carry a 200-pound strain throughout, for if just one inch was weak, it could mean losing the whale. In the marine world this rope was considered the best, with each strand having seventeen yarns. Every whaleboat contained two tubs of this spirally coiled line, each measuring over 200 fathoms or 1,200 feet in length. The rope ran out very rapidly once the harpoon to which it was attached struck the whale. The light weight of this rope helped to prevent tangles—tangles that could mean the loss of limbs or life.

Rope often had to be remade to suit the various needs of the ship, and this panbone-and-wood rope winder, which was made on board an unidentified vessel, helped do just that. Individual strands of the rope were attached to the panbone rods, and when these rods were turned by the handle, they would twist the strands into a length of rope. Old rope was untwisted by a reverse cranking, and then it would be used as oakum, the name of unraveled rope used for caulking seams. Machine-made rope became available in the nineteenth century, which made the rope winder obsolete, for an even stronger and more reliable type of rope was produced.

SERVING MALLET,
panbone,
H. 2", W. 1", L. 6½". (Peabody Essex Museum)

With a name like serving mallet one might expect that this piece of panbone scrimshaw would have something to do with food, but that is not the case. A serving mallet was involved in the final step of a three-step process that protects rope from chafing against the vessel or another rope, and guards it against wear and weather. The first step, called worming, filled the spiral grooves between the strands of the rope with spun yarn. This was followed by parceling, which wrapped the same piece of rope with strips of tarred canvas in an overlapping manner. Then followed the two-man job of serving or whipping the piece of rope, which was usually done with spun yarn. The mallet's rounded head has a concave groove along one side, which was carved to match the size of the rope. This groove was called the score. While one man held the yarn and gave the rope the initial wrapping, the second man tightened the yarn by revolving the mallet around the rope. This process was called riding the rope, and it was often used to cover a splice in the rope.

FID,
1867–1871, whalebone,
H. 1¾", W. 1¾", L. 11¾". (Peabody Essex Museum)

FID,
1855, ivory,
H. 1", W. 1", L. 10½". (Peabody Essex Museum)

These carrot-shaped sailors' tools, usually made of a hardwood such as lignum vitae or bone, were strictly utilitarian and consequently have little decoration. Ranging in size from 8 inches to 20 inches or more, fids were employed for inserting thimbles into prepared rope, reaming out grommets, splicing rope, working knots, and for opening holes in a canvas sail because sailmakers preferred spreading the threads of the canvas rather than cutting a hole in it. The point of the fid, which could not be too sharp or it would snag the yarns, had to be protected, for if it became damaged a ragged point could ruin a sail by catching or tearing it. Thus a smooth surface was most important. Fids were stored in a rack that allowed the implements to hang through holes, but not permitting the points to touch a surface. Fids like these two were most often handmade and therefore individualized. The scrimshander of the lower one inscribed it with the date 1855 and some linear decoration. The whalebone, round-capped fid came from the bark *Said Bin Sultan*, which sailed out of Salem in 1867. This vessel was named after the ruler of Omar and Zanzibar who favored trade with the West, particularly the United States, with which he signed a treaty of amity and commerce in 1833.

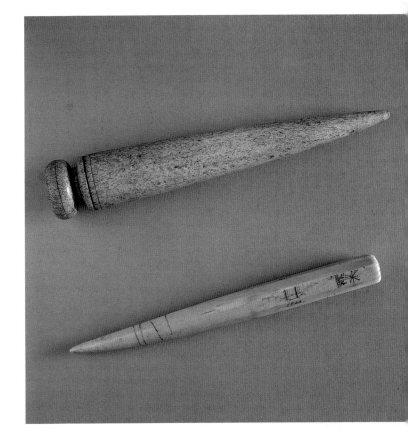

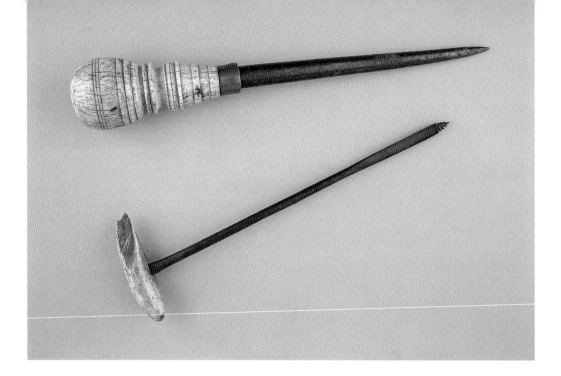

MARLIN SPIKE,
panbone, metal,
H. 1¾", W. 1¾", L. 11". (Peabody Essex Museum)

GIMLET,
bone, metal,
H. 1", W. 3", L. 9½". (Peabody Essex Museum)

A marlin spike is a metal version of a fid, but a marlin spike should not be confused with the smaller sail pricker. A tool of the rigger, as opposed to the sailmaker who used a fid, a marlin spike had a longer round head upon which to pound an iron or steel shaft that tapered to a point. The head on this example is handsomely turned and is panbone. The marlin spike was used to open parts of rope for splicing, to penetrate twists on strands for knotting, and acted as a lever in tightening the seizings on the shrouds and clues of sails. Sizes of this tool varied greatly from six to twenty-four inches.

The common ship's gimlet was designed for making small holes or for starting holes for wooden screws. This gimlet, with its ivory-tooth handle, is typical of the T-shaped boring tool. Although this example measures only nine and one-half inches in length, others were known to measure over three feet. In diameter, the shaft with its spiral twist at the tip is one of the smallest boring tools. Because of its length and small diameter the shaft often broke.

BELAYING PIN,
panbone,
H. 1½", W. 1½", L. 14½". (Peabody Essex Museum)

Belaying pins, such as this typical panbone example, were a portable implement designed as a substitute for a cleat and meant to secure a rope in the ship's rigging by means of wrapping an S-turn around it. Each pin, whether on board a whale boat or the mother ship, was earmarked for a particular rope. A long narrow board with a line of holes drilled into it was secured inside the gunwale opposite each mast. This was called a fife, and belaying pins were placed in these holes. The size of the belaying pin, which could be as long as twenty inches, depended on the amount of coil to be hung from it. Made of wood, bone, or metal, the pin had a raised, carved section near the center to prevent the tool from slipping through the fife. Rounded at the top, the pin tapered slightly to an almost flat bottom. Besides their maritime function belaying pins were also handy for making one's point in a fight.

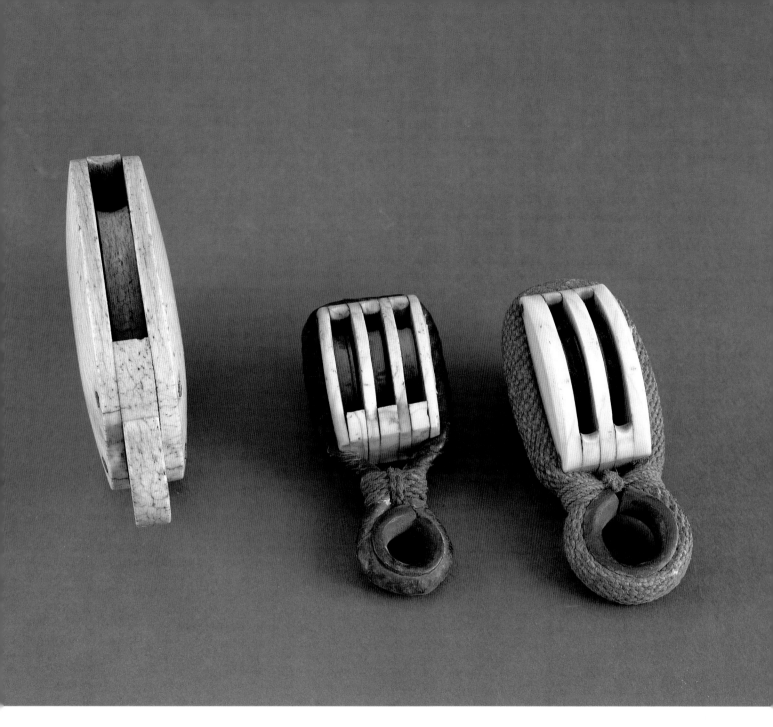

SINGLE BLOCK,
bone, metal,
H. 1¼", W. 3¼", L. 6". (New Bedford Whaling Museum)

TRIPLE BLOCK,
ivory, metal, leather, rope,
H. 2", W. 2¼", L. 4½". (New Bedford Whaling Museum)

DOUBLE BLOCK,
ivory, metal, rope,
H. 1¾", W. 2¼", L. 4¾". (New Bedford Whaling Museum)

Blocks, which were common working implements on whaling vessels, amplified the mechanized strength of the lines being used. These blocks were visible on masts, yards, sails, and elsewhere in the rigging. Only three of the many sizes and shapes of blocks are illus-trated here. The single, double, and threefold examples shown are all "made" blocks, meaning that they are composed of several pieces, while "mortised" blocks are carved from one piece. Any specialty blocks also had to be handmade. The wheel inside the block is called the sheave, and its concave outer rim is known as the score of the sheave. The wide, exterior planes, here not plainly visible, on the block's left and right sides are labeled the cheeks. These cheeks have a center hole that holds the third major part of the block—the pin, which runs through both the sheave and the outside shell. Whether the block has one, two, three, or more sheaves, they all turn on this one pin or axis. The pin, shell, and sheave in turn are all bound in place by a rope or wreath that fits securely into an indentation (not seen here), and connects to a rope ring called the block strop. The latter is seen on two of these blocks and is the means by which they can be hung. Ivory and bone blocks were actually used on whaling vessels.

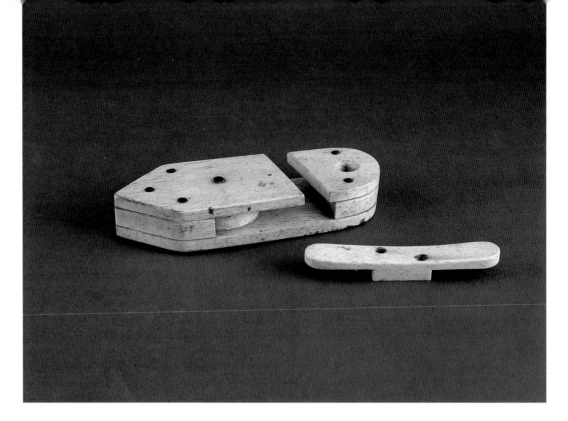

SNATCH BLOCK,
bone, metal,
H. 1½", W. 3", L. 9¼". (New Bedford Whaling Museum)

CLEAT,
bone,
H. ¹¹/₁₆", W. ¹⁵/₁₆", L. 6¼". (New Bedford Whaling Museum)

Like all blocks, the snatch block was a form of pulley. Whalebone examples held together with metal rivets, such as this one, were actually used on whale ships. Unlike single, double, or triple blocks, a snatch block has an opening on one side. This is where the bight or loop in a rope, as opposed to the tail end, was occasionally fixed.

The purpose of a cleat was to secure any variety of ropes on board a sailing vessel. Lines could be hitched to a cleat whether it was attached to the ship vertically or horizontally. Older cleats can be dated because they have a more pronounced curve in the arms. Those made before the nineteenth century were nailed or bolted down but after the invention of the screw, cleats were screwed into a base. Although most cleats have two arms, one-armed versions were also made.

THIMBLE EYE,
whalebone, rope,
H. 1", W. 3", L. 3¼". (Peabody Essex Museum)

Some refer to this rope-strapped whalebone thimble eye as a rigging eye. Most were constructed of iron but on all of them, the iron or whalebone was hollowed on the outer surface to hold rope. The roping is prepared first, greased with tallow, and then with the aid of a fid the eye is inserted. It was imperative for the rope to fit snugly, for this scrimshawed implement was used in rigging and mooring lines. A shackle may be placed through the thimble. A thimble eye prevented rope from swinging too far from its center of action, or it acted as a guide for a rope. Thimble eyes were also seen on a whaleboat's backstay lashing.

26

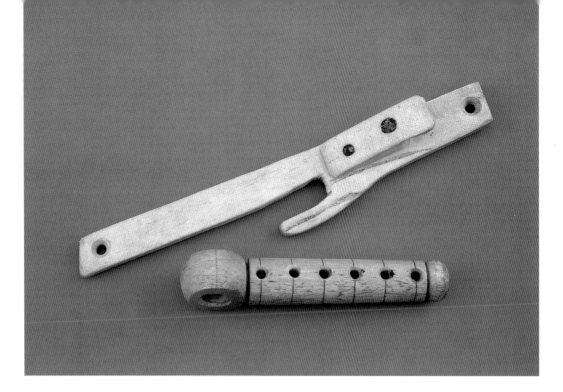

SNOTTER RELATED,
whale skeletal bone, copper,
H. 1", W. 1¹¹/₁₆", L. 10¹/₈". (The Kendall Whaling Museum)

EPHROE BLOCK,
whale skeletal bone,
H. 1', W. 1⁷/₁₆", L. 6". (The Kendall Whaling Museum)

The long, odd-shaped implement is affiliated with a snotter, but is not a snotter itself. Because of its small size, it would have been used on a whaleboat rather than the ship. Secured to the upper portion of a mast, this would have held the snotter and prevented it from slipping downward. The snotter was a short piece of rope with an eye end that was intended to receive the lower end of the sprit and keep it in place.

Now obsolete, the ephroe block, which was usually made of wood, had a series of holes set in a line that extended the edge of an awning. The large swiveling top hole was used for securing the piece to a permanent part of the ship. Thin lines were inserted through the smaller holes and the two ends of each of these lines extended to the awning, the top lines extending to the farthest point and the lowest lines going to the closest points. Ephroe blocks also stretched standing ends of running rigging.

HARPOON TOGGLE PATTERN,
after 1848, bone, brass,
H. 5⁵/₈", W. 1³/₈", D. ¹¹/₁₆". (Mystic Seaport Museum)

SWIVEL,
ivory, metal,
L. 2³/₄", Diam. ⁷/₈". (Mystic Seaport Museum)

Both of these small scrimshawed objects had definite functions for the whaler. The pointed device is a pattern for a harpoon toggle. The toggle itself was invented in the 1840s by a black whalecraft maker named Lewis Temple. His idea was to have a harpoon that entered the whale more easily, and when it was sufficiently in the animal the detachable, hinged head or toggle would, under stress, turn at a right angle to the shank of the harpoon. Consequently, the harpoon would more likely hold fast to the whale. Many such toggles would be needed during the course of the hunt, thus making this bone pattern a necessary and much appreciated item.

The ivory swivel would have most probably been used in the rigging. The two links fit together in such a way that the two lines or ropes tied to either end could turn freely and independently, thus helping to prevent kinks in the line.

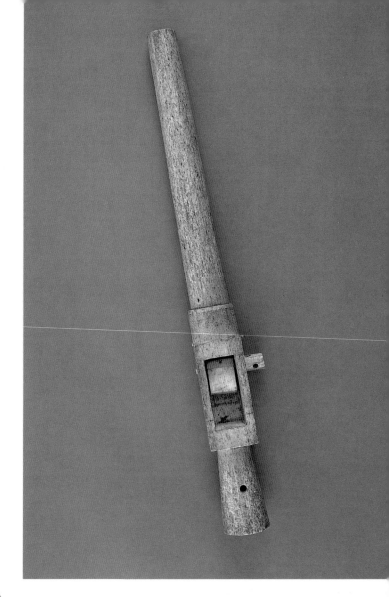

MODEL OF A DARTING GUN,
bone,
H. 1¹/₂", W. 2", L. 14⁵/₈". (New Bedford Whaling Museum)

The panbone model of a darting gun shown here may have been made by its inventor, Eben Pierce, a New Bedford man who patented this device in 1865 and began manufacturing it in 1873. The darting gun was mounted on a harpoon and when it entered the whale far enough, a mechanism went off that triggered an explosion that killed the whale. The harpoon and the gun were then released and reeled in by the lanyard attached to the gun. Used primarily in Arctic waters, the darting gun made ice whaling much more feasible because when an ordinary harpoon struck the whale, the animal would often disappear under the ice, never to be found. The explosive device in the darting gun killed the whale before it could swim under the ice.

HOOPS,
bone, copper,
H. ⁵/₈", Diam. 6⁵/₈"; H. ⁵/₈", Diam. 6¹/₁₆"; H. ⁵/₈", Diam. 6¹³/₁₆". (New Bedford Whaling Museum)

CHOCK PINS,
bone,
H. ⁷/₁₆", W. ¹¹/₁₆", L. 7³/₄"; H. ⁷/₁₆", W. ¹¹/₁₆", L. 7⁹/₁₆". (New Bedford Whaling Museum)

These diminutive hoops most likely are ryers, also spelled wryers, intended for casks six to eight inches in diameter that were stored in the areas between larger casks. It is also possible that these hoops were used on a gaff-rigged vessel to guide the ropes when sails were being furled or rolled up.

There is no doubt about the purpose of chock pins. They were a safety device used in the prow of whale boats. The harpoon line ran from its tub up the center of the boat to a leaded groove in the bow that was called the chock. Once through the chock the line came back to the harpoon held in the hand of the whaler. To keep the line from jumping the chock, chock pins were inserted over this line to keep it in place. Despite this precaution, many lives were lost when flying harpoon lines unexpectedly entangled a whaleman and pulled him into the sea.

Miniature chock pins were worn by proud harpooners who wanted the world at large to know just what position they held while at sea. On Nantucket, desirable and eligible maidens looked down on seamen who had not earned the right to wear such miniature pins.

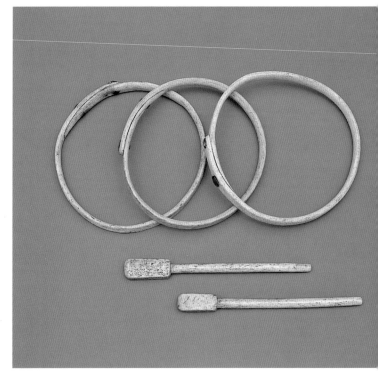

COOPER'S CROZE,
bone, copper,
H. 2⁷/₈", W. 4⁵/₈", L. 6". (Mystic Seaport Museum)

No whaling vessel left port without a cooper on board, for he had the unending task of making and mending casks, which were filled with supplies outbound and were refilled with whale oil on the return. In an industry where leakage could be costly, it comes as no surprise then that the cooper commanded a substantial lay.

The cooper's croze made a groove on the inner side of a barrel's staves. This groove was cut at a designated spot near the end of the staves and was meant to hold the head of the cask. The nail-like piece or cutting part, called the croze iron, was fitted into the top of the long stem, known also as the post. This vertically adjustable post was secured to the semicircular portion of the tool by means of a wedge that allowed for various distances between the croze groove and the end of the stave. Thus when the tool is turned along the inside of the staves a groove is made. The size of the croze depended on the size of the barrel. Few coopers had the luxury of owning a scrimshaw croze like this one, which may well have been a replacement for a broken croze.

CASK-MARKING TOOL,
ivory, ink, metal,
L. ⁷/₈", W. 1⁵/₈", L. 6". (New Bedford Whaling Museum)

Because of the value of the whale oil they held, casks were made of the very best materials. Their sizes were adapted to conform to the dimensions of the vessel's hold. When the ship was heading out to sea, these casks often held drinking water. Leakage meant that repairs and adjustments were often necessary. The cask-marking tool was employed both in the making and repairing of the oil barrels. This instrument allowed the cooper to scribe a line with the sharp spur that was parallel to the edge of a stay or head. While one part of the instrument rode along the edge, the cooper would push down on the tool, thus leaving the mark at the prescribed distance. This non-adjustable cask-marking tool belonged to Gibbs and Jenney, ship owners operating out of Fairhaven, Massachusetts. In 1860, one of their fleet, the *Syren Queen,* lost five men to scurvy on a voyage to the Davis Strait in the North Atlantic.

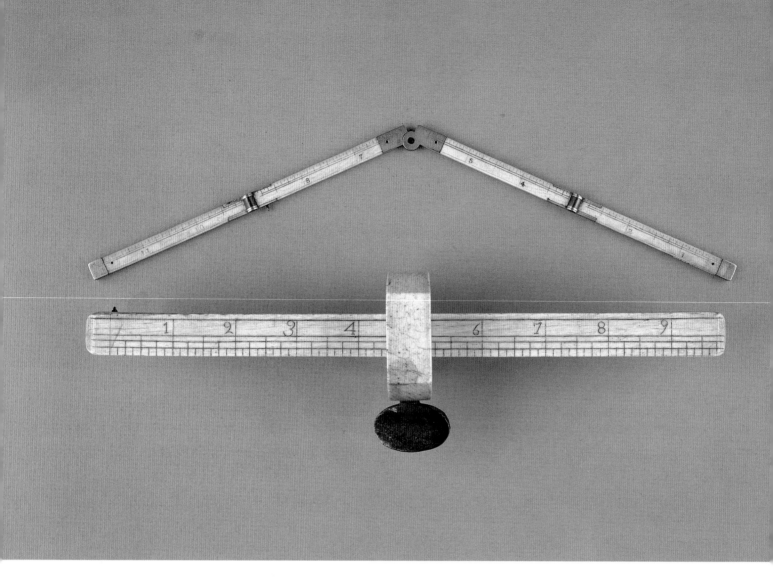

FOLDING RULE,
ivory, metal, coloring,
H. 1¹/₂", W. ¹/₄", L. 12". (Peabody Essex Museum)

MORTISE GAUGE,
panbone, iron, coloring,
H. 3", W. 3", L. 10". (Peabody Essex Museum)

The twelve-inch ivory hinged rule is a fine example of utilitarian scrimshaw. The metal fittings at specified intervals allow the ruler to fold for easy storage. On board a ship, where space was always at a premium, a folding rule was a definite asset. Traditionally, these rules were constructed of boxwood, but this scrimshander ably substituted ivory. Note the difference in coloration between the ivory of this rule and the panbone used in the mortise gauge.

This scrimshawed panbone mortise gauge with its iron thumbscrew is just one of many types of existing gauges. The ship's cooper manipulated this tool to mark two parallel lines at either end of a barrel where a top and bottom were to be inserted. The slide adjusts to the proper distance desired from the end of the staves; then the thumbscrew would be tightened to insure accuracy. The mortise gauge would be turned around the inside of the end of the staves, where its projecting spikes—hidden in this photograph—would leave the precise parallel lines. The marked space would then be hollowed out for the lids.

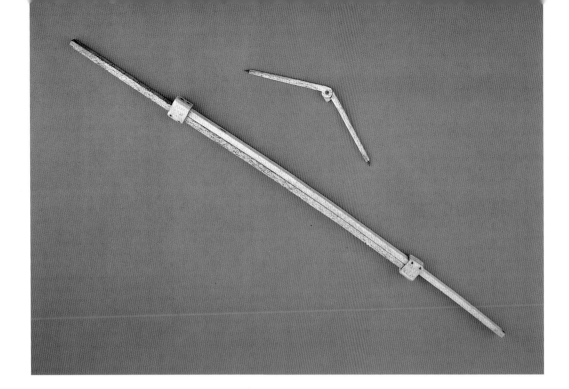

DIVIDERS,
whale skeletal bone, steel, copper,
H. ³/₁₀", W. ³/₄", L. 6¹/₈". (The Kendall Whaling Museum)

INSIDE MEASURING ROD,
1856, whale skeletal bone, walrus ivory, copper, black ink,
H. 1¹/₈", W. 1³/₈", L. 27³/₄", extends to 53¹/₈". (The Kendall Whaling Museum)

Although the proper name for this bone tool is a dividing compass, small examples were usually referred to as dividers. Consisting of two straight legs of equal length that were connected at one end by a movable joint, the main purpose of a divider was to take measurements and to scribe arcs and circles. Used by coopers, shipwrights,

and woodworkers, a dividing compass varied in size from five inches to twenty-four inches in length, with the large examples used for scribing the outline of a barrel head onto wood.

There are two types of inside measuring rods: the gauge rod for determining the number of gallons needed to fill an empty container, and a wantage rod for determining how many additional gallons are needed to fill a container. Wantage tools were employed in coopered barrels and this is a form of just such a tool. The barrel would be brought on deck and placed on its side so that the bung hole was on top. The rod would be inserted perpendicularly down to a point where the extension is just under the stave. When the rod was withdrawn from the barrel, it would be noted where the oil was highest on the rod, thus telling how much more was needed to fill the barrel.

STRAIGHT RAZOR,
whalebone, brass, metal,
H. ¹/₄", W. ³/₄", L. 8¹/₂". (Peabody Essex Museum)

SAILOR'S KNIFE,
whalebone, metal,
H. 1", W. 1", L. 7". (Peabody Essex Museum)

Both the straight razor and the sailor's knife pictured here would be well used, personal items. In both cases it is highly likely that both blades were contained in different cases when they were new. If the original case had been damaged or broken, a scrimshander would, rather than throw away the razor or knife, personalize the piece by carving a new covering. The straight razor, with its manufactured blade marked "of the best quality," has a replacement bone handle incised with decoration reminiscent of gentle ocean waves. The sailor's knife would most probably be on his person at all times, thus becoming almost an extension of the man. This whalebone handle with its incised crosshatching and diagonal slashes personalized and identified the owner. In addition to its usual purposes, sailor's knives were employed in eating, and were also the first tool used in scrimshawing. Both of these instruments show real signs of wear.

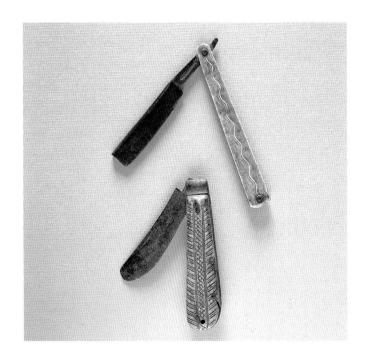

31

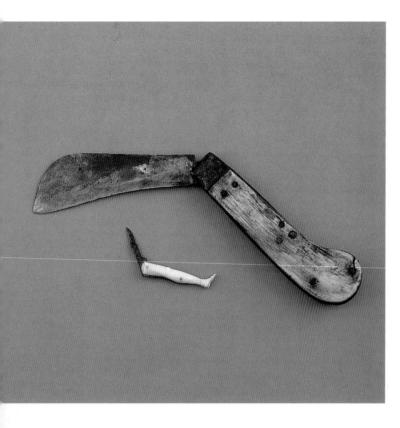

SAILOR'S CLASP KNIFE,
bone, steel,
H. $^{11}/_{16}$", W. $1^3/_8$", L. $8^5/_8$" when opened.
(The Kendall Whaling Museum)

PEN KNIFE,
walrus ivory, steel,
H. $^1/_4$", W. $^3/_8$", L. $2^{11}/_{16}$" when opened.
(The Kendall Whaling Museum)

It was assumed that every sailor carried his own clasp knife, the name for any knife with a blade that closed into the handle. This was a seaman's own personal possession. If lost, a new one could be purchased from the ship's store. In 1858, aboard the *Canton*, clasp knives cost fifty cents each even though the ship's owners purchased them for two dollars a dozen. Rarely considered a carpenter's tool, the clasp knife was employed on rope work, rigging, scrimshaw, and as a weapon.

This pen knife with its scrimshawed leg-shaped handle is a miniature version of the sailor's most common tool. As in the case of the clasp knife, the steel blade was probably imported, for American manufacturers could not compete with the Europeans, who had cheap access to the then-necessary hand labor needed for producing these knives.

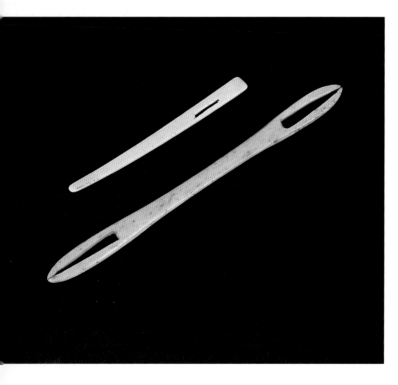

NETTING NEEDLE,
bone,
H. $^1/_{16}$", W. $^1/_4$", L. $3^1/_8$". (Mystic Seaport Musuem)

NETTING SHUTTLE,
bone,
H. $^3/_{32}$", W. $^3/_8$", L. $5^1/_8$". (Mystic Seaport Museum)

Netting predates nineteenth-century whalers by many centuries. Part of a sailor's equipment would be the tools for the making and mending of nets. Although this needle and this shuttle are bone, others were made from steel, wood, and ivory. Nets were inserted where a sail rubbed a mast or chafed against ropes. They were more commonly used under the bowsprit or in other spots where seamen might need to be caught if they fell. Obviously, then, these nets needed knots that were both firm and immovable. Their size and strength depended on their given purpose. The length of the needle depended on the coarseness and width of the piece being worked. The yarn would have been inserted through the hole in the needle and secured tightly. The shuttle would not have had yarn trailing behind it, for the yarn was wound around the body of the shuttle through its forked ends, thus enabling the yarn to be passed over, under, and around the netting without a chance of its tangling.

SEWING THIMBLE,
bone,
H. ⁷/₈", W. ³/₄", L. ³/₄". (Peabody Essex Museum)

In addition to the making and maintenance of sails, men on board whalers needed to sew in order to repair their worn or torn overalls, shoes, hammocks, or tobacco pouches. To replace the worn items with new ones from the ship's slop chest was too costly. Many seamen became quite adept at the art of sewing because, in part, it broke the monotony of the extended voyages. This bone tailor's thimble measures less than an inch long, but it was perfect for protecting the finger and for pushing the needle through fabric. Most thimbles made for men did not have the crown or cap. Thimbles were only one sewing implement made for use at sea. Scrimshanders also produced needle holders, spools, and ditty boxes, which held their sewing gear. One sailor's superstition held that sewing in the rain was a harbinger of continued foul weather.

PERSUADER,
Attributed to James Martin, 1864, walrus ivory, brass, wood,
H. 1⁵/₈", W. 2¹/₄", L. 16¹/₂". (Mystic Seaport Museum)

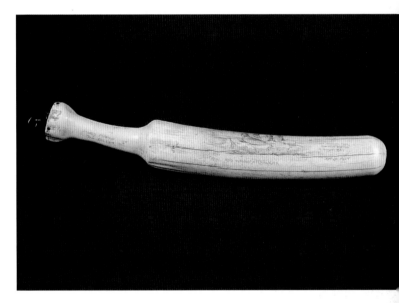

The inscription on this object tells us that it belonged to James Martin and was used during his 1864 voyage out of New Bedford, Massachusetts, to Hudson Bay on the ship *Morning Star*. For in addition to whale oil and baleen, some seamen pursued both the seal and the walrus while in the Arctic. The fur and the oil from these creatures were economic staples. This large club, called a persuader or a billet, was used to subdue the animal. Although a billet is usually a hardwood club, in this case it was scrimshawed from the tusk of a walrus.

LOG-BOOK STAMP,
sperm-whale ivory, residual black ink,
H. ⁹/₁₆", W. 1³/₁₆", L. 2⁵/₁₆". (The Kendall Whaling Museum)

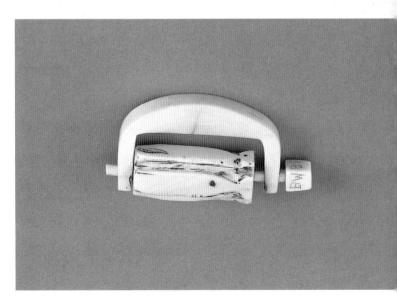

Included in the information placed in a ship's log book, which was usually kept by the first mate, was an account of whaling activity— how many whales were seen, how many captured, how many were lost or escaped, the amount of oil collected, dates and names of boats. This was done pictorially, using the whale form or parts of it to record the information. Some mates actually drew these pictures freehand, while others relied on a scrimshawed stamp made of ivory, wood, bone, or a combination of these materials. Stamps became popular and were also used to depict other things such as an anchor for a port made by the whaler, or a moon for sky watching. This rare, revolving, four-sided stamp on a C-clamp shape depicts four types of whales, with each identified by initials. Shown is a bowhead whale initialed BW. The other three images are the sperm whale labeled S, a finback with BF, and a humpback initialed BH.

FISH JIG,
ivory, lead, metal, cord,
H. 1 1/2", W. 2", L. 5 3/4". (Peabody Essex Museum)

If time allowed, and fish were on the run, whalemen often threw in a fishing line. The catch provided a pleasant relief from the diet of salt horse and beef or pork pickled in brine. This fish jig with its ivory shank was an adequate substitute for a rod and reel. The lead sinker attached to the cord served to give additional weight when cast out. It also ensured that the hook would turn upward when the fish was caught. Sometimes the line was on loan from the ship's carpenter, who had an entirely different use for it. He would apply chalk to the line and then stretch it between two points, securing it at both ends. When snapped against the surface, a corresponding straight line of chalk would thus be transferred, leaving a temporary straight line for the carpenter's use.

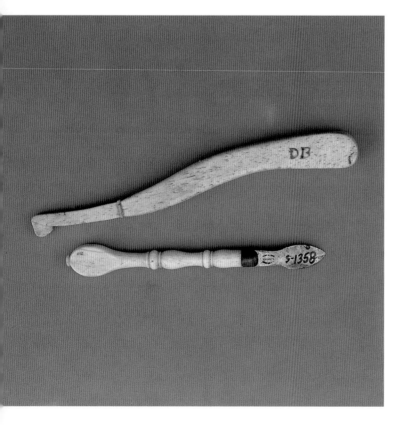

MACKEREL SPLITTER,
whale skeletal bone,
H. 7/16", W. 15/16", L. 7 3/16". (The Kendall Whaling Museum)

KNIFE ERASER,
c. 1859, bone, brass, steel,
H. 3/8", W. 3/4", L. 5 11/16". (The Kendall Whaling Museum)

When whalemen fished from their whale boats, they often caught different kinds of mackerel. It was after the catch that the mackerel splitter or split knife was put to work in a two-man operation. The seaman with the mackerel splitter would begin "dressing" the fish by splitting the fish down the back. A second man would clean out the gibs or entrails, rinse the fish in salt water to remove the blood, and then salt the catch before layering it in barrels. Lively conversation and song sometimes accompanied this operation that left the men with sore fingers and hands. This initialed tool does not have its cutting blade.

The knife eraser was also called an ink eraser or steel eraser. This tool eliminated mistakes and overrun lines whether drawn or written, for the steel tip scraped the ink off the paper. This tool was patented in March 1859.

LAP DESK,
ivory, ebony, metal, glass, fabric, wax inlay,
H. 3⁷/₈", W. 8⁵/₈", D. 14¹/₄". (Mystic Seaport Museum)

Space on board whaling vessels was always at a premium. The captain's quarters, though spacious by comparison with other living quarters on board, utilized all available space. If a desk was provided, it would have been set against an upright partition called the bulkhead, and this writing desk would have been placed upon it. Above the desk would have been a ship's compass so that the captain would know, even in his cabin, where his ship was headed.

This very elegant ebony and ivory portable lap desk could have been made by a whaling captain, or perhaps for a whaling captain by a mate or a seaman. The latter was often the case, since favors for the boss never hurt—even then. When the lid of the box was flipped back, it revealed a suitable writing area including ink bottles and spaces for quills and paper. The desk has particularly beautiful ivory inlay on the outer surfaces. Notice the patriotic escutcheon.

KNUCKLES,
bone,
H. 1⁷/₈", W. 2⁷/₈", L. 5¹/₄". (New Bedford Whaling Museum)

DAGGER WITH SHEATH,
bone, steel, twine.
Dagger: H. ³/₄", W. 1", L. 15".
Sheath: H. ¹/₂", W. ³/₄", L. 11¹/₄". (New Bedford Whaling Museum)

Some might think that the bone implement with four holes pictured here was a fairlead that was made to control lines running through the holes in order to keep them from going adrift and becoming confused with other lines. Because there is no opening at the base for attaching the piece to a mast or shroud, it is unlikely that it is a fairlead. It is probably a version of brass knuckles with the holes intended to hold four fingers. The rectangular base acted as a palm re-enforcement, thus strengthening the blow. These knuckles were carried by seamen to help protect them when they entered foreign ports. Being light and brittle, bone knuckles were not as effective as those made of brass.

A sheathed dagger was employed for both work and self-defense on board. Before 1866, it was part of the standard outfit for all foremast hands. Riggers wore them on their belts along with a marlin spike and a grease horn. Because these daggers were so often used as weapons, they were banned on board in 1866 to protect fellow seamen and their officers. Although this scrimshawed example is partially homemade, others were available from the ship's slop chest or store. In 1858, sheathed daggers sold for 25 cents aboard the ship *Canton*, double the cost that the owner had paid.

CAT-O-NINE-TAILS,
whale skeletal bone, twisted lines,
H. ⁷/₈", W. 1¹/₄", L. 32"; handle 12¹⁵/₁₆".
(The Kendall Whaling Museum)

On whaling ships, corporal punishment was the usual means of discipline. Although often just, brutality on board was almost universal. Lesser offenses resulted in being ironed, which meant being handcuffed with a stick tied across the mouth. Flogging was the worst punishment. Here a cat-o-nine-tails, commonly referred to as the cat, was put to a seaman's backside. Composed of nine strands of rope or leather knotted at the ends and tied to a handle of rope, wood, or bone, the cat's lashes were extremely painful. Although flogging was declared illegal on board United States whalers in 1850, it continued in lesser degrees through 1865 when it ceased altogether. Floggings were meticulously recorded in the log books, which noted both the number of lashes and a description of the cat-o-nine-tails. This was done as protection for the captain against any later legal action. Such legal action was the right of a flogged man, although the cards were usually stacked against him, for most lawyers he had access to would have been paid off by the captain.

BUCKET,
panbone, wood, paint, metal,
H. 18½", W. 12", L. 12". (Peabody Essex Museum)

This painted bucket from the bark *Lancer* with its panbone swing handle played a role in a maritime tradition. Few whalers took part in this tradition because holidays and special occasions were rarely observed on whaling vessels. It was always up to the captain whether the custom of "crossing the line" was observed. For those seamen who had never crossed the equator, "crossing the line" was a rite of passage from "greenhand" to "old salt." The implements needed to become a Son of Neptune were a bucket, a speaking trumpet, an oversized wooden razor, and a porpoise fork. The initiation would be performed by the crew and overseen by the captain and his mates. All greenhands would be locked in the forecastle until Neptune arrived, at which time they were introduced and returned to the forecastle. Then, blindfolded, they would be brought forth one by one and be seated, and then a piece of wood covered with tar and grease was forced into the mouth of each. When Neptune, holding the porpoise fork, asked each man's name, a speaking trumpet would replace the wood, but it would have been filled with sea water. After having answered three inane questions affirmatively, the grease and tar would be shaved off their faces with the wooden razor. This would be followed by a dunking in salt water. After shaking hands with Neptune, the greenhands were now considered part of the brotherhood of sailors.

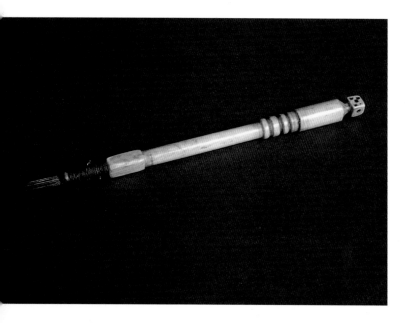

TATTOO NEEDLE,
ivory, steel, coloring, twine,
L. 6", Diam. ³/₈". (Mystic Seaport Museum)

Examples of tattooing are known to date as far back as Ancient Egypt, but it was not until the late-eighteenth and early-nineteenth centuries that Europeans and Americans became fascinated by tattoos. Sailors and adventurers to eastern and southeastern Asia and Oceania were the first to sport tattoos in our society. Tattoos soon became a rite of entry into manhood or an emblem of accomplishment. A full-rigged ship decorating a sailor's arm in the nineteenth century signified that he had sailed around the fearsome Cape Horn at the bottom of South America.

It is possible that the scrimshander who carved this piece was also a tattoo artist. The gaming die on the finial of this eight-needled instrument was also seen in tattoo art.

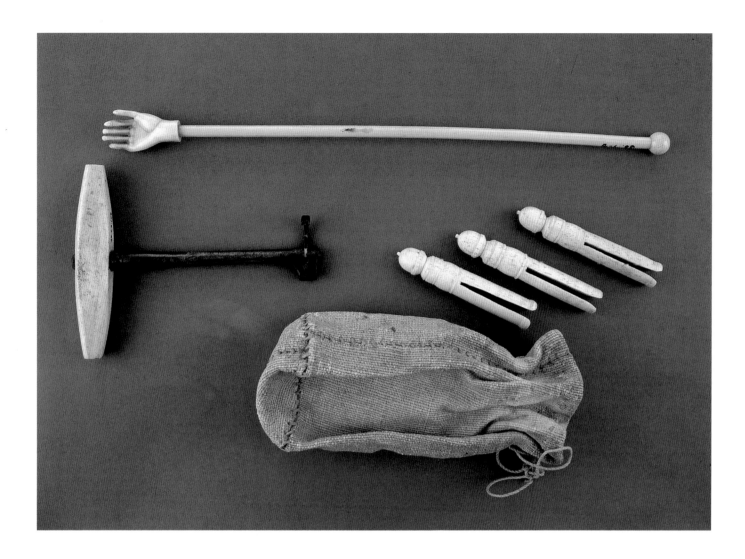

BACK SCRATCHER,
ivory,
H. ³/₄", W. 1", L. 14¹/₈". (New Bedford Whaling Museum)

CLOTHESPINS,
bone,
L. 3³/₄", Diam. ⁵/₈";
L. 3⁷/₈", Diam. ⁵/₈";
L. 3⁷/₈", Diam. ⁵/₈". (New Bedford Whaling Museum)

TOOTH EXTRACTOR,
bone, metal,
H. ³/₄", W. 4⁵/₈", L. 6". (New Bedford Whaling Museum)

With the quantity of vermin on board, a back scratcher was no luxury item on a whaler. The delicately carved hand on this example would

have brought much welcome relief from hard-to-reach itching.

Clothing soaked with perspiration, salt water, whale oil, and grease was washed only on Sundays, and not in fresh water. Sea water, ashes, and even urine were used as cleansers, leaving much to be desired by modern standards. The washed garments, already ragged from wear, were hung to dry on the spanker boom with the aid of clothespins handsomely carved from bone. And the wind shredded them even more.

Although whaling ships did have a medicine chest, it was extremely elementary. The medically untrained captain usually acted as the doctor. Malnutrition and scurvy often caused teeth problems, such as a tooth broken at the gumline from biting into hardtack. This tooth extractor with its bone handle would have been screwed onto the tooth while the sailor held onto the bench he sat upon and endured countless yanks until the tooth came out. If that wasn't enough, the sailor had to pay for the extraction.

CHAPTER THREE

For Use at Home

While the securing of whale oil and/or baleen was the reason for the lengthy voyages, it was far from being a full-time occupation from the moment of departure until the return to home port. The time that was actually consumed by whaling would best be described as being infrequent. Often the ship took months to enter the grounds, the place where the whales were thought to gather, and just arriving at this point did not guarantee action. In fact, weeks could be spent spotting the creatures in what was supposed to be their current habitat.

As a result, there were huge intervals of time when the seamen were left to their own devices during the course of a day. This did not affect their wages because a peculiar form of payment had been established in the whaling business. Whalers were not paid a regular salary; instead, their pay was based on a pre-set share in the profits. This "lay," as it was termed, varied from quite a large portion for the captain to almost minuscule shares for a greenhand or inexperienced seaman. Although incentive played a part in this, a larger role was played by luck.

Nevertheless, all this empty time ran against the grain of hard-working Yankees who preferred not to be idling about. A variety of pastimes were employed to end such inactivity. Dancing, singing sea shanteys, whittling, reading (if one was literate), and gamming, the term used for visiting with other vessels at sea, were all enjoyed, but scrimshawing was the most popular pastime. Because scrimshaw was so time consuming and demanded such intensive care it was an ideal method of keeping hands and minds occupied. This was a diversion that had no deadlines or competition, other than a probable desire for peer admiration.

Another explanation for the popularity of scrimshaw was the nature of the men themselves. When the long whaling journeys began, most of the sailors were solid and respectable, coming from stable home lives. The long voyages, however, precluded any notion of continuing such a normal life. So the sailors' gifts of scrimshaw were a balm for the separa-

tion from their homes. They truly were tokens of love for those held dear. As whaling continued, these family men generally decreased in number, except for the captains and some career mates. They were replaced with more varied types.

Another important factor was the availability of the raw material for scrimshawing. In addition to being costless, whale ivory, whalebone, and baleen lent themselves to artistic use. Ivory was hard, baleen flexible, and bone had size. The woods used were the pine and cedar left over from the carpenter's supply, or such exotics as ebony, sandalwood, mahogany, or teak that might be obtained during the voyages.

Unlike scrimshaw made for use on board, the pieces meant for those at home had a decidedly feminine aspect, for although this scrimshaw was also utilitarian it now needed to be visually pleasing to the women. Thus aesthetics played a role as the decorative qualities of the pieces enhanced the useful. This function of the decorative enhancing the useful was a common principle in the folk arts of that period.

Although factories began producing consumer goods about 1850, scrimshanders continued to turn out a variety of items in quite a wide range. For sewing there were crochet, netting, and knitting needles, thimbles and sewing boxes, and bodkins. These implements helped women to complete their tasks and also display their skills at a time when housekeeping was so time consuming that most women remained at home. Even after the invention of the sewing machine about 1850, handwork was still a very necessary accomplishment.

Because the preparation of food demanded long hours and because most housewives took pride in their daily cooking, kitchen utensils were a popular type of scrimshaw. Therefore, the sailors created useful and attractive rolling pins, butter molds, food choppers and meat mallets, corn huskers and apple corers, potato mashers and food paddles, nut picks, and the ubiquitous jagging wheels. There were also other household items such as clothespins, button hooks, glove stretchers, rulers and yardsticks, boot jacks, and pickwicks. All these were made by the whalers to ensure their memory at home while they were away.

Many of the items listed above would certainly have been useful both at sea and at home, but those used on the ship would have had a more rugged appearance and less decoration. One fascinating aspect of the creation of scrimshaw was the rare use of a lathe. When one examines many scrimshaw objects, it appears incredible that the pieces were not turned on a lathe. Instead, the sculptural turned pieces were fashioned only with knives and chisels, and in some cases they even surpass what could have been accomplished on a lathe.

A final point to be made is that the scrimshaw objects were small enough to be worked on in the space allotted the ordinary seaman, so they did not require much raw material.

All these everyday objects handmade by ordinary whaling people add another important facet to our understanding of the maritime culture of nineteenth-century America. The importance of scrimshaw was first recognized by the pioneering Peabody Essex Museum in Salem, Massachusetts, which began buying scrimshaw in 1907, rather than waiting for donations. It is significant that the earliest scrimshaw purchased by the museum was utilitarian, and the first three pieces bought were all household items.

DARNING EGG,
elephant ivory, wood, black coloring,
H. 1¹⁵/₁₆", W. 1¹⁵/₁₆", L. 6". (The Kendall Whaling Museum)

THIMBLE,
sperm-whale ivory, red sealing wax, black ink,
H. ¹/₂", W. ⁵/₈", L. ¹¹/₁₆". (The Kendall Whaling Museum)

Darning eggs were used for plain sewing that was needed in every home to keep socks, gloves, and other clothing in good repair. Darning was done before the holes occurred, which accounts for the proverb "a stitch in time saves nine." The darning egg was placed under the worn part of the fabric and held tightly to it, thus giving a firm and smooth foundation for the sewing. Made of ivory, bone, glass, or wood, darning eggs usually had a handle and needed to be lightweight.

The original meaning of the word thimble was thumb stall. It is worn on the thumb, first finger, or middle finger to help press a needle through cloth and to protect fingers from being pricked by the sharp end of a needle. Thimbles come with or without tops called domes. When there is no dome, the side is used, as it would be with this example. The tiny indentations on the side are referred to as the knurling. Ivory thimbles, common in the nineteenth century, were usually topless, one piece and decorated on the knurled siding. Thimbles like this example were often given as tokens of love or esteem in the nineteenth century.

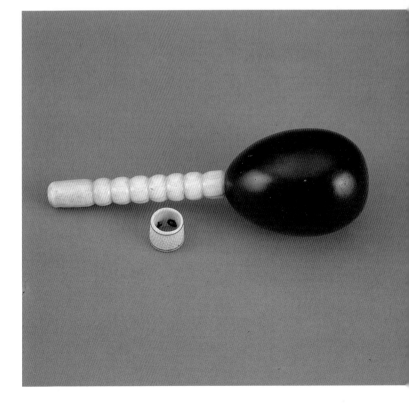

THREAD REEL,
after 1850, bone, brass, wood, paper,
H. 6¹/₄", W. 4³/₄", L. 6³/₈". (New Bedford Whaling Museum)

THREAD WINDER,
ivory,
H. ³/₃₂", W. 1³/₁₆", L. 1³/₁₆". (New Bedford Whaling Museum)

THREAD WINDER,
ivory,
H. ¹/₁₆", W. 1¹/₄", L. 1¹/₂". (New Bedford Whaling Museum)

THREAD WINDER,
ivory,
H. ¹/₈", W. 1¹/₄", L. 1¹/₄". (New Bedford Whaling Museum)

This ornately carved ferris wheel-like thread reel is permanently attached to the sturdy base, but the wheel itself and the spools can be removed. It is possible to date this piece of scrimshaw to the second half of the nineteenth century because it was not until 1850 that thread was sold on disposable spools. Another innovation was the notch on the spool into which the thread could be tucked to keep it from unwinding. The ten spools on this reel have their original Clark & Company labels, but the thread, due to age, has changed from white to brown. Reels like this example were very popular toward the end of the century.

The three delicate thread winders included in this photograph held thread for sewing and embroidery. Generally, it was silk thread that was put on the winders, for it was sold only in skeins until well after cotton thread could be purchased on spools. These small, flat winders kept the delicate silk from snagging, and their indented edges kept the thread from falling off. Thread winders also provided an easy way to store small amounts of thread. Sailors also used them, but on board they were called spiders. Because these sewing implements were used continuously in unchanged forms over a long period of time it is hard to date them precisely.

THIMBLE CASE,
ivory, red coloring,
H. 1⁵/₈", Diam. 1". (Mystic Seaport Museum)

There has also been a long history of thimbles in ornamental cases being given as presents, and this was especially true in the nineteenth century. An acorn-like shape was a very popular design for these cases that were made to protect the thimble. As much work went into making the case as for the thimble itself. Making a screw-on top was no easy task, especially in the small size of this case, which has been ornamented with a red scroll design.

TRACING WHEEL,
post 1868, ivory, steel,
L. 5⁷/₈", Diam. ⁵/₈". (Mystic Seaport Museum)

This sewing tool, called a tracing wheel or pattern tracer, was used to transfer the outline of a pattern placed on top of fabric. The rowel, a small wheel with sharp projecting points, would be set in motion by pushing the handle over the pattern. The points would pierce the pattern and make small prick marks on the material underneath, thus allowing the sewer to cut an exact replica. The carver of this scrimshawed handle made attractive, simple turnings without marring the long uninterrupted shaft that was necessary to provide a proper hand grip.

An August 28, 1868 advertisement in *Harper's Bazaar* gives us a rough idea of the date of this tool. The reader is informed that this recently invented device, called a copying wheel, could be purchased for 25 cents.

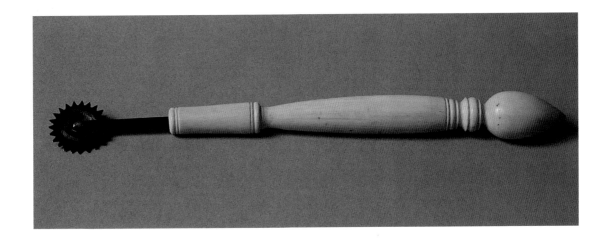

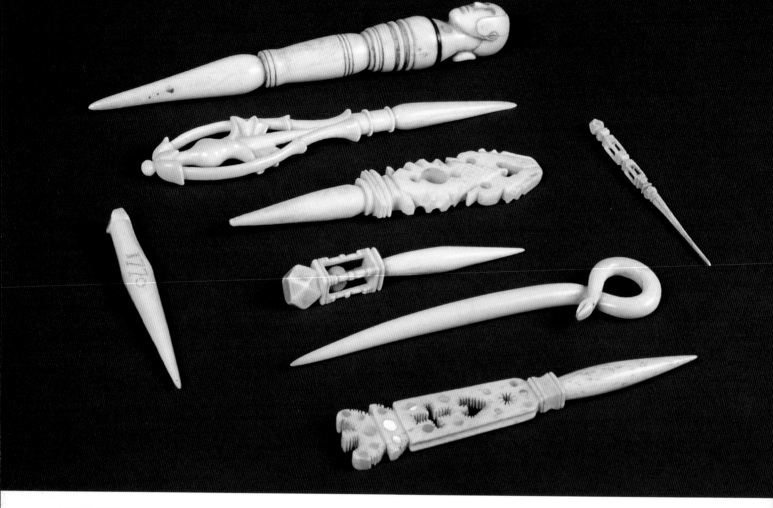

BODKIN,
ivory, baleen, inking,
L. 6½", Diam. ¾".

BODKIN,
ivory,
L. 3⅜", Diam.⅜".

BODKIN,
dated 1770, ivory,
L. 3", Diam. ⅜".

BODKIN,
ivory,
L. 5¹¹⁄₁₆", Diam. 1⅛".

BODKIN,
ivory, ink,
L. 5", Diam. ⁵⁄₁₆".

BODKIN,
dated 1770, ivory,
L. 3", Diam. ⅜".

SEWING BOX,
whalebone, pine, cotton, black and blue ink, metal,
H. 7¾", W. 8¾", L. 11½". (New Bedford Whaling Museum)

BODKIN,
ivory,
L. 4⅝", Diam. 1".

BODKIN,
ivory,
L. 4⅞", Diam. ⁵⁄₁₆".

(All pieces are from the collection of Mystic Seaport Museum)

A mariner would know at once the usefulness of a bodkin, for its function was similar to the sailor's marlin spike or fid that was used for making holes in canvas or for working knots. Like all bodkins, these eight examples were carved from a solid piece from a tooth, slab, or jawbone. This short (three to five inches), straight, or curved implement could have the form of a blunt needle with a long eye that was used for threading cord, tape, or ribbon through holes or casings, or it could have a sharp point for making holes in fabric or for eyelet embroidery. An unrelated use was that of a hair ornament. The bodkin may even have preceded the needle. Remember that ribbons, cords, and laces fastened garments together until sometime in the nineteenth century, when machine-made buttons and metal fasteners came into existence. As is handsomely illustrated by these eight ivory examples, bodkins were often intricately carved. Here we have a sculptured head, delicate carving, fretwork, a movable ball in a cage, a sinuous snake, inlay, and a very early bodkin dated 1770.

Sewing boxes, such as this elegant, large oval example, were primarily a nineteenth-century item. In earlier times, women kept their needlework tools in the deep, spacious pockets of their skirts or in decorative bags. When fashions changed, these pockets and bags were no longer part of the daily costume, and the much more practical sewing box came into being. As can be seen from the work of this highly skilled scrimshander, these boxes were much more than just a container, they were art objects to be prominently displayed, as well as used. A variety of things, depending on the woman's specific sewing interest, would have been kept in the box, but the basics included scissors, a thimble, bodkins and stilettos, a needle case, and thread. On the top of the sewing box is a pincushion made of heavily quilted fabric surrounded by a scalloped frame decorated with a flowing vine border. Sewing boxes had varying degrees of decoration, but this is certainly a superlative example. This exquisite creation is made from a piece of panbone bent into an oval and held together with thirteen carved rat tails and small metal rivets. Indeed, the rivets have been used as a decorative device all around the box. In addition to the beautiful construction the box is decorated with a large American ship and four smaller boats that have been engraved at the left, and with a tropical scene at the right.

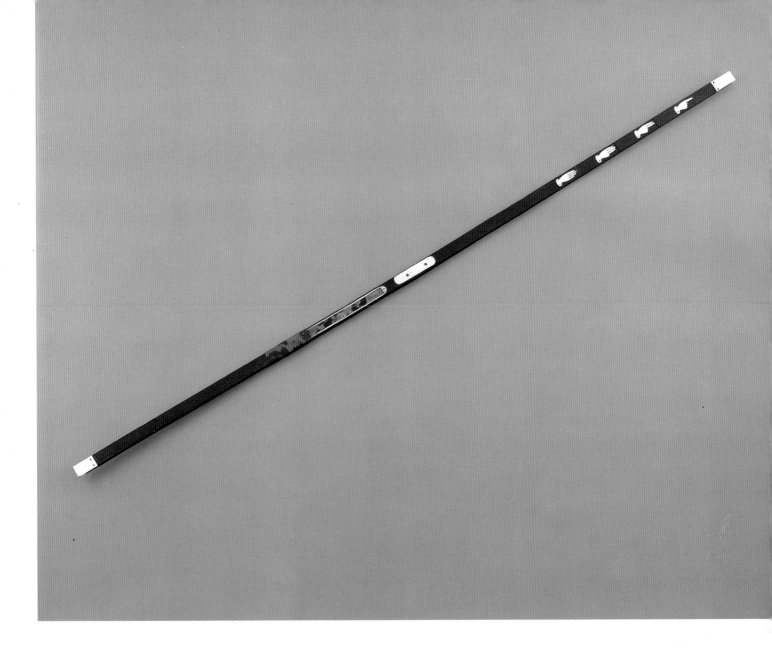

SEWING STAND,
ivory, woods, tortoise shell, coloring, cloth,
H. 14", W. 9¼", L. 8⅞". (New Bedford Whaling Museum)

Handmade sewing stands of various sizes and forms were traditional gifts to sweethearts and wives from their men folk in the nineteenth century. Scrimshanders had the advantage of having access to exotic woods, ivory, and bone to be used in the construction and the inlays of their stands. Even though more store-bought clothes were available and machines were replacing some handwork, women of all classes continued to sew, both as a way to maintain and repair their fabrics and as an outlet for their creative talents. The upper portion of this stand has a revolving tier that enabled thread to be displayed, stored, and easily selected. The handmade ivory spools probably show that commercial spools were not yet available, so the top of the reel needed to be lifted off, the ivory spool removed from the shank, wound with thread, and then replaced. The four drawers in the lower section housed various needlework accessories, while the tops of the two front corner posts provided pincushions. The coloring in the grooves of the turned ivory highlight the work as do the various shell and wood inlays.

MEASURING STICK,
ebony, ivory, tortoiseshell, brass,
H. ³⁄₁₆", W. ⁹⁄₁₆", L. 36". (New Bedford Whaling Museum)

This measuring stick is clearly different from the modern yardstick. Although it contains thirty-six inches, the form of this piece is most unusual. In the early nineteenth century a yardstick might be only divided into four quarters of nine inches each. One quarter might be divided into two equal sections and another quarter into four nails, a nail being 2¼ inches long or one-sixteenth of a yard. This handsome rule has the right section of nine inches divided into four hands, showing one, two, three, or four fingers, and each hand represents one nail measuring 2¼ inches. In other examples the nail is represented by the letter N. Measuring fabric by nails was passé by the 1830s. The name "Mrs. H. G. Wing" that is inscribed on the ivory plate in the center indicates that the rule was intended for home use. Some sticks warp, thus causing faulty measurements, but the scrimshander avoided warping by using ebony, a very hard wood. The tortoiseshell inlay on the left side of the rule probably indicates that the ebony had been damaged at some point, and this repair enhances the stylishness of the piece.

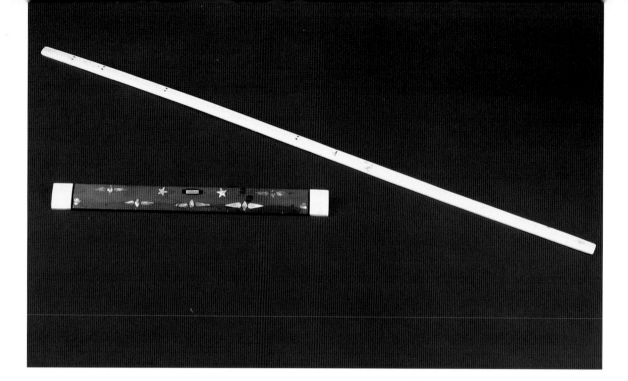

RULER,
ivory, wood, abalone, mother-of-pearl,
H. 7/16", W. 1 3/8", L. 15 1/8". (Mystic Seaport Museum)

YARDSTICK,
before 1856, bone, metal,
H. 1/4", W. 5/8", L. 35 3/4". (Mystic Seaport Museum)

This very decorative ruler has inch marks scribed on one of its edges. Because of the decorative inlays of abalone and mother-of-pearl, this ruler with ivory tips may have been used more as just a straight edge than as a ruler.

Homemade yardsticks were the norm at the turn of the nine-

teenth century. Another generation would pass until machine-made yardsticks came into being. Housewives would use yardsticks for measuring yardgoods and other domestic uses. Because of shrinkage, ivory and bone rules were not always accurate. This bone example, which is beveled along one edge, has shrunk a quarter of an inch. One form of calibration for fabric measurement was by 1/6, 1/8, 1/12, and 1/16 of a yard. The black dots on this yardstick are set at 18", 9", 4 1/4", and two at 2 1/4", thus using increments of a half, a quarter, an eighth, and a sixteenth of a yard. By 1856, the 36-inch yard was standardized. The rule of thumb for dating such measuring sticks is the more regular the calibrations, the later the date. This example most probably dates from the first half of the nineteenth century.

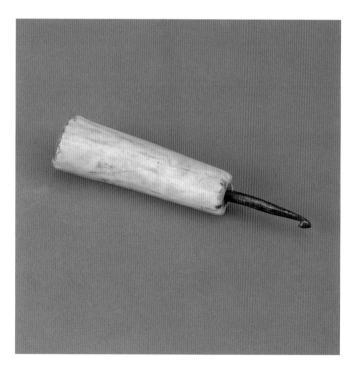

RUG HOOK,
bone, steel,
H. 3/4", W. 13/16", L. 4 3/16". (The Kendall Whaling Museum)

This rug hook is a simple crochet-like hook with a bone handle. Short lengths of material were held beneath the rug's foundation fabric of linen, hemp, or burlap. The hook, inserted through the top of the fabric, gathered a loop of the decorative yarn and pulled the loop up through the fabric. This process would be repeated innumerable times until the decorative surface of the rug was completed. Hooked rugs began to appear in American homes in the 1840s, but by this same time sailors were known to have already produced mats and rugs by looping lengths of rope into old sail canvas. So this rug hook could well have been made either for a lady's or sailor's sewing kit.

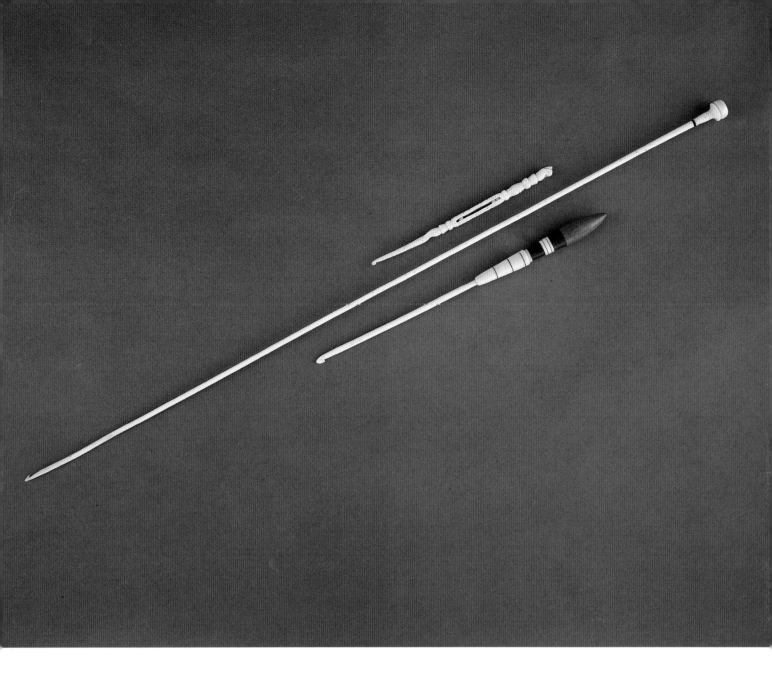

CROCHET HOOK,
c. 1840–1900, bone,
H. ¹/₄", W. ⁵/₁₆", L. 5¹/₂". (New Bedford Whaling Museum)

CROCHET HOOK,
c. 1840–1900, bone, ivory, baleen,
L. 21³/₈", Diam. ¹/₂". (New Bedford Whaling Museum)

CROCHET HOOK,
c. 1840–1900, ivory, wood, ink,
L. 8³/₄", Diam. ¹/₂". (New Bedford Whaling Museum)

These three scrimshawed crochet hooks date from 1840 or after because crocheting did not arrive in the United States until the 1840s. Although crochet is a French word meaning "little hook," it came to America via Ireland. At first, hooks like these were all hand-made, but by the latter part of the nineteenth century they were being mass produced. As we see here, hooks came in many sizes, but size was not as important as the shape of the hook, which is similar to that of a barb on a fishing hook. In addition to having to be firm and smooth, which is why old used crochet hooks were preferred, they also had to match the gauge of the thread. The gauge varied widely because any size of thread could be used. Wool usually called for large bone hooks. Crocheting enjoyed a great popularity because the necessary skills were easy to learn and the materials used were inexpensive. We are left to wonder how anyone could effectively control a crochet hook that was almost two feet long like the center hook.

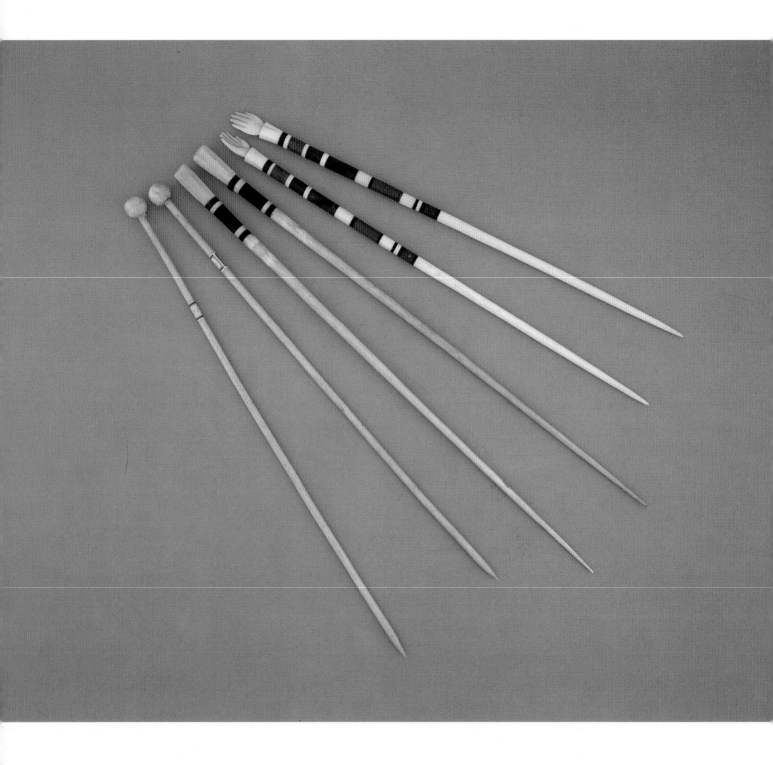

KNITTING NEEDLES,
bone,
H. ¹/₂", W. ¹/₂", L. 11¹/₂". (Peabody Essex Museum)

KNITTING NEEDLES,
bone, wood,
H. ¹/₂", W. ¹/₂", L. 11¹/₂". (Peabody Essex Museum)

KNITTING NEEDLES,
ivory, wood, baleen,
H. ¹/₂", W. ¹/₂", L. 11". (Peabody Essex Museum)

The earliest knowledge of knitting dates back to the Coptic tombs of the fourth century, and it was considered a masculine occupation up through the late Middle Ages. In most households knitting was done out of necessity, even after factories produced machine-knit clothing in the early nineteenth century. These three pairs of scrimshawed needles all have decorative tops: one pair with knob ends, another with baleen inlay beneath inverted finials, and a third pair with wood and baleen rings under carved hands. These tops, however, serve a useful purpose, for they prevent the knitting from slipping off the needle. When such a top exists the needle was sometimes referred to as a knitting pin.

KNITTING-NEEDLE SHEATH,
bone, metal,
H. ¹/₂", W. 2", L. 3¹/₄". (Peabody Essex Museum)

KNITTING-NEEDLE SHEATH,
bone, metal,
H. ¹/₄", W. 1³/₄", L. 2¹/₄". (Peabody Essex Museum)

Produced chiefly as a folk craft, these scrimshaw objects, which are totally out of fashion today, are not easily identified. In the early part of the nineteenth century many people still relied on homemade clothing, and a knitting needle sheath helped speed up the process if the piece was being knitted. Historically, this object was called a knitting-needle sheath. It is a misnomer, for a sheath is chiefly familiar as a case or a covering for a dagger or sword, but in this case the sheath only holds the tip of a knitting needle. The knitting-needle sheath was tucked into a belt, sewn onto an apron, or pinned on clothing at the knitter's right hip. A hole in the top of the small shaft attached to the sheath gave support to the inserted needle held by the right hand, thus freeing the fingers of this hand to work the yarn more quickly at the opposite tip while maintaining a steady needle. Stitches were also kept from sliding off a double-ended needle. Obviously, such needles were not the large ones used for heavy yarns. These bone sheaths, one having a heart on heart, and the other lavished with intricate pierced work, were typical of those given as love tokens by sailors who wanted to show off their carving skill. Other examples were produced in wood, ivory, and brass.

TATTING SHUTTLE,
c. 1875–1878, ivory, ink,
H. ⁷/₁₆", W. ¹³/₁₆", L. 2¹/₂". (Mystic Seaport Museum)

NETTING NEEDLE,
ivory,
H. ¹/₃₂", W. ⁵/₃₂", L. 2⁷/₈". (Mystic Seaport Museum)

During the nineteenth century, women with leisure time often tatted. It was said that this type of needlework showed a lady's hand to great advantage. The tatting shuttle had only three pieces: an oval top and a bottom that were both convex on the outside and flat on the inner side, and whose pointed ends nearly touched. The third piece, a center section that was small, short, and thick, joined the top and bottom together. Thread was wound onto the shuttle through the pointed ends, which were closely aligned at the tips to prevent the thread from unwinding too quickly. The dimensions of a shuttle were not particularly important beause the size of the tatting did not depend on the size of the tool. The shuttle, a form of needle, created patterns and trimmings entirely in themselves. To create the lacelike textile called tatting all one needed was the shuttle and thread, and the work could be stopped and started at any moment without harming the work. This shuttle is made of ivory with ink decoration, others were bone, tortoiseshell, and mother-of-pearl.

Like the tatting shuttle, the netting needle was familiar to scrimshanders who did similar work in knotting and net making. Decorative netting did not exist until the eleventh century, long after utilitarian netting was established. This ivory netting needle, like all others, is split at each end for the winding of the thread and has a small hole at one end to secure the thread. Using netting in conjunction with a mesh foundation, women created doilies, shawls, and antimacassars.

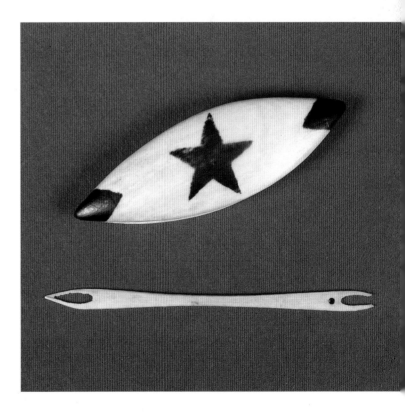

51

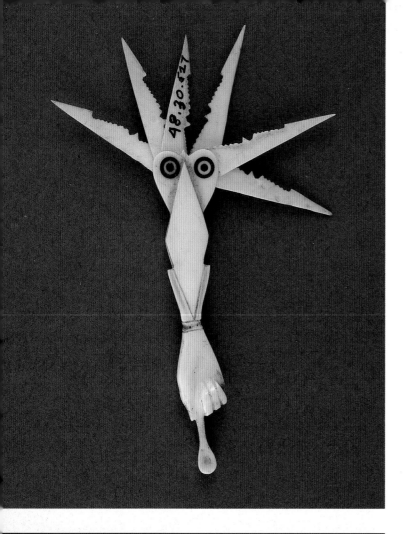

DRIZZLER,
ivory, brass, black ink,
H. ¹/₄", W. ¹/₂", L. extended 3¹/₂". (New Bedford Whaling Museum)

This piece of scrimshaw will probably be puzzling. Now totally obsolete, the drizzler originated at the court of Versailles where ladies used it to pick gold and silver thread out of old clothing and furnishing fabric. Also called parfilage or raveling, it was never widely popular. In the nineteenth century the drizzler was used to save silk thread by picking at the fabric with the various jagged blades. And what was the function of the tiny spoon held by the carved hand? Before thread was machine-twisted it often needed to be waxed to keep it from tangling or to prepare it for stringing beads. This wax was obtained by inserting the spoon into one's ear. An adverse effect of drizzling was the destruction of old and valuable needlework.

SWIFT,
bone, metal, coloring,
H. 18¹/₂", W. at base 5¹/₂", extended diam. 14¹/₂". (Peabody Essex Museum)

A swift was unquestionably the most difficult scrimshaw object to create. Only a few scrimshanders tried to make a swift, for in addition to basic artistry the carver also had to have an exacting sense of mechanics. After the panbone had been sawn, cut, and sliced to make the dozens of slats, and slabs had been carved and turned into the larger component parts, the intricate assemblage of all the parts still had to be accomplished. The swift had to open and shut in a fashion similar to that of an umbrella. This movement took place on a central rod called an axis spoke. The strips were often joined with metal rivets as is seen here, or by knotted ribbons. A thumbscrew was set on the lower shaft to keep the swift in a desired position. If the swift did not have a permanent base another much larger screw, in this case carved in the shape of a fist, was created to attach the swift to a table. The yarn winders were often topped with a small cup to hold the ball of yarn, such as here, or with a pincushion. This fine example has red bands on its post, and a scrimshawed box (not in illustration) for storage. The lady at home, to whom the swift was sent, would wrap a skein of yarn tautly around its extended frame. This frame would rotate as the yarn was wound into a ball by the owner.

SWIFT, ▶
ivory, bone, wood, shell, metal, silk, ink, wash,
H. 21", W. at base 6⁷/₈", extended diam. 16". (New Bedford Whaling Museum)

All swifts were complicated and intricate, but even the simplest of them had more than one hundred parts, so the scrimshander also had to have some engineering ability. The wheel or cage revolved around the axis spoke or center spindle, and it was composed of ribs joined by rivets and knotted fragments of silk. This cage had to move both up and down the center spindle and in and out from it to perform the function of the swift correctly. The correct carving of the individual parts did not necessarily ensure their workability. This swift stands on a base doubling as a small sewing box, and it has posts for spools of thread, four cups at the corners for wax or thimbles, and a supply drawer. The exquisite turnings highlighted with colored wax are enhanced by the pierced front of the drawer and images of ships on each side of the base. Because swifts were so fragile, many of them ended up as a pile of pieces, so it was always a question whether it was preferable to enjoy a swift as sculpture or to use it as a yarn winder.

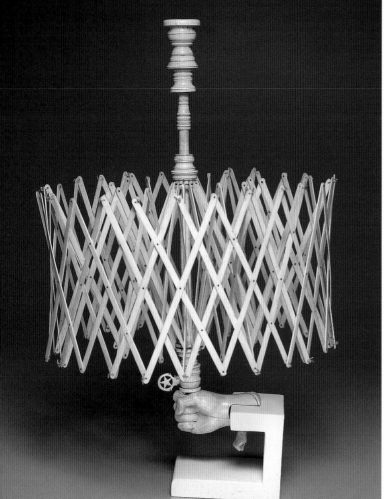

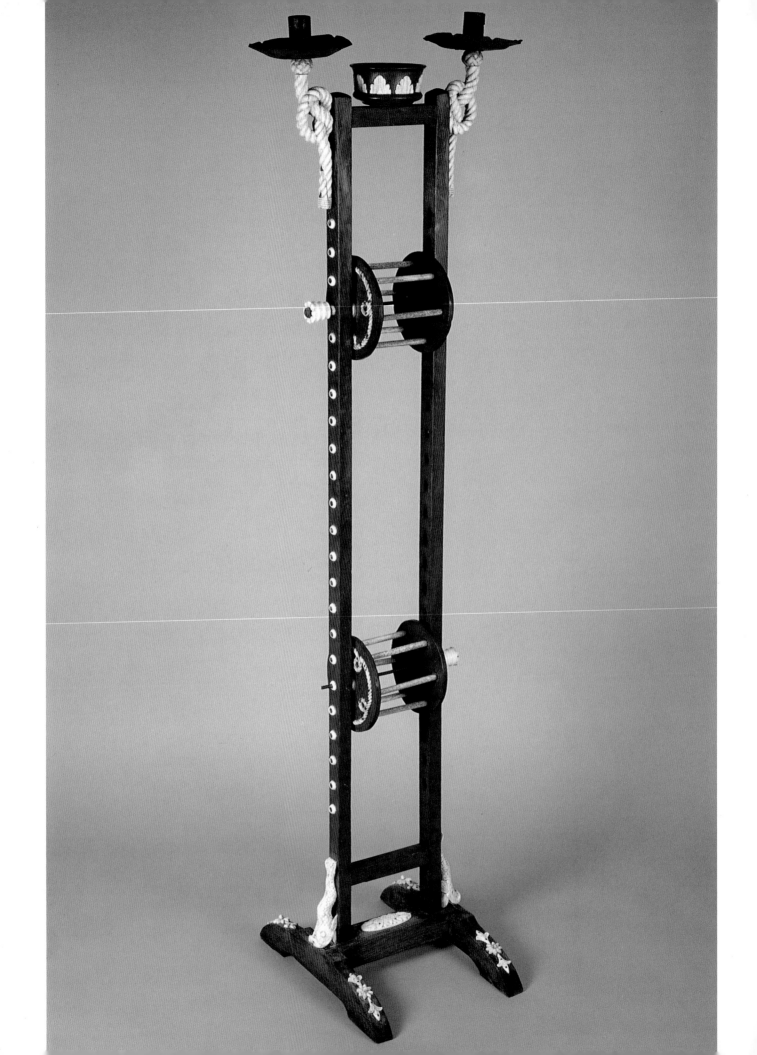

◀ SQUIRREL-CAGE SWIFT,
bone, wood, ivory, metal,
H. 44", W. 8³/₈", L. 11⁹/₁₆". (Mystic Seaport Museum)

This swift has quite a different shape from the more familiar type of yarn winder. Known as a squirrel-cage swift, it is both larger and less portable than most swifts. The name derives from the fact that the two adjustable reels resemble the cage that a squirrel was sometimes placed in and kept rotating by its continuous running. The ivory knobs on the sides of the stand hold the reels in place. The reels can be adjusted according to the length of the skein of yarn by removing the knobs and placing them in the appropriate holes encircled by ivory. The yarn is placed on the outer surface of the reels, which rotate with the pull of the knitter as she winds it into a ball. The outstanding feature of this swift is the pair of carved-bone rope and turks-head knot candlesticks at the top. The bone-rope motif is repeated on the sides of the reels. The scrimshander further embellished this swift with bone leaf carvings on the ball cup, carved sea creatures that decorate the upright supports, and more leaf designs on the feet. This is a most extraordinary example of scrimshaw.

YARN WHEEL,
whale skeletal bone, sperm-whale ivory, red sealing wax, black ink,
Diam. 22", Depth 6". (The Kendall Whaling Museum)

This is a yarn wheel, which is also called a niddy-noddy. The yarn wheel was generally used to wind spun yarn into skeins rather than to wind skeins into balls, which was the purpose of a swift. The scrimshander appropriately preserved a nautical theme by creating this niddy-noddy to resemble the helm of his ship. The result is a delicate and handsome example of mariner folk art.

MEAT MALLET,
whalebone,
H. 1¹⁵/₁₆", W. 3³/₈", L. 9¹/₂". (Mystic Seaport Museum)

FOOD CHOPPER,
whalebone,
H. 1", W. 5³/₄", L. 6⁷/₈". (Mystic Seaport Museum)

In Herman Melville's *Moby Dick* there is mention of the cook using a meat mallet on whale steak. More often, however, the mallet would have been used to try and save some second-rate cut of meat that may have begun to spoil. Many whalemen complained of this in journals and letters. Most meat pounders were wooden and were used before cooking to improve the poorer cuts of beef, pork, or lamb. The side of the mallet with crosshatching shown here was used for tenderizing, and the opposite plain side was used for flattening.

Other names for the whalebone food chopper were mincing knife or just mincer. When used on fruit, suet, sausage, and the like, the chopper usually had an accompanying bowl, for the cook would not want the blade of the chopper to roughen the interior of the bowl used for dough. Both these examples of scrimshaw are well proportioned and their simplicity of form is aesthetically pleasing.

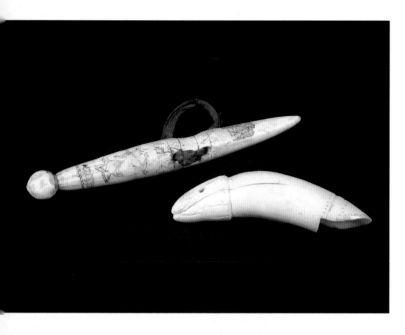

CORN HUSKER,
bone, leather, coloring,
L. 4³/₄", Diam. ⁹/₁₆". (Mystic Seaport Museum)

APPLE CORER,
ivory,
L. 3¹/₆", Diam. ¹¹/₁₆". (Mystic Seaport Museum)

This bone corn husker, also known as a husking pin or husking hook, fits over the thumb by means of its narrow leather strap. Although there were numerous types of corn huskers, their purpose was basically the same: to remove the outer covering of the ear of corn. It was a kitchen tool, for it was really only good for husking a small quantity of ears of corn.

Apples played a much more important role in the American diet in the eighteenth and nineteenth centuries than they do today. For that reason apple corers, such as this ivory fish-shaped example, were quite common. In 1803, an inventor received a patent for an iron corer, and silver apple corers were known to grace the tables of the well-to-do.

POTATO MASHER,
bone,
H. 1¹/₂", W. 1¹/₂", L. 9¹/₄". (Peabody Essex Museum)

BUTTER PADDLE,
bone,
H. ¹/₂", W. 3¹/₂", L. 10³/₄". (Peabody Essex Museum)

Bone potato mashers were unusual, for most were made of wood. Wire mashers with wooden handles became available after 1850. Like all such mashers, this simply turned example is an odd form of a pestle used in the kitchen on both vegetables and potatoes. A common kitchen utensil in the eighteenth and nineteenth centuries, it was also known as a potato beetle; beetle meaning to beat or ram. Due to thrift, lack of storage space and of refrigeration coarse staples like potatoes were served often, keeping the cost of a meal on board a ship in 1850 to less than nine cents a man.

Such luxury items as butter, when available, were meant for only the captain and the mates. The hands in the forecastle, eating off a tin plate, and drinking from quart cups, tasted no butter on their hardtack. A bone butter or lard paddle such as the one shown was meant to be used by the womenfolk back home. After churning, the butter would be placed in wooden trays and worked with this paddle to rid it of excess water. Then the same paddle packed the butter into a tub.

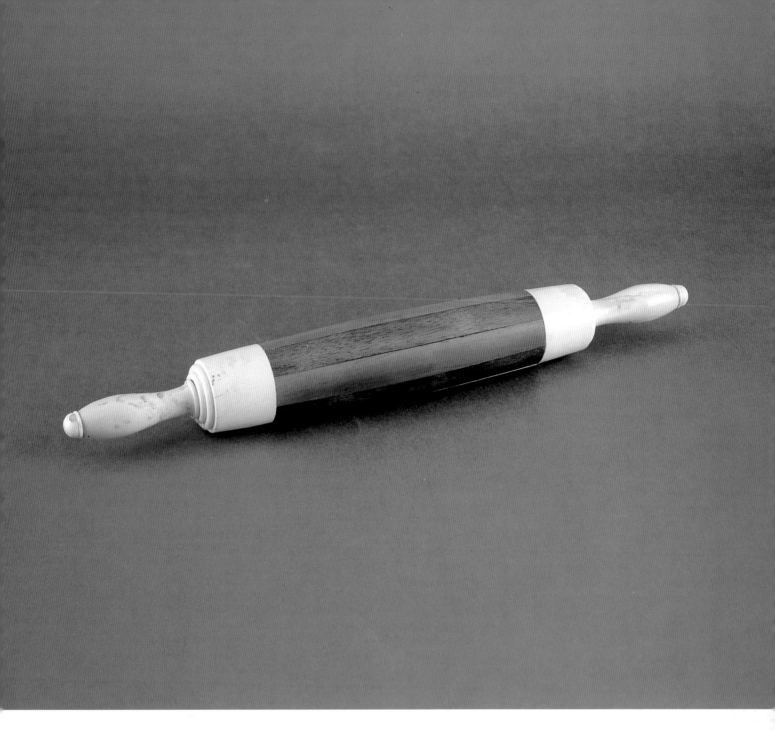

ROLLING PIN,
ivory, wood,
L. 17^{1}/$_{2}$", Diam. 2^{1}/$_{4}$". (New Bedford Whaling Museum)

If, like a scrimshander, you had to soak bread in your hot coffee or
tea so that the worms in the bread were scalded to death and consequently rose to the top of the cup to be skimmed off, it is quite possible that you would have visions of tasty pies, pastries, and crackers.
The scrimshander might then busy himself making a rolling pin for
his loved one. Early rolling pins were one-handled, thus allowing
one hand to push with the handle, while the other hand pressed
down on the pin. By whaling times, most rolling pins had handles at
both ends, and the scrimshanders often made rolling pins from
exotic hardwoods like lignum vitae and with turned ivory ends.
Rolling pins similar to this handsome example were often given as
wedding presents along with jagging wheels.

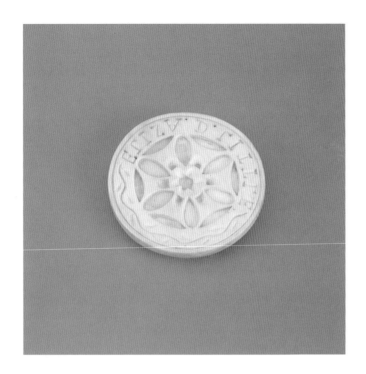

BUTTER MOLD,
attributed to Joseph C. Little, c. 1847–1861, sperm-whale ivory,
H. ³⁄₈", Diam. 2³⁄₁₆". (The Kendall Whaling Museum)

Butter molds and cookie prints are often confused. Both were similar in size and both were found in nineteenth-century kitchens. The cookie print was a flat, circular disc usually stained from molasses and other ingredients. Butter molds, popular until the 1860s when factories began producing dairy products, identified the maker if she were selling her butter and usually had some sort of decorative design. Most had handles and were cup shaped or boxed. They were quite clean from repeated washings in the dairy. Due to its identifying name "Eliza D. Little" and its cleanliness, this piece of scrimshaw is believed to be a butter mold. The attribution of this butter mold is based on the fact that Eliza D. Little was the wife of Joseph C. Little.

SADIE PATTERSON'S JAGGING WHEEL,
dated 1861, New Bedford, Massachusetts, ivory, metal, wood,
L. 5⁷⁄₈", Diam. 1⁷⁄₁₆". (Mystic Seaport Museum)

MARY HOWLAND'S JAGGING WHEEL,
dated 1847, Nantucket, Massachusetts, ivory, ebony, steel, brass,
L. 7¹⁄₂", Diam. 1⁵⁄₈". (Mystic Seaport Museum)

JAGGING WHEEL,
ivory, brass, steel,
L. 6³⁄₄", Diam. 2". (Mystic Seaport Museum)

Eighteenth- and nineteenth-century American menus were filled with pies, which in some circles were known as the Queen of the Yankee Cuisine. Pies today are primarily thought of as a dessert, but in earlier days meat and mince pies were eaten at all three meals. Consequently, seamen yearned for the tasty pies from home ovens and had to make a severe adjustment to what was served on board. Good cooks were a rarity at sea, and so most problems on board revolved around the food, and it is no wonder that scrimshanders carved jagging wheels to help preserve memories of those homemade pies. Sadie Patterson's 1861 whale-tooth-shaped jagging wheel (middle) and Mary Howland's 1847 example (bottom) most assuredly were gifts from homesick seamen. The outer rim of the wheel hub on the top example in the illustration leaves no doubt about what was on the carver's mind. It reads in reverse "Good Pie Well Made." These simple devices—also known as crimpers, pastry jaggers, gigling irons, pie trimmers and pie sealers—cut pastry, pie strips, and cookies, fluted pie edges, and sealed piecrusts to prevent leakage. Some had two, three, or four tines on one end to prick air holes in the crust. Keeping the wheel clean of food fragments had to be a tiresome job and perhaps this is the reason that jagging wheels are seldom used today. Scrimshanders carved more of these imaginative and highly decorative pieces than any other kind of kitchen equipment. Many examples were executed in ivory.

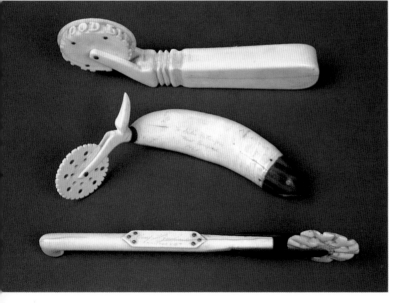

DIPPER,
bone, wood, coconut, metal, ivory,
H. 3¹/₂", W. 3¹/₂", L. 14". (Peabody Essex Museum)

CORKSCREW,
bone, metal,
H. 1", W. 3¹/₄", L. 4¹/₄". (Peabody Essex Museum)

NUT PICK,
bone, metal,
H. ¹/₂", W. ¹/₂", L. 4¹/₄". (Peabody Essex Museum)

The coconut-bowl dipper was a popular scrimshaw item and many had, as this one does, a bone heart-shaped ferrule. The creator of this graceful and well-designed implement obviously had secured the coconut and the exotic hardwood in warmer climates. Coconut dippers lasted much longer when used to scoop up dry substances such as flour or coffee rather than when used for liquids.

Until 1858, when the screw cap was invented, the cork was the major bottle stopper, so corkscrews were a necessity. This tooth-handled corkscrew is particularly interesting because the spiral is carved ivory, not metal.

During the nineteenth century meals often ended with nuts, as reflected in the familiar expression "from soup to nuts." Thus a nut pick was meant for table use. After the nut had been cracked open, the meat would be picked out of the shell. Most nut picks were probably not as decorative as this example with its carved column and dog's-head finial.

JAGGING WHEEL,
bone, metal,
H. ¹/₂", W. ¹/₂", L. 7". (Peabody Essex Museum)

JAGGING WHEEL,
after 1845, bone, copper,
H. ¹/₂", W. 1¹/₄", L. 4³/₄". (Peabody Essex Museum)

JAGGING WHEEL,
ivory, metal,
H. 1", W. 1¹/₂", L. 5". (Peabody Essex Museum)

Jagging wheels are a kitchen tool with at least a shank or handle and a revolving fluted or jagged wheel. Although none is found on these examples, a fork may also be attached. The wheel was always made from one piece, but the handle could be one, two, or three pieces joined together. No pictorial engraving was done on jagging wheels. Most were made of bone; many are ivory; and some are wood and metal. These three disparate wheels illustrate the diversity of form; the elegance and grace of the running dog are in stark contrast to the plainness of the simple bone handle holding a wheel made from a copper penny dated 1845. The ivory rings on the third example suggest a love of whittling for its own sake. Jagging wheels required both skill and experience and required hours of difficult carving and were not tackled by novice scrimshanders.

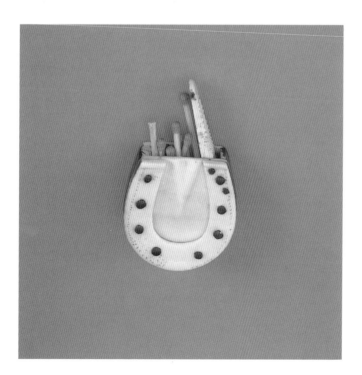

MATCHBOX,
walrus ivory, silver, stain,
H. ⁹/₁₆", W. 1⁹/₁₆", L. 1¹¹/₁₆". (The Kendall Whaling Museum)

We, of course, do not think about it today because we switch on a light, turn on the stove, or flick on a lighter, but matchboxes were quite essential in the nineteenth century. Before Zippos, Bics, and packets of paper matches, wooden matches—much smaller than those used today—were needed to light the oil lamps, and the matchboxes were made of various materials. This scrimshawed-ivory example is small enough to fit in a pocket. The lid ensured that the matches would remain dry. The horseshoe form, with its silver rivets, was a familiar shape, as well as being a traditional symbol of good luck.

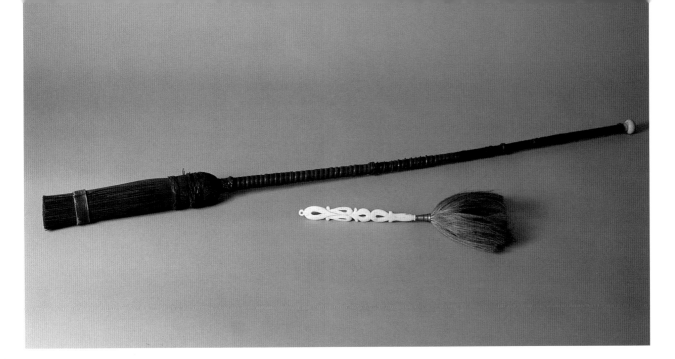

HEARTH BRUSH,
before 1870, baleen, ivory, wood,
L. 46", Diam. 2¹/₂". (Mystic Seaport Museum)

WHISK BRUSH,
whalebone, horsehair, brass,
H. ⁵/₁₆", W. handle 1", L. 14¹/₂". (Mystic Seaport Museum)

Nineteenth-century homes used many different kinds of brushes that were designed for specific purposes. This long baleen, ivory-tipped hearth brush has stiff bristles for keeping the stone or brick floor of the fireplace free of ash and embers. Household fires were a continual danger and demanded constant attention. Because this brush uses so much baleen, it most probably dates from before 1870, when baleen was commanding its highest commercial prices. A frugal Yankee whaling captain would not have given away such a valuable commodity easily. The unknown scrimshander did remarkable interlacing and weaving of the baleen strips on the handle and top of the brush.

Because a whisk brush is meant for quick, sweeping motions, the broom of this whalebone piece is both loose and pliable. The decorative bone handle has been carved with great elegance, and the small loop at the top ensured easy hanging.

PICKWICK,
bone, metal,
H. 3", W. 1¹/₂", L. 1¹/₂". (Peabody Essex Museum)

PICKWICK,
ivory, brass,
H. 3³/₄", W. ¹/₂", L. 1¹/₂". (Peabody Essex Museum)

With whaling came oil lamps, and with oil lamps came pickwicks. At the start of the nineteenth century these were interrelated products. The two-sectioned pickwick had a base intended to keep it from falling over whether at home or on a ship, and a top that held a long, thin metal pick of iron, steel, or even brass. The pagoda-shaped bone example decorated with multiple turnings on the left and the bell-shaped ivory one on the right both performed identical duties: to pick a wick. Thus, if a wick in an oil lamp had burnt down, or if a brighter light was desired, the stylus would be inserted into the wick and with an upward tug, pulled it up. Pickwicks became outmoded with the invention of the manual wick control that was attached to the lamp.

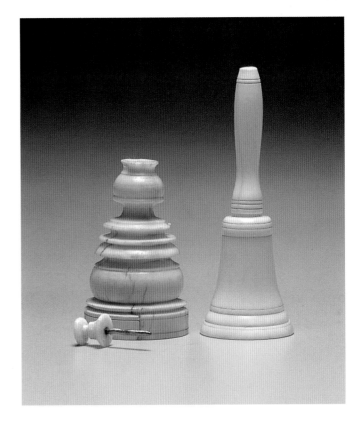

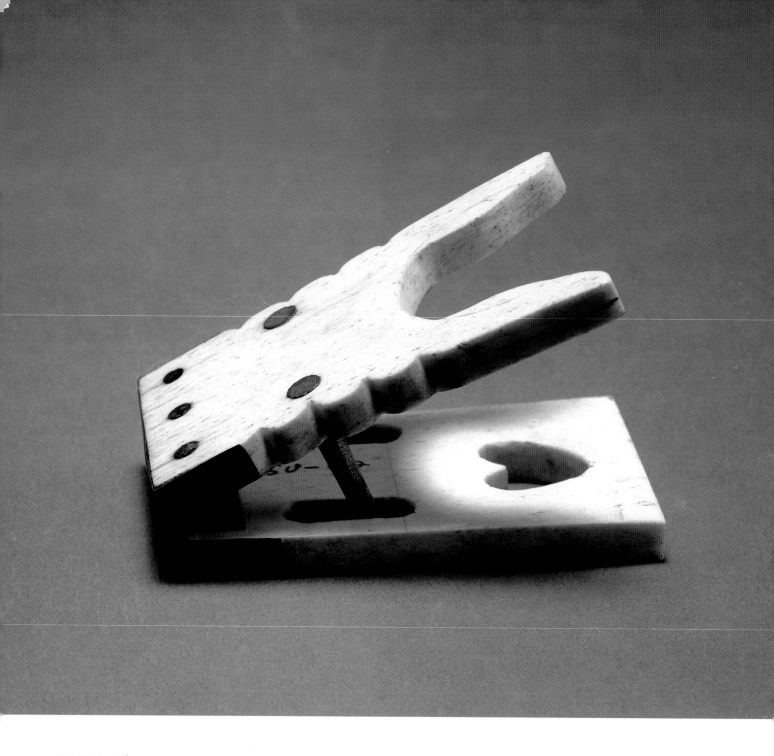

BOOT JACK,
whalebone, copper, brass,
H. 3", W. 2½", L. 4⅜". (New Bedford Whaling Museum)

Today, most people would have no use for a boot jack, but in the nineteenth century when shoe leather was rough and sizes were more general, boot jacks were quite practical. A boot could be difficult to remove by hand, but by placing the jack on the floor and inserting the back of the heel into the elevated section with the cutout "U" shape, one could pull one's foot out of the boot without much problem, and the boot remained in the jack. Because of the size of the "U" shape, it is probable that this folding jack was meant for a lady's boot. The heavy slabs of whalebone are softened by the carved designs.

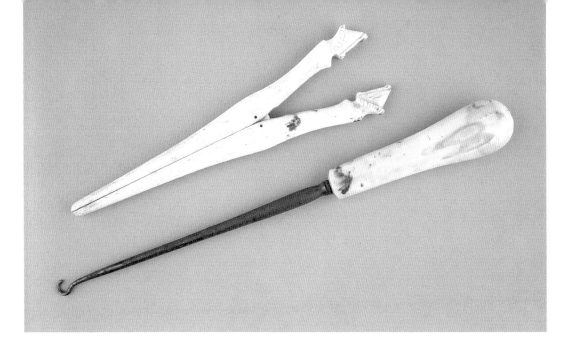

GLOVE STRETCHERS,
bone, metal,
H. ¹/₂", W. 2", L. 7". (Peabody Essex Museum)

BUTTONHOOK,
bone, metal,
H. ³/₄", W. 1¹/₄", L. 10". (Peabody Essex Museum)

The two scrimshawed articles shown here were undoubtedly designed for women's use. The Y-shaped bone implement was used to stretch gloves after they had been washed. While the wool, leather, or kid gloves were still damp, the pincer-like shaft would be inserted into the fingers, and then gentle pressure on two handles would separate the two halves of the shaft, thus stretching the glove finger back to its original size. The hooves carved on the tips of the handles remind us that those who rode or drove horses often protected their hands with leather gloves.

Before the mass production of factory-made clothing, buttons and buttonholes were not always uniform in size. Sometimes a button needed extra help in getting through a buttonhole with the help of a buttonhook. Fine clothing was often put together with many small covered buttons on sleeves, shirt or blouse fronts, and shoes. The small metal hook at the end of the shaft was inserted through the buttonhole. It grasped the back of the button and was then pulled through the buttonhole. The plain, utilitarian bone handle was carved by a scrimshander who had made handles for his own tools and knew the importance of a good grasp.

CLOTHESPINS,
bone,
L. 4⁷/₈", Diam. ¹⁵/₁₆";
L. 2³/₄", Diam. ⁷/₁₆";
L. 7¹/₄", Diam. 1";
L. 3⁷/₈", Diam. ¹¹/₁₆". (New Bedford Whaling Museum)

Clothespins appeared shortly after the introduction of hemp rope, which provided clotheslines. Prior to this, wet laundry was draped on bushes and placed on the grass. Clothespins remained a homemade item until the latter part of the nineteenth century when they began to be manufactured. Because they were handcrafted, there was no uniformity, so the pins came in a variety of shapes and lengths. As seen in these four examples, the degree of turning and the individualized styling reflect the maker's intention of producing objects that were simultaneously utilitarian and attractive. One whaler is known to have turned out three dozen pins. After all, what good is just one? Remember also that clothes washing in the nineteenth century was not done with the frequency that it is today.

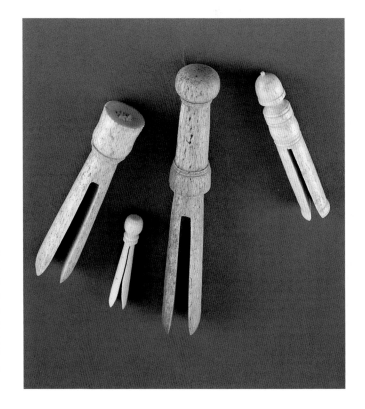

CHAPTER FOUR

Made to Be Seen

Whenever it may have started, it seems that since time immemorial individual craft workers have enjoyed making things for themselves, their families, and their friends. At the beginning of the nineteenth century handwork was still the norm. The coordination of hand and eye and pride in one's work meant that craftsmen were making, repairing, and maintaining those things that were not only strictly utilitarian but also those that were more purely ornamental. Thus craft in many instances was transformed into folk art. All this, combined with the elaborate taste associated with the Victorian era, set the stage for the art of scrimshandering.

Scrimshaw was an integral part of daily life on board a whaler. It provided an emotional outlet that was both physical and mental at the same time. As a social diversion one may consider it as paralleling its female counterpart, the quilting bee.

Scrimshaw is an American variant on the art of carving ivory, and the specialness of this type of carving labels it, at least in the beginning, as being specifically Yankee. This mostly masculine art form was created and perfected by the estimated 150,000 to 200,000 whalemen. Captains, mates, and seamen were all involved in scrimshaw, for it was nearly universal among whalemen for nearly eight decades. As whaling began, prospered, and declined, so did scrimshaw.

This form of self-expression is believed to have been associated more closely with the Yankee whalemen than with the foreign crews that came to replace them, although the foreigners certainly made scrimshaw too. There was some trading of scrimshaw among whalers, and there were pieces that were bartered in foreign ports, but for the most part the scrimshaw, if it was not made for use by the sailor, then it was destined to be gifts. There was no reward other than the pleasure of having completed a piece, and the joy received from giving it to a loved one. It made sense that scrimshaw was not created for sale; if the time involved had been factored in, the cost would have been prohibitive. How interesting that this almost totally noncommercial work should have been juxtaposed with the very commercial world of whaling!

Scrimshandering had many reasons for holding the interest of whalemen. In addition to the utilitarian objects produced for the home and the ship, it kept their hands busy, adept, and limber and their minds clever and original. This art form thus became testimony to the dexterous hands and creative minds of these men. It was thoroughly ingrained in their minds that idleness was just not acceptable; one had to be productive during waking hours. Scrimshaw filled the bill: the raw material was at hand, enormous periods of free time existed, and a useful object could be made. Patience also played a major role, for it was needed during the making of each object, but also from piece to piece so that skills could be continually improved. None of the skills needed to fashion bone and ivory would have been a result of formal training. These untutored artists learned not from a text but from a combination of natural inclination, peer example, and trial and error.

In the making of utilitarian scrimshaw, the ship's cooper and the carpenter, both trained craftsmen, may have given the scrimshanders needed tips in joinery, turning, carving, and inlay, skills employed in various degrees on certain pieces. Through experience, the individual qualities of bone and ivory would become evident to the carvers. The designer would learn to appreciate the fine, hard grain of ivory. Cut and sliced ivory could be used for inlay in boxes, for teething rings, and for larger pieces like candlesticks and picture frames. Speckled whalebone also had special qualities to be studied if the carved hunks, slats, and bands of bone were to be successfully used in work boxes, wastebaskets, and buggy whips. The size of panbone allowed it to be sliced into thicknesses from an 1/8 inch to 1/4 inch. Other considerations included color, age, and the effect of light. Flaws, cracks, and chips in the raw material also often had to be dealt with.

Many of the woods employed for the bottoms of ditty boxes and work baskets, the sides and tops of trinket boxes, for inlays, games, and furniture would already have been familiar to the seamen. Ebony and lignum vitae would have been easily identified, but unknown types were simply put to use. With his self-acquired knowledge the scrimshander was only limited in his creativity by his desire and inventiveness, his skill, and that most important ingredient, patience. So a risk factor was always present.

When we consider the great variety of scrimshaw to be found in the "made to be seen" category, it is evident that the decorative arts were important to whalemen. Although they certainly would have never used the term "decorative arts," the ornamentation on these useful objects reveals a greater degree of skill and sophistication than do the hands-on tools already illustrated.

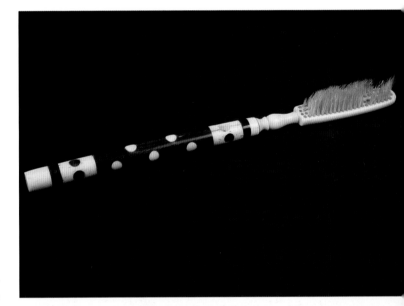

TOOTHBRUSH,
ivory, natural bristle, unknown material,
L. 7", Diam. ³/₈". (Mystic Seaport Museum)

Although it is small in size, this toothbrush boasts a very lively design. Rarely did a personal necessity receive such attention. The scrimshander knew this would not be a display piece, but that did not prevent his creating an elegant object. The handle, solidly shaped for holding, is enhanced with bandings and is punctuated with black and white polka dots. Note also the delicate turning that leads to the bristles. Imagine the tediousness of making the bristle inserts. The worn bristles and the missing circular inlay makes clear the age of the piece, yet it retains a sense of modernity that surely in reproduction would make it a consumer's delight.

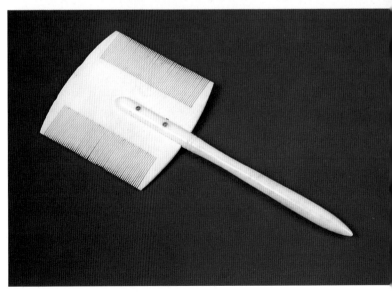

COMB,
ivory, metal,
H. ³/₁₆", W. 1¹/₂", L. 3⁹/₁₆". (Mystic Seaport Museum)

The almost miniature size and the very fine teeth of this ivory comb indicate that it was probably meant to comb a baby's hair. Although not quite four inches long its two parts are in total harmony with each other. The simple, slightly curvilinear one-piece handle, with its two turnings at the point where the comb is inserted into the shaft, fits snugly over the double-sided comb.

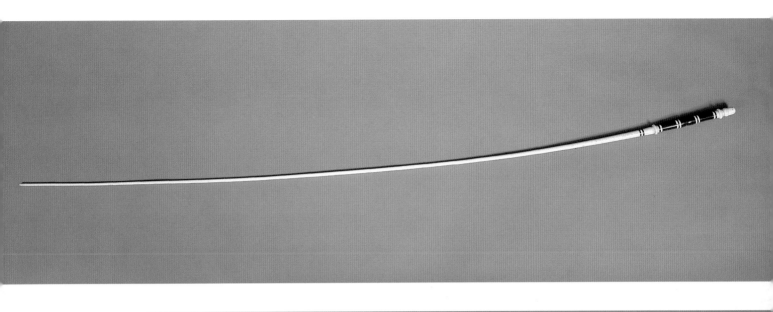

BUGGY WHIP,
wood, ivory, baleen, bone,
L. 72", Diam. 1". (New Bedford Whaling Museum)

Inasmuch as the horse and buggy was such a universal mode of transportation in the nineteenth century, one might suppose that scrimshawed buggy whips would be common. However, they are extremely rare objects. A possible explanation of their rarity is due to the fact that the whips needed to be long and flexible, so there was probably a lot of breakage of the bone. This splendid example is six feet long, and it has a gracefully turned handle of ivory, wood, and baleen joined to a long, thin strip of shaped panbone. The length of the whip meant that a captain or a mate was the maker, for only they would have had the room to work on and store such a piece.

POSSIBLY A PIPE STAND,
wood, walrus ivory, sperm-whale ivory, clay pipes,
H. 12", Diam. 8¹/₆". (The Kendall Whaling Museum)

There has been a good deal of discussion about the intended function of this piece of scrimshaw. Similar objects in other collections are thought to be stands for various tobacco accoutrements. It is quite possible that the long ivory cups in the second tier from the top were made to hold matches, while the next two levels were ideal for holding pipes, as seen in the illustration. The ivory carvings at the base, which are reminiscent of the davits that held whale boats on the ships, also seem suited for holding pipes. Whatever may be the true function of this piece, both the ivory and the unidentified wood, which probably came from some foreign port, are meticulously turned and carved, the result of much time and effort.

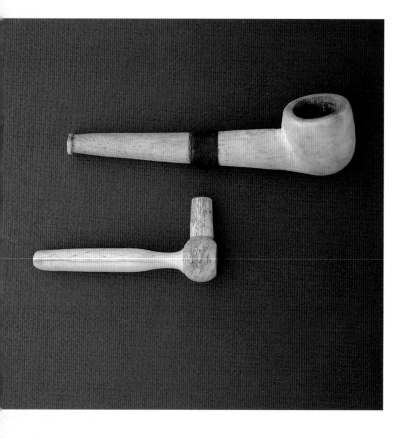

TOBACCO PIPE,
bone, metal,
H. 1¼", W. 1", L. 4¼". (Peabody Essex Museum)

OPIUM PIPE,
bone,
H. ¾", W. 1½", L. 3". (Peabody Essex Museum)

Tobacco pipes and less frequently opium pipes, along with such pipe accoutrements as tampers and picks, were scrimshawed items most often carved to be used by their makers. Ivory was never used for pipes because the heat supposedly had an adverse affect on them. Tobacco was popular with whalers, with some men using over 100 pounds during a three-year voyage. While working, men chewed tobacco, but during their off periods it would be smoked. A whaling crew was divided into two watches of four hours on and four hours off, with two-hour periods (one for each watch) called the dog watch. These ran from four to six and six to eight in the evening and were meant for rest and relaxation. It was then that pipe smoking was prevalent. Besides being a form of relaxation, tobacco helped take away the misery caused by the food. The ship's owners, knowing the tastes of their crew, sold tobacco at very profitable rates that were often charged against the purchaser's lay.

Although most sailors had little knowledge of it, opium was found by and introduced to whalers who ventured into Oriental ports. Sailors have always been willing to try a new, exotic—and even dangerous—pastime. This two-piece pipe is pierced from one end to the other so that the smoker can draw on the opium vapors.

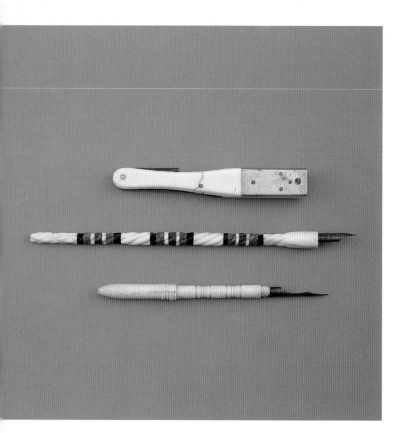

QUILL PEN CUTTER,
ivory, steel,
H. ½", W. ⁹⁄₁₆", L. 4". (The Kendall Whaling Museum)

PEN HOLDER,
walrus ivory, wood, steel,
H. ⁵⁄₁₆", W. ⁵⁄₁₆", L. 6¹¹⁄₁₆". (The Kendall Whaling Museum)

PEN,
whale skeletal bone, steel,
H. ⁵⁄₁₆", W. ⁵⁄₁₆", L. 4¾". (The Kendall Whaling Museum)

Nineteenth-century desk supplies were familiar to scrimshanders who made them as gifts, probably in the hope that they would encourage letter writing to the news-starved whaler. Before today's ball points, old fountain pens, and still older steel pen points, quills were what were dipped into ink to compose letters. These quills had to be both sharp and the right size to avoid blotching the page, and it was quill pen cutters, like the example at the top of the illustration, that served just this purpose. After the quill pen came the pen holder, in which a steel nib could be inserted as seen in the handsome middle piece. Because pen points broke or wore down, a supply of extra nibs was kept on hand and inserted into the holder as needed. This pen holder with its inlaid woods and in the style of a spiral narwhal horn carving is exceptionally attractive. As steel points improved, pens such as this simply turned model at the bottom with its rounded end were scrimshawed with built-in nibs.

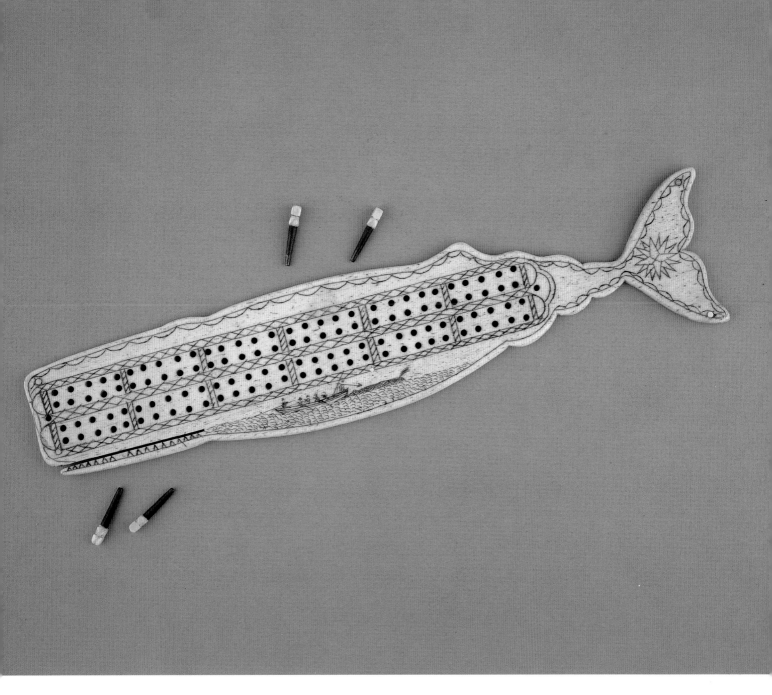

CRIBBAGE BOARD,
bone, wood, coloring,
H. 1", W. 2¹/₂", L. 11¹/₂". (Peabody Essex Museum)

Cribbage, a card game for from two to four players, is based on various combinations that count for points. To keep track of these points one uses a cribbage board with its rows of holes into which pegs are inserted. Although it is not tremendously popular now, cribbage was in the nineteenth century a widely known pastime both at home and at sea. This extremely well-planned and well-executed board is quite rare. Most bone or ivory cribbage boards were a product of the Eskimo trade. Seamen in the Arctic would trade goods for such pieces. Because of its overall whale shape and the engraved illustration of a whaleboat with a harpooner attacking a whale, it is highly probable that this board was made by a whaleman. Additional support for this attribution is that a sperm whale with teeth in the lower jaw is depicted. The compass rose engraved on the tail is additional proof, for it is not an Eskimo design.

CHECKERBOARD,
bone, baleen, wood, ivory, copper, brass,
H. 2¹/₄", W. 15⁵/₈", L. 14³/₄" (New Bedford Whaling Museum)

The time for recreation on a whaleship was the second dog-watch that ran from six to eight in the evening. Boxing was discouraged by the captains, but scrimshandering, checkers, dominoes, cards, cribbage, and chess were not. This folding checkerboard set on its box reflects two of these pastimes. The thirty-two whalebone squares and thirty-two wooden ones are framed by strips of baleen, and the outer borders are alternating bands of wood and bone. The reverse side has a backgammon board composed of ivory, bone, baleen, and wood. The stakes for seamen using such gameboards were usually tobacco. Such a handsome piece may well have been meant for the parlor when its maker returned to home port.

ALPHABET LETTERS (124),
c. 1820, bone, black ink,
H. ¹/₈", W. ¹¹/₁₆", L. ¹/₂". (The Kendall Whaling Museum)

DOMINOES (28) IN BOX,
bone, wood, red and black ink,
Box: H. 1¹/₁₆", W. 1¹/₂", L. 2¹¹/₁₆";
Dominos: H. ¹/₈", W. ¹/₂", L. 1¹/₁₆". (The Kendall Whaling Museum)

These bone and black-inked letters were not meant just for children. Many seamen were illiterate and used these scrimshaw letters to learn the alphabet and spelling. Enclosed in a wooden box with "Abc" inlaid on the top, these 124 letters form more than four complete alphabets to be used for study or word games. One side of each block shows a capital letter, while the reverse side shows the same letter in lower case. Alphabets also appear on scrimshawed horn books and are often found on children's blocks in folk portraiture.

The twenty-eight whalebone dominoes with black ink dots are very small and fit neatly into a box with a sliding top shaped like a domino. The box is so small that it could easily be stored. Other scrimshawed dominoes are larger and are sometimes backed with ebony.

PARASOL, ▶
ivory, baleen, brass, steel, wood, silk, mother-of-pearl,
H. ¹¹/₁₆", W. 1³/₄", L. 36⁷/₈". (New Bedford Whaling Museum)

Although we do not know the maker of this scrimshawed parasol, we can be certain that it was intended for somebody special. The Yankee lady who received this gift undoubtedly used it with great pride, for such a time-consuming present took infinite patience and both mechanical and engineering ability to complete, similar to the talents needed to produce a swift. From the hanging ring of the handle with its intricate turning and carving to the elegantly pointed ivory tip everything indicates precision work. The unseen baleen ribs with their identically sculptured ivory tips were attached to a painted wooden shaft. Whether the scrimshander purchased the patterned silk material and assembled it on the frame or whether the recipient did it, we do not know. We do know that the mother-of-pearl button closure is a replacement.

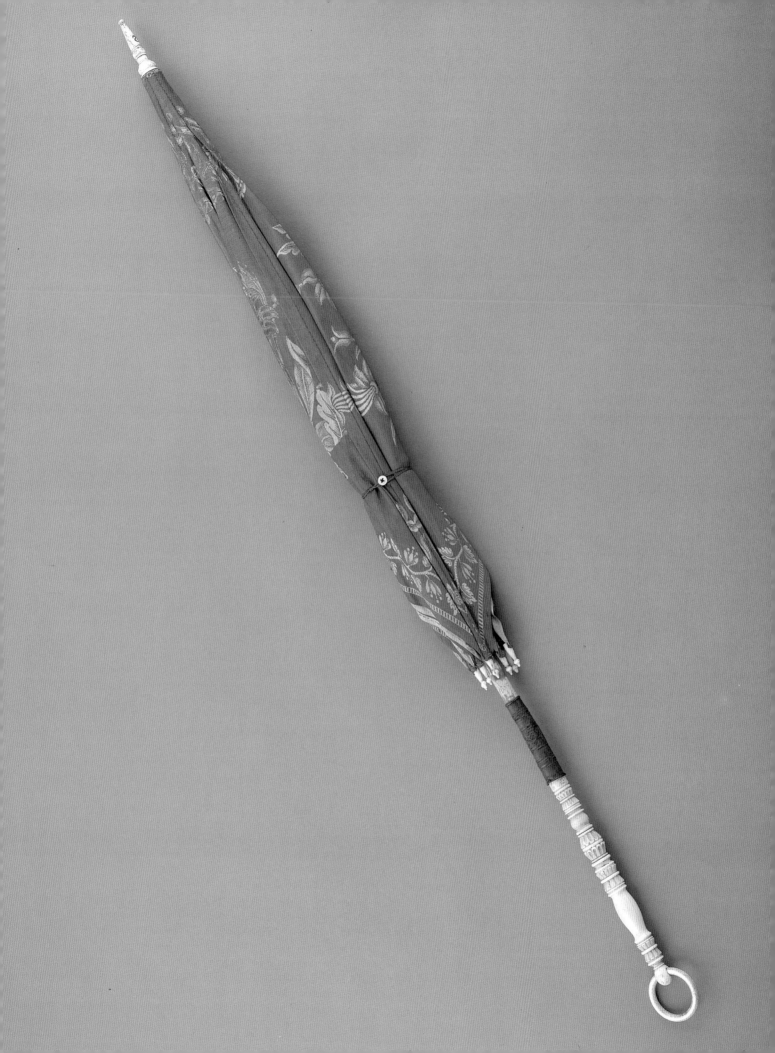

DOLL CRADLE,
bone, woods,
H. 7½", W. 6¾", L. 13". (New Bedford Whaling Museum)

TOY TOP,
bone, paint,
H. 2¾", Diam. 1⅝". (New Bedford Whaling Museum)

DOLL BED,
bone, twine,
H. 7", W. 8⅞", L. 12⅜". (New Bedford Whaling Museum)

Although a variety of toys was being manufactured in the nineteenth century, many doting fathers continued to make gifts for their children. In New England it was common practice for carpenters to cre-

ate toys as a sideline. In the beginning of the century, young girls were encouraged to play with dolls, for it was felt that doing so would train them in child care and housekeeping. These two quite different examples of doll furniture were considered both educational and playful. The attractive cradle with its bone rockers and borders also has a variety of subtle inlays on its sides. The doll bed is a working miniature. The twine support for a mattress can even be tightened. The folk art portrait engraved on the footboard is a very special feature of this elegant piece. The small top was more apt to be a boy's toy even though the alternating red and black numbers from one to twelve have an unknown purpose. These beautifully designed and constructed playthings are rare, not because few were made, but because the survival rate of toys, which were actually played with, was understandably low.

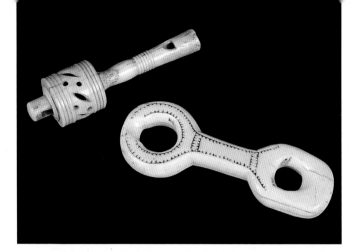

RATTLE/WHISTLE,
bone,
L. 3¹³/₁₆", Diam. 1". (Mystic Seaport Museum)

TEETHING RING,
ivory, coloring,
H. ⁵/₈", L. 1¹/₂", W. ³/₈". (Mystic Seaport Museum)

Many mariners made sailor's whistles, so it is no surprise that a child's version would appear as scrimshaw, and this example has a rattle attached. The hollow handle provides the whistle, while the filigreed and symmetrically turned cage for the rattle is slipped onto the end. This working toddler's toy, although made of bone, is quite similar in design to one made of silver about 1750 by the Philadelphia silversmith, Philip Syng, Jr.

The ivory teething ring has a hand grasp perfectly suited to a baby's fist. The design of minute triangles decorating the piece is worn just enough to show that it was obviously used by a child.

TEA STRAINER,
coconut shell, walrus ivory,
H. ³/₁₆", W. 4³/₁₆", L. 4¹/₄". (The Kendall Whaling Museum)

SUGAR TONGS,
bone, tortoiseshell,
L. 4¹/₄". (The Kendall Whaling Museum)

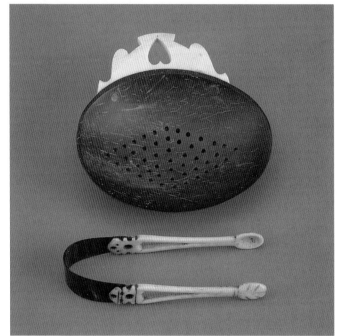

Both of these delightful pieces were used for the correct serving of tea before the invention of the tea bag. Popular since our Colonial period, loose tea was brewed in a teapot. The tea strainer would then be held over or placed upon a teacup to catch any loose tea leaves that might be mixed in with the tea when it was poured from the teapot. A decided advantage of the coconut-shell bowl of the strainer was that tea stains would closely match the color of the shell and become unnoticeable. Silver and pewter tea strainers of the time are very similar in design to this example.

Before granulated sugar or sugar cubes were commonplace, sugar was purchased in the form of a loaf and then was cut into lumps that were grasped by sugar tongs like this pair. The flexibility of tortoiseshell, which probably came from Caribbean waters, allowed the tongs to bend as the arms clasped the sugar. The tips of the handsome bone arms are carved with a leaf design.

SHAWL PIN,
ivory, metal, possibly wax,
L. 4¹/₂", Diam. ⁵/₈". (Mystic Seaport Museum)

SHAWL CLIP,
elephant ivory, metal, unidentified substance,
H. ¹/₄", W. ³/₄", L. 3". (Mystic Seaport Museum)

SHAWL CLIP,
ivory, metal, unidentified substance,
H. ¹/₄", W. ³/₄", L. 3". (Mystic Seaport Museum)

Drafty nineteenth-century homes made shawls a necessity. They were also used for brief outdoor journeys. Because most shawls had no buttons they were constantly slipping off the shoulder. However, this illustration shows handsome solutions to the problem. The pin with the polyhedron ivory tip inlaid with an unidentified substance is most unusual and highly decorative. The two clips offer another solution. Similar in size, one clip features ivory on top, and the other has burnished metal. Both are enhanced with beveled edges and have mottled circular pegs joining the pieces. These are unusual items for a scrimshander to make, but perhaps they had been specifically requested.

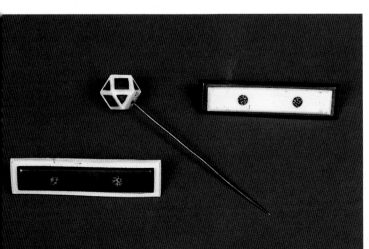

PICTURE FRAMES,
1850–1875, walrus ivory, tortoiseshell, wood,
H. ⁷/₁₆", W. 2¹/₄", L. 3¹³/₁₆";
H. ¹/₂", W. 2¹/₄", L. 3¹³/₁₆". (The Kendall Whaling Museum)

The Civil War greatly increased the popularity of photography, for it produced likenesses that were cheaper, faster, and much more realistic than painted portraits. Consequently, there was great growth in this field in the last half of the nineteenth century. The small, elegant ivory frames enclose the photographs in ovals. The delicate tortoiseshell hanging rings are attached to the frames with small, plainly turned ivory knobs. The children's photographs may well have been a welcome reminder to a whaling captain of his family back home, or it is possible that the ivory frames hung in a front parlor.

WASTE BASKET,
whale skeletal bone, wood, metal,
H. 14⁷/₈", Diam. 10¹/₂". (The Kendall Whaling Museum)

Waste baskets in general are designed to be severely functional, but this cannot be said of this handsomely decorative creation. The fragility of this piece indicates that it was probably designed to be used for waste paper at a desk. The design of the twelve side slats with ogival finials that match the delicate feet suggest that they were carved with the aid of a template. The undulating hoops at top and bottom that are attached to the slats with small metal rivets are beautifully carved. Like most scrimshawed containers this waste basket has a wooden base, which is inlaid with a six-pointed bone star.

TOWEL ROLLER,
bone, wood, metal,
H. 2½", W. 2½", L. 16". (Peabody Essex Museum)

Although it looks like a rolling pin, this is actually a towel holder with stationary handles flanking a free-moving center section. It is the wooden center section that prevents this being a rolling pin, for the wood is both pitted and uneven—very undesirable qualities for preparing dough for baking. In the nineteenth century most middle- and lower-class homes did not have individual hand towels by the pitcher and wash basin, the pump in the kitchen, or the barrel on the porch. This holder would be placed in a sturdy rack, and toweling would be sewn end to end, thus forming a ring that would revolve around the holder as each person washed and dried his hands. A real advantage of the holder was that the towel never fell to the floor or was misplaced.

CANDLESTICK,
ivory, wood, mother-of-pearl, coloring,
H. 8¼", W. 3⅜", L. 3½". (Mystic Seaport Museum)

Ivory candlesticks were not new to whalers; they were part of a tradition originating in England. The fact, however, that these seamen fished for sperm whales that supplied the oil that produced sperm-oil candles meant there was a close connection between candlestick and candlestick maker. It was an indirect way of promoting their own product. Sperm-oil candles were so highly regarded that as far back as 1750, a Benjamin Crabb of Rehoboth, Massachusetts, was granted a monopoly to make these candles as long as he agreed to train five others to do the same. A mixture of aestheticism and utilitarianism is evident in this handsome object. The ivory shaft, although cracked, is elegantly turned; however, it is the wood and ivory base with its small acorn finials and mother-of-pearl circular inlays that draws attention to the candlestick.

WATCH HOLDER,
ivory, bone, woods, mother-of-pearl, brown and black ink, mirror,
H. 29", W. 5¾", L. 9". (New Bedford Whaling Museum)

Before the wrist watch, men had pocket watches, but when they were not being carried they were often placed in a watch holder. In addition to this scrimshawed version, folk-art watch holders were also constructed in chalkware, redware, and plain wood. Although we do not know who made this extraordinary creation, we do know that it came from the brig *Sarah Louisa*, which was captained by the New Bedford whaler Ray Green Sanford on a voyage lasting from August 1838 to June 1840. The watch, of course, is dwarfed by the architectural housing that is a masterful example of an artisan having created beyond necessity. The multitiered, towering, and patriotic construction uses mahogany as its primary wood. A single drawer in the base acts as a foundation for the first tier where a woman holding a liberty cap on a pole stands in front of an impressive door between two elegant windows. The second level houses a niche holding an American eagle on a stand, and a mirror backlights this carved emblem. Finally, on the third tier is the case for the watch. Each level is adorned with small carved busts, posts with finials, and a variety of inlays. The result is a magnificent and significant tour de force of the art of scrimshaw.

CLOCK,
whalebone, metal, coloring, string,
H. 8¼", W. 4", L. 5¾". (Peabody Essex Museum)

FOOTSTOOL,
wood, ivory, bone, brass,
H. 7", W. 6½", L. 10". (New Bedford Whaling Museum)

Clocks and navigational tools were the most sophisticated techno-logical products of colonial America, thus setting a standard for the forthcoming century, when Connecticut became known as the cen-ter of the clockmaking industry in the United States. Clocks had been expensive, and it was not until the 1830s that machine-made clocks came on the market. Inexpensive brass movements, which put an end to wooden works, were hardier than those made of wood and were not affected by dampness. By the 1850s, there was a demand for low-priced clocks.

All of this makes the scrimshawed clock shown here a fascinating timepiece. Constructed almost entirely of whalebone, one of the few metal parts is inscribed "New Haven, Conn . . . Jero," meaning that it had originated in another form and was probably broken. In the same manner that he altered broken tools, the scrimshander took those parts that worked and then skrimmed the rest in order to create this intricate working clock. The small bone hammer in the shape of a whale's tooth that is poised to strike the gong is yet another example of the whaler's imaginative resourcefulness.

Footstools of this size were a popular household item in the nine-teenth century. Women would place their feet on them while sitting to protect them against the cold floors of houses that had no central heating. The inlaid ivory initials on either side of the eight-pointed star are undoubtedly those of the giver and the receiver, and the bone hearts on the skirt probably indicate that they were a couple—not mother and son, or sister and brother. The bone hearts, dia-monds, and borders that outline the skirt of the footstool provide an elegance to the whole that is emphasized by the round ivory feet.

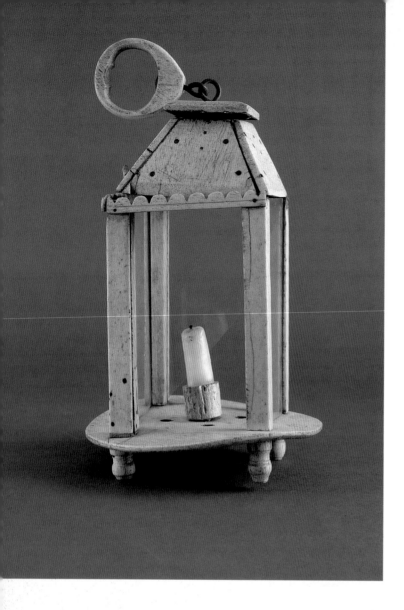

LANTERN,
bone, metal, glass,
H. 11½", Diam. 8". (New Bedford Whaling Museum)

Spermaceti oil taken from the head of the sperm whale produced the finest candles. This oil, which needs hardly any refining, was even stored in separate casks. Because of their cost, it is unlikely that a ship's forecastle was lighted with such candles. Except for the scalloped border on the lower edge of the dome and the slightly carved feet, the emphasis on this scrimshawed lantern is utilitarian. It was constructed so that it could either stand on a table or hang by means of the large whalebone ring resting on the dome.

BIRD CAGE,
whalebone, metal,
H. 21", W. 16", L. 16". (Peabody Essex Museum)

In Herman Melville's *Moby Dick* a lost bird alighted on the *Pequod* and was captured. Soon a scrimshawed cage became its home on board. Another example of a scrimshawed aviary is shown here complete with its perch post, food and water holders, a removable waste tray, a hanging device, and rounded bone bars. Flame finials top the four corner posts. Exotic birds were sometimes purchased in warm-climate ports while the whalers were on shore leave. These living souvenirs were brought back to the ship and became companions and mascots. Often, when the whaling ship was far from land, these birds had free run of the vessel, but when land was near, they were placed in cages. Few birds actually arrived in home ports, for some would have escaped, while others would have died from the change in locale. In 1902, when the ship *Kathleen* was sinking and had to be abandoned, the captain's wife, a Mrs. Jenkins, saved only her warm clothes and her caged parrot.

COAT AND HAT RACK,
hardwood, ivory, narwhal tusk, metal,
H. 90⅜", W. 32", L. 32". (Mystic Seaport Museum)

The narwhal, which may have played a role in the unicorn myth, is a species of Arctic whale which, except for the tusks, has no commercial value. The long, twisting horn that tapers to a point is really a modified tooth that grows out of the left side of the upper jaw to a length of six to ten feet. Whalers usually got those tusks from the Arctic natives. These tusks are very hard and are quite difficult to carve, and consequently they are rare in scrimshaw. This extraordinary coat and hat rack is set on a wooden base with ball feet; the turned wooden shaft is outfitted with turned ivory pegs to hold hats. The four narwhal tusks rise out of the ball feet and are supported midway with a horizontal ivory brace. Three of these tusks are similar in size, but the fourth one towers majestically at just over ninety inches to help make this a memorable scrimshaw showpiece.

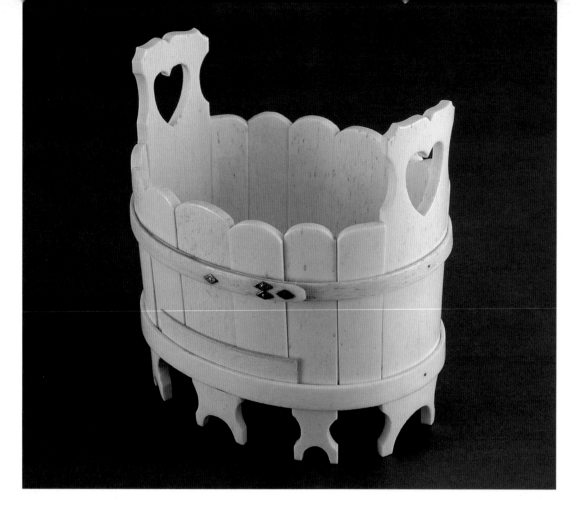

TUB,
whale skeletal bone, ivory, brass, copper,
H. 7⅝", W. 6¼", L. 8". (The Kendall Whaling Museum)

One might easily assume that a ship's cooper scrimshawed this tub,
for it has staves and hoops similar to those of an oil barrel. The tops
of the thick slabs of whalebone with its visible grain are reminiscent
of a picket fence. The heart shapes in the handles indicate that
this was a gift to a loved one. The hoops are joined by attractive
diamond-shaped copper and brass rivets, while smaller rivets attach
the hoops to the handles. Unlike most boxes and containers, this tub
has an ivory bottom instead of the usual wooden one. Victorian
objects similar to this example were meant to hold letters, sewing
equipment, or other paraphernalia.

HANGING POCKET,
bone, metal,
H. 7½", W. 5½", D. ¾". (Peabody Essex Museum)

Hanging wall pockets were utilitarian knick-knacks that the
Victorian era found indispensable in the last part of the nineteenth
century. Nothing just was; everything had to be placed in something.
Large wall pockets held daily newspapers and myriad weekly and
monthly publications. Others were designed for correspondence
that needed to be answered. Because of its small size this example
may well have been intended to hold recipe cards in the kitchen.
The creator of this pocket joined his sections with metal pegs that
were larger than usual. The design of the back includes the ubiquitous heart in the center. The wave-like rim of the front gives an
appropriate nautical feeling to the piece.

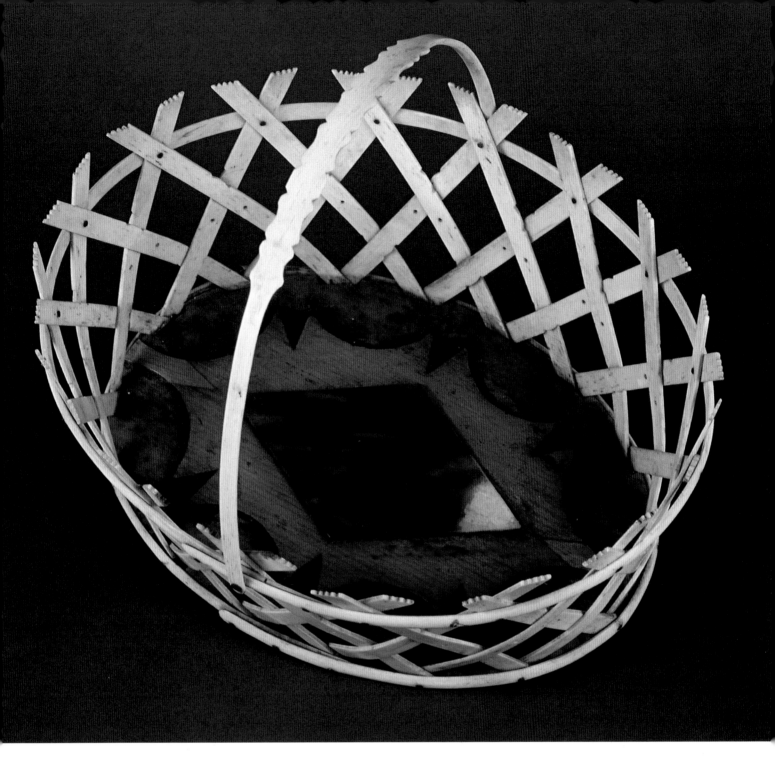

WORK BASKET,
whalebone, wood, horn, metal,
H. (with handle up) 7⅝", W. 7⅝", L. 9⅛". (Mystic Seaport Museum)

The work basket pictured here may have been used to hold sewing or knitting, or even to display fruit. It is a triumph of delicacy. To produce the decorative siding, bone was sawn, cut, and sliced into strips. These thin strips were then interlaced and joined by tiny metal pegs to upper and lower rounded bone hoops to form the lattice work. The scrimshander may well have seen a similar design executed in redware pottery of the time. The decorative notches on the tops of the slats and on the center of the handle add much to the beauty of the piece along with the handsomely designed base with its diamond-shaped horn inlay.

MINIATURE CHEST OF DRAWERS,
bone, ivory, wood, tortoiseshell,
H. 14½", W. 14⅜", D. 6¼". (New Bedford Whaling Museum)

This outstanding miniature chest of drawers was probably intended
to be placed on top of a full-size chest to hold jewelry. Without its
decorative ivory inlay and bone carving it would really be quite plain,
so it is easy to appreciate the magic of the skilled scrimshander and
the beauty of his work. The handsome wood used in this special
piece is enhanced by the decoration of stars, diamonds, long tear-
drops, drawer pulls, and classical columns created with bone and
ivory. The recipient of this cabinet had to have been enchanted by it,
just as we are today.

DITTY BOX,
bone, wood, coloring, metal, tortoiseshell,
H. 3", W. 6", L. 8". (Peabody Essex Museum)

Scrimshanders certainly did not invent the oval box, but they used
the form many times, for it was not cumbersome and was easy for
the hand to grasp. Ditty boxes, like this example, could be used for
toilet articles or for sewing paraphernalia. Still others might contain
tools for mending nets. To construct the sides of the box a thin broad
slice of panbone was boiled to make it pliable, and then bent into the
oval shape. The ends of the panbone were next fastened to a flat base
when still soft so that when the panbone cooled and dried, it would
retain the oval shape. The panbone box shown was made in traditional fashion with a wooden top decorated with inlay and engraved
motifs on the panbone sides, which include a ship, American flags, a
harp, and a building.

DITTY BOX,
before 1850, baleen, wood, metal,
H. 4", W. 5", L. 6½". (Peabody Essex Museum)

Every right whale and bowhead whale that was captured had a mouthful of baleen. Before about 1850 baleen had little commercial value, and it was distributed to the scrimshanders, who called it whalebone, even though it was not actually bone. After 1850, baleen's importance to the manufacture of busks, umbrellas, hoops, whips, carriage springs, and suitcases, to name just a few items, meant that scrimshanders were no longer given the baleen. Many found this fibrous, tough material difficult to work, and because of its color and hardness undesirable for engraving designs. One of the rare qualities of this oval box is its baleen top, for most baleen containers have both wooden tops and bottoms. The baleen box illustrated is remarkable for the houses and trees engraved on it, and this village scene may well have been a fond recollection of his hometown by the scrimshander.

PUZZLE BOX,
walrus ivory, whale skeletal bone, tortoiseshell, beech, pine, mahogany, ebony, mirror, metal,
H. 3⅜", W. 6⅝", L. 11⅛". (The Kendall Whaling Museum)

From the earliest years in the Colonies Americans produced boxes for holding everything from salt to Bibles. By the Victorian era, due to a mania for neatness and safe keeping, even more types of boxes were being made. This puzzle box, rare because of its large size, is an example of just one form that whalers scrimshawed. The secret of opening this puzzle box is knowing the right order in which to twist the knobs on the top, which are reflected in the mirror. When the correct combination has been found, the bone cog wheels on the inside of the lid move to release the latch. The box is a handsome and fascinating example of safe storage.

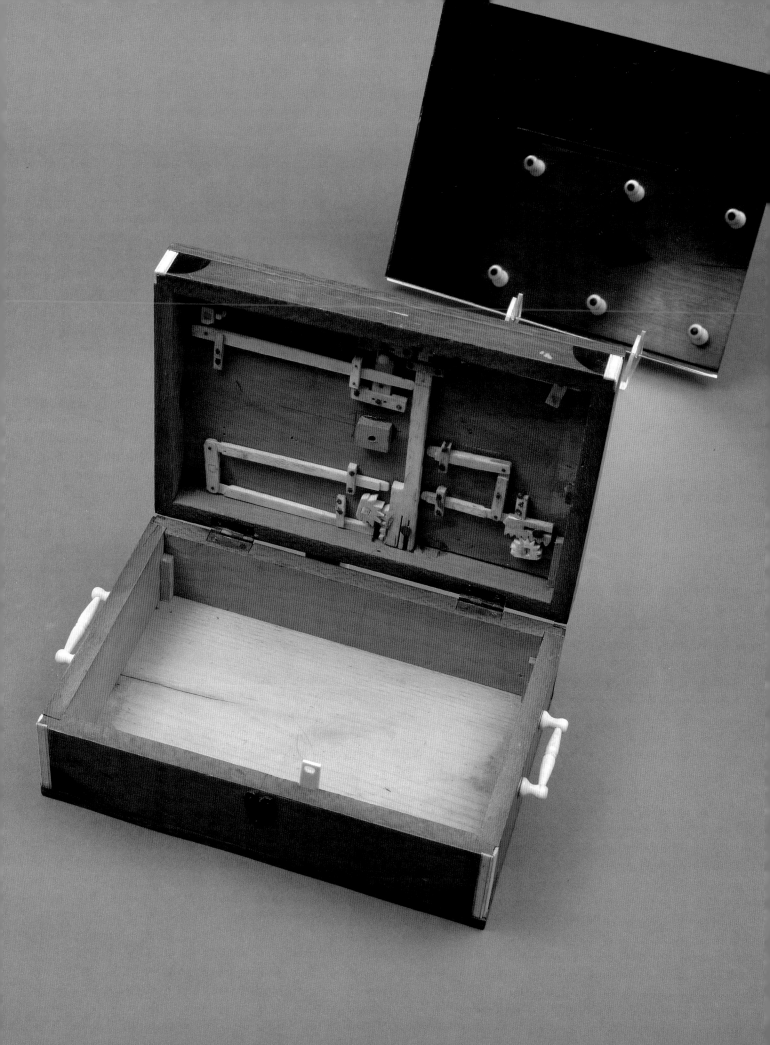

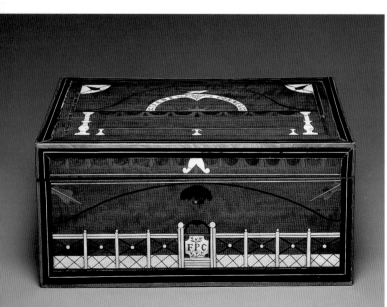

BOX,
bone, wood, ivory, baleen, metal,
H. 5⅝", D. 6½", L. 8¾". (New Bedford Whaling Museum)

Due to the Victorian mania for having all kinds of containers for storage, there are many scrimshawed wooden boxes with ivory and bone inlay. This is a marvelous example of such work. The focal point of the top is the inlaid ivory arc, which itself is inlaid with wooden letters spelling "Jane Cornell." The front of the box boasts a beautiful ivory fence with a gate bearing the initials "FPC," which presumably refer to the scrimshander, who very possibly was also her husband. The inside of the box not only has more fine marquetry, but also has an exquisite ivory eagle hovering over an American flag atop a pole. Two hands on either side of the flagpole draw our attention to the patriotic symbols. It is a great piece.

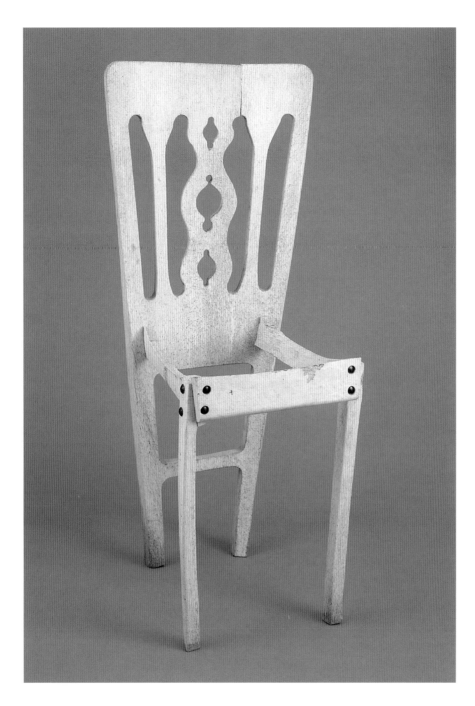

CHAIR,
panbone, metal,
H. 40½", W. 17¼", L. 16½". (The Kendall Whaling Museum)

Sometimes the vertebrae of a whale were used for the seat of a chair, but it is very rare to have an entire chair made of panbone. This armless chair has only six parts, the largest piece of which forms the back, rear legs, and the stretcher. From the wide plain crest rail the back of the chair tapers inward as the legs approach the floor. The three-piece seat frame was designed to hold an upholstered seat then becoming fashionable for straight-backed side chairs. In contrast to those in the rear, the front legs are straight. This piece is a simple country version of the Chippendale style.

CHAPTER FIVE

Known and Supposed Makers

Anonymity and folk art often go hand in hand, and in the field of scrimshaw this fact is all too true. Most scrimshaw, whether it originated in the captain's quarters or in the forecastle, was unsigned and undated. Indeed, it is a very rare piece that has been identified by either the maker or the vessel on which it was made.

Scrimshaw's personal aspect played a major part in this situation. The object was to be used by the creator or given to close friends or relatives. Because everyone involved knew who made it, there simply was no need to sign the work. This was especially true if a scrimshawed tool was made for self use: "I made it; I know it; I use it. Why sign any name?" Consequently, the idea of signing a piece of scrimshaw occurred in only a very small percentage of scrimshawed objects. These men were not concerned with self glorification, or with posterity's admiration. In fact, the majority of carvers did not think of their efforts as even having artistic value. After all, does a woman sign the dress she has just sewn?

For the most part scrimshaw's anonymity remains permanent, for without a signature it is quite difficult to identify work. Until fairly recently there has been a historic lack of research resulting in only a minimal amount of satisfactory documentation. Few thought that discovering identifications was a worthwhile quest. This lack of interest continued until the 1960s.

Fortunately, there has been a real change and current investigation is uncovering artists' identities and their dates. However, this scholarly research must still be considered to be in an early stage, so there is much to be determined and much false information that needs to be corrected. A major researcher in this field is Dr. Stuart M. Frank, Director of The Kendall Whaling Museum and author of *Dictionary of Scrimshaw Artists*. Thanks to his ongoing efforts we have a compilation of all known or attributed scrimshaw artists.

Problems exist in this new interest of identifying the scrimshaw carvers, because, as of yet, there is no accepted standard. One person or institution may have different guidelines from another for determining what is positive identification and what is an attribution. For the purposes of this chapter, the author is relying on the word of the institution that owns the scrimshaw.

Other considerations that need to be taken into account include the fallibility of some existing records and the invented stories that have arisen due to the lack of substantial verification. Furthermore, researchers need to keep in mind that scrimshanders took carving ideas from one another so freely that individualism is often hard to pinpoint, especially in the utilitarian scrimshaw. Still, style can be a lead. More definitive aids are provenance and that rare signature. To give some idea how rare proper identification is, this author personally reviewed 3,294 works of scrimshaw and found that only fifty-nine of these pieces could be attached to a name, and due to multiples only twenty-nine separate carvers came to light.

Dating scrimshaw is also a difficult task because within the time span of American whaling, artistic styles were not ascribed to specific periods. A different approach must often be taken. We know, for example, that thread did not become available on disposable spools until 1850, which means a thread stand with spaces for disposable spools must date after 1850. Because crocheting did not arrive in the United States until the 1840s, Yankee scrimshawed crochet hooks date from that point on. These could be first steps in the search for the maker.

Even a name or initials on scrimshaw do not necessarily indicate the maker. They might very well be the name or the initials of the intended receiver of the work. On the other hand, such a name has been known to be that of the maker, and then not one other bit of information could be found out about him.

Currently, there seem to be more attributions than positive identifications. Attributions comprise the assigning of a maker's name to a work of scrimshaw without having positive proof, but still there is good reason to believe that the piece came from the hand of a specific seaman. Attributions also are derived from provenance, labels, and intense research. An identified work might be compared to an unidentified object and because of similarities this could lead to another attribution.

Sometimes enough similarities in style or motif can be found among pieces that lead us to suspect strongly that they came from the same carver, even though no name accompanies them. In such cases, which usually involve carved teeth, a label such as the "Eagle Portraitist" will be assigned to the group.

Because the names of scrimshanders are so rare, proper identification adds to the object's importance. Interest in it is heightened, because a sense of personal history has been added to the provenance. The absence of a maker's name, on the other hand, does not diminish the value of an exceptional work of scrimshaw.

The known or attributed makers of the scrimshaw pictured in this section do not cover every known utilitarian object they produced. Many of these whalemen carved numerous pieces, indeed so many that it precluded their inclusion in the chapter. Also, some weak attributions have been omitted.

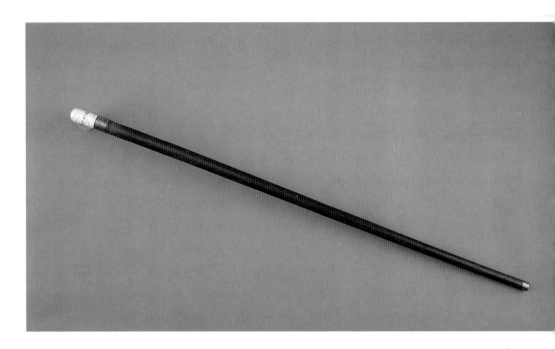

CANE,
attributed to William W. Allen, c. 1851–1854,
wood, brass, walrus ivory, silver, black ink,
H. 1", W. 1", L. 34½". (The Kendall Whaling Museum)

It is assumed that this simple, plain wooden cane with a brass tip and "L" shaped walrus-ivory handle was handcrafted by William Allen. Though no written records state this, the inscription "Wm. W. Allen" on the outside of the handle supports this belief. The real mystery seems to be the word "Minden" written on the silver cuff at the point where the shaft joins the handle. No explanation of this is currently available, but it might be the name of a subsequent owner.

Allen was born in Fairhaven, Massachusetts, and went to sea as a young man in 1836, moving up the ladder from crew in 1840 to second mate in 1849. From 1851 to 1854, he kept the journal for the *Alfred Gibbs* out of New Bedford. In addition to being a whaleman, Allen was also known as a ship owner and a merchant. Even with this information, we know very little about this Yankee scrimshander.

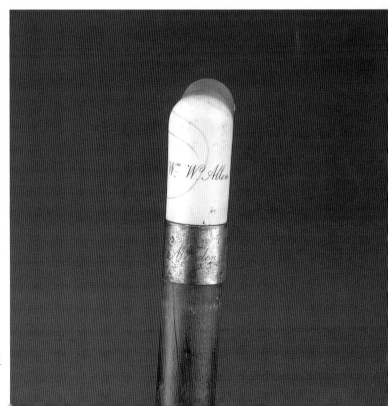

SEALING STAMP,
James Harris Beetle,
ivory, red and black wax,
L. 3⅝", Diam. 1⅜". (New Bedford Whaling Museum)

Knowledge of this scrimshander comes from a later family member. James Harris Beetle was the father-in-law of Captain Asa Russel Gifford, who in turn was the grandfather of Marion Schuh, the sole survivor of that whaling family. In a handwritten letter to the New Bedford Whaling Museum dated December 10, 1979, this 82-year-old woman identified and made arrangements to donate the very attractive sealing stamp. Miss Schuh also informed the museum that the "J.H. Beetle" on the stamp came from the Eastville section of Cottage City on Martha's Vineyard, which today is Oak Bluffs. The reverse lettering on the stamp arcs around the top of a miniature ship under full sail. Six small stars occupy the bottom portion of this boldly turned and scribed ivory seal. Red wax lines the scribing on the top knob while black wax is used for the same purpose on the central portion.

SWIFT,
Thomas Burdett,
1851, ivory, bone, wood, silk, red wax, abalone, metal,
H. 16¾", Diam. when closed 2¾"; box: H. 3¾", W. 4⅛", L. 17¼".
(New Bedford Whaling Museum)

Thomas Burdett followed in his father's footsteps and was a whaling captain. He kept whaling in his family by marrying the daughter of a whaling captain from Maine. Born in Nantucket, he began his career in 1833 at age nineteen. On his very next voyage he was hired on as first mate. Burdett sailed out of New Bedford as a whaling captain and out of Boston as a merchant captain, crossing easily from one field to the other. We know that he took seven voyages on at least four vessels each lasting about four years in length, and it was on one of these that this swift and its box were made. His granddaughter, Emma L. Burdett, who knew her grandfather, donated this piece to the New Bedford Whaling Museum along with a handwritten note stating that it was carved on the ship *Statira* out of new Bedford while on a whaling voyage. Burdett also made a sewing box.

SWIFT,
attributed to Stephen C. Christian, c. 1835–1851, whale skeletal bone, sperm-whale ivory, silver, red sealing wax,
H. 17", Diam. 14". (The Kendall Whaling Museum)

New Bedford women all aspired to be the recipient of a scrimshawed swift, and New Bedford whaler Stephen Christian fulfilled this desire for his wife Abigail, even spelling out her name in silver rivets on the back of the beautifully carved hand that holds the swift. This handsome piece has a well-turned shaft with scribing inlaid with red sealing wax, a well-porportioned cup at the top for the ball of yarn, and ribs joined both by rivets and ribbon.

Young Christian went to sea at the age of fourteen, thus embarking on a thirty-year career all on New Bedford vessels—first as crew, then officer and mate, and finally master. For the period from 1836 to 1839 he kept the journal for the ship *Frances*. This talented scrimshander died on land in 1864.

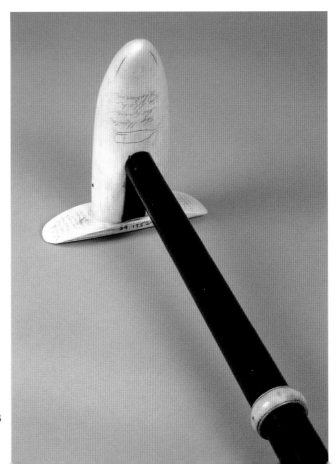

GAVEL,
attributed to James M. Clark, 1835–1845, whale ivory, wood, coloring, brass,
H. 5½", W. 4⅞", L. 15". (Mystic Seaport Museum)

This scrimshawed gavel can only be attributed to James Clark, inasmuch as the inscription or supporting papers do not say "made by." The inscription on one side of the whale tooth reads "Ship Mentor/New London/James Clark/Whaleman." This in all probability means Clark, who was at sea from 1835 to 1870. He also has a swift attributed to him. The *Mentor*, built in New York in 1810, was only one of several vessels that Clark went to sea on. He climbed the ranks to become a whaling master for some twenty-four years. Two of his ships were lost to the Confederates during the Civil War.

93

SWIFT,
Silas Davenport, c. 1840–1860, sperm-whale ivory, whale skeletal bone, ebony, wood,
H. 18", Diam. 2⅞". (The Kendall Whaling Museum)

The American whaleman Silas Davenport was born in Sharon, Massachusetts, in the early 1820s. At sixteen he began a career of whaling that lasted for almost a quarter of a century. All his voyages were out of New Bedford, and he always served as crew. During that time he made this swift shaft that is quite unlike other swifts of that period, for it is made primarily of wood. The unassembled ribs, which are not shown here, are made of ivory and are quite intricately carved. From 1863 to 1865 Davenport fought in the Civil War as a private in the Union Army. Next he became a cobbler, then a bookbinder before dying about 1894.

SWIFT,
attributed to William Cottle, 1840, whale skeletal bone, metal, ribbon, yarn,
H. 21½", Diam. of base 6½". (The Kendall Whaling Museum)

DITTY BOX,
attributed to William Cottle, c. 1850, baleen, wood, metal, red and blue coloring,
H. 3½", W. 5¾", L. 8". (The Kendall Whaling Museum)

William Cottle sailed out of the port of New Bedford on the *Hector* while still a teenager. By the time of the second of the three voyages he made on this ship he was the second officer. While on the first venture Cottle scrimshawed a swift for his girlfriend. On the underside of the base one reads "Like a Phoenix Risen/Ship Hector 1840," and there is depicted on the swift a phoenix-like bird flying out of fire. Inlaid on the top of the base is the name "Julia A. Look," Cottle's sweetheart back on Martha's Vineyard. Cottle was nineteen and Julia was sixteen. Eight years later in 1848, they wed and all future scrimshaw made for his wife bore the name Julia Ann Cottle. This includes the ditty box pictured that is engraved with naval scenes. Subsequently, Cottle became the first mate on one ship and then the captain on two others. During this period he scrimshawed a letter stamp and a letter opener for Julia. After his final voyage on the *Eugenia* he retired in 1859.

LETTER SEAL,
attributed to Edward Cory, c. 1841–1851, sperm-whale ivory, wood, L. 4⅝", Diam. ¹⁵/₁₆". (The Kendall Whaling Museum)

All evidence suggests that this letter seal was scrimshawed by Edward C. Cory. The seal with the reversed lettering E.C. Cory also has a mariner's anchor carved into it. When the seal was used, hot wax, most often red, was melted on paper, and when this was done the base of the seal was pressed down upon the wax leaving the imprint of the seal. On envelopes it was applied over the flap to ensure privacy. On important documents seals accompanied the signature.

Although born in Rhode Island, Cory was a New Bedford whaler known to have been active from 1832 to 1854. On three vessels he served as crew, and on the fourth he was the captain. It is believed that he carved this seal while master of the *South Carolina* when whaling in the Indian Ocean.

BODKIN,
Charles H. Durgin, 1861–1862, walrus ivory, tortoiseshell, red and balck coloring, L. 3⅝". (The Kendall Whaling Museum)

BODKIN,
Charles H. Durgin, 1861–1862, walrus ivory, red and black coloring, L. 4". (The Kendall Whaling Museum)

BODKIN,
Charles H. Durgin, 1861–1862, walrus ivory, brass, L. 4¼". (The Kendall Whaling Museum)

These three bodkins were carved by Charles H. Durgin, a carpenter/cabinetmaker born in New Hampshire in 1841. At about the age of twenty-one Durgin followed his brother and took to whaling out of New London. These bodkins were made during his first voyage on the bark *Monticello*. Although the pointed ends are similar in size and shape, it is the tops that give each its individuality. The square cap of the first is inlaid with red and black dots above a nicely turned upper section inlaid with tortoiseshell. The polyhedron top of the second bodkin also has colored dots. The third example has inlaid brass dots on the turned and carved shank topped by a handsome symmetrically shaped orb.

Durgin's second journey on the *Monticello*, 1862–1865, like the first, was to Arctic waters, which accounts for the use of walrus ivory. Both times the vessel remained for the winter, but on the second voyage Durgin kept a journal, which is primarily devoted to his free-time activities. Durgin noted that he had produced some forty napkin rings, about twenty bodkins (simple and complex), six boxes, a banjo, and some canes. These were done not only for himself but also for family and friends, including other whalers who admired his work. On one occasion he traded his work for walrus ivory from a captain of another vessel.

CIGAR HOLDER,
Elihu Gifford, 1872, ivory, mahogany, metal, H. 11", W. 9¼", L. 5½". (New Bedford Whaling Museum)

On page 27 of *A Visit to the Museum of The Old Dartmouth Historical Society*, published in 1932, it is reported that this quite extraordinary, statuesque cigar holder was made in 1872 by Elihu Gifford of Dartmouth, Massachusetts. The ivory and mahogany were worked aboard the *Cape Horn Pigeon*, and the piece was presented by Gifford to his captain, George O. Baker. It was Baker who gave the cigar holder to the Historical Society, now the New Bedford Whaling Museum. On that voyage, which ran from 1872 to 1876, Gifford was a mate. Later he was a New Bedford captain; subsequently, he sailed out of San Francisco as captain on five expeditions. Confusion has arisen because a Captain Charles Gifford also sailed from San Francisco.

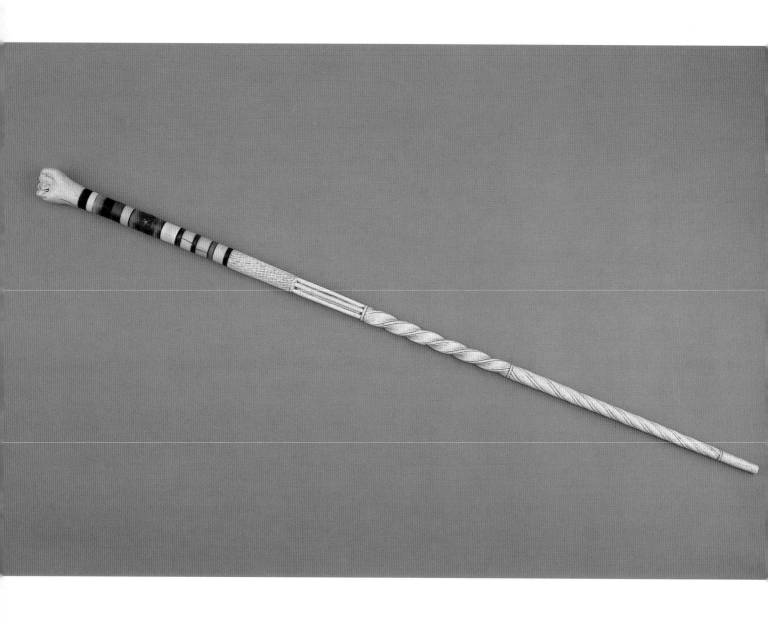

CANE,
attributed to Joseph Hersey, c. 1843–1851, whale skeletal bone, whale ivory, baleen, wood,
L. 36". Diam. ¹⁵/₁₆". (The Kendall Whaling Museum)

Joseph Hersey, born in New York, was employed as both an officer and a captain on whale ships out of Provincetown, Massachusetts. From 1843 to 1851 Hersey kept five journals on these vessels. In one dated 1843, while aboard the *Esquimax*, he writes about a lathe being made specifically to be used for scrimshaw. It was probably at this time that this cane, a particularly handsome example of the genre, was carved. From bottom to top, the four-part shaft displays two types of spiraling, carved columns, and a section of crosshatching before joining the seventeen circles of mixed baleen, wood, and ivory that culminate in a fine clenched-fist handle. In his highly decorative journals Hersey writes about how others continually asked him to engrave their scrimshaw, which he cheerfully did. Other pieces of his scrimshaw, which he writes about, have yet to come to light.

JEWELRY BOX,
Alonzo Herendeen, 1884, sperm-whale ivory, tortoiseshell, baleen, sandalwood, mother-of-pearl, velvet, pencil, metal, H. 3¾", W. 4½", L. 12½". (The Kendall Whaling Museum)

Here is one of those all-too-rare scrimshaw objects possessing full information about its origin. On the bottom of the jewelry box is written "Made from sandal wood from the Island of Juan Fernandez, South Pacific Ocean, by Captain Alonzo O. Herendeen, ship *James Arnold*, 1887." But who is "A.P.H.?" The inlaid mother-of-pearl initials undoubtedly are those of one of the womenfolk at home. Herendeen climbed the ladder from fourth mate, boatsteerer, and cooper, to second mate, then mate, and finally captain. Although he was born in Cape Cod, he sailed out of Dartmouth and New Bedford, Massachusetts.

JEWELRY BOX,
James Hyland, 1842, walrus ivory, baleen, mahogany, wood, metal, H. 3", W. 3⅝", L. 9¾". (The Kendall Whaling Museum)

Although the top of this decorative jewelry box has an inlaid eagle and "E Pluribus Unum" on it, it is the underside that is important to us. Inscribed in wooden letters is "This box made by James G. Hyland. 1842 Born Setuate Mass 18 8 Thes letters made in 1871." Between "by" and "James" is a masonic emblem. The missing numeral in the birth date causes confusion about Hyland's age. It can be safely assumed that he was born early in the nineteenth century. The inlaid hearts, mixed with circles and diamonds of wood, ivory, and baleen, suggests this was a gift to a loved one.

Hyland rose through the ranks to become captain of two vessels out of New Bedford. During his last voyage he became sick and died shortly after reaching homeport.

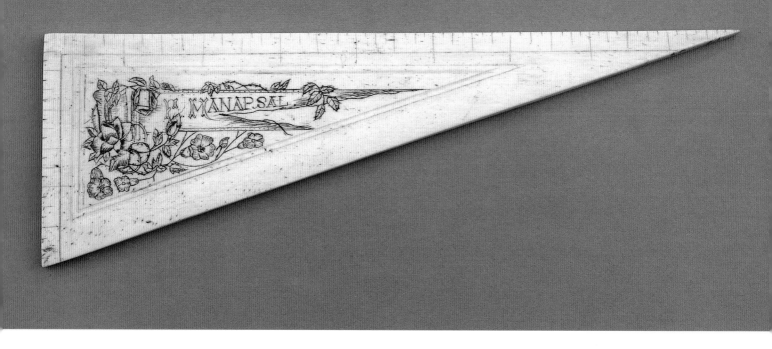

DRAFTSMAN'S TRIANGLE,
Faustino Manapsal, 1906, whale skeletal bone, black ink,
H. ¼", W. 2⅞", L. 8⅞". (The Kendall Whaling Museum)

Faustino Manapsal was employed as a steerage boy on the *Alice Knowles*, which sailed out of San Francisco on a voyage from 1906 to 1907. We do know that this job, which was ranked higher than the cabin boy but lower than the cook, was secured by an outfitter who arranged such employment for greenhands and seamen. Called a crimp, the man received money for this service, which was somehow taken from the hired-man's lay.

Little else is known about Manapsal other than what is found on this handsomely constructed and embellished draftsman's triangle. Because scrimshanders were known to sign their handmade tools we assume he was the maker. The measurement markings on the triangle pale in comparison to the name engraved with the elaborate flowering vine. The engraving on the reverse side includes bunting, a book, sword, gun, pen, inkwell, envelope, paper, and the date 1906, which marks this as a late example of scrimshaw.

SEVEN LOG-BOOK STAMPS,
Kettle, 1840–1860, mahogany,
A to G H. 1", W. ¹¹/₁₆", L. 2⅜", 2¼", 2¼", 2³/₁₆", 2¹/₁₆", 2¼", 1¾".
(The Kendall Whaling Museum)

Only a last name, Kettle, is scratched onto the back of one of these seven mahogany log-book stamps, and there are no extant journals in which they were used to help further identify the man. It is known that three men with that name went whaling: James, who was from Boston and was born about 1820; Jacob S.G., from Schenectady, New York, and who at the age of forty-two in 1866 sailed out of New Bedford on the *Orray Taft*; and William who sailed out of Fairhaven, Massachusetts, on the *Joseph Maxwell* in 1848. Because of residual ink on these stamps, we assume they were actually used in a log book to record whaling activity. The rectangular space on each whale's mid-section held such statistics as dates, types of whales, whether or not whales were successfully captured, and the number of barrels of oil a whale furnished. More research that is continually being done by such scholars as Stuart M. Frank, Director of The Kendall Whaling Museum in Sharon, Massachusetts, may eventually reveal more specific identification about Kettle.

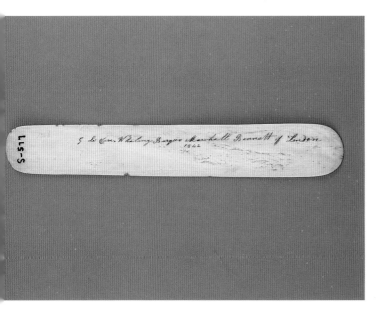

BUSK,
George Le Cluse, 1842, whale skeletal bone, black ink,
H. ⅛", W. 1¾", L. 12³⁄₁₆". (The Kendall Whaling Museum)

The back of this busk, which is inscribed "G. Le Cluse, Whaling Barque Marshall Bennet of London, 1842," is of greater interest than the front, which is carved with the word LOVE, a carrier pigeon, a full portrait of a man and woman in a doorway, and a bust of a woman with "Remember Me" over her head. This is because the inscription identifies the maker, Le Cluse, an Englishman born in London in 1812, who was descended from a French family. His only contact with whaling began in 1839 when, at age of twenty-six, he signed on the English ship *Marshall Bennet* as the ship's armourer. During this voyage, which ended at the beginning of 1843, he also made two other busks. On his return to England, Le Cluse took up tinsmithing.

DIPPER,
John C. Marble, c. 1857–1860, sperm-whale ivory, coconut shell,
ebony, metal,
L. 13", Diam. 4¼". (The Kendall Whaling Museum)

Because of extant journals, papers, letters, and a sketch book, much is known about John Marble. Born in New Bedford, Marble began whaling as a greenhand at the age of nineteen. By his fifth voyage in 1843, he was already a captain. Marble interrupted his whaling career, which had emanated out of many different eastern ports, after his son died. Because he had not been at home when his son died, Marble decided to stay close to the hearth and did shore-bound maritime work. With the arrival of another son, Captain Marble, along with the baby, his wife, and his brother, set out whaling once again. He died aboard the *Awashonks* with his family in attendance in October 1861.

Many pieces of scrimshaw were in the possession of Marble's family, but after an examination of their oral and written history, it was determined that only the dipper illustrated had been made by Marble. The plain bowl has a well-designed ebony and ivory handle.

WORK BOX,
attributed to A.P. More, 1860, pine, mahogany, sandalwood, wood, walrus ivory, metal,
H. 4¾", W. 6⅝", L. 12¾". (The Kendall Whaling Museum)

The *Triton* sailed out of New Bedford on a three-year voyage beginning in 1857, but A.P. More was not listed on the original crew list. At some later date and port, More signed on and during that time produced this work box marked inside "A.P. More to Lilie Hathaway Jan. 14 1860 Bk. Triton." On the lid eight walrus-ivory diamonds and eight sandalwood diamonds surround a large center diamond. The mahogany veneer is further enhanced by a small wooden heart on the front where a key escutcheon would normally be.

LETTER STAMP,
attributed to Harris Pendleton, c. 1825, whale skeletal bone,
H. ⅜", W. 2", L. 2⅞". (The Kendall Whaling Museum)

LETTER SEAL,
attributed to Harris Pendleton, c. 1825, whale skeletal bone,
L. 4¼", Diam. ⅞". (The Kendall Whaling Museum)

The whalebone letter stamp with "H. Pendleton" and the letter seal initialed "H°P" with top and bottom arcs filled with Xs, both done in reverse lettering, are different from other scrimshaw shown in this book in that the scrimshander was hunting fur seals, not whales. Harris Pendleton, to whom these pieces are attributed, was born in Stonington, Connecticut, in 1786, a town known more for fur sealing than whaling. Pendleton's extended family was in the seal-hunting business and he soon joined them. It is recorded that in 1821 he captained the *Hero* on a sealing expedition to the Antarctic.

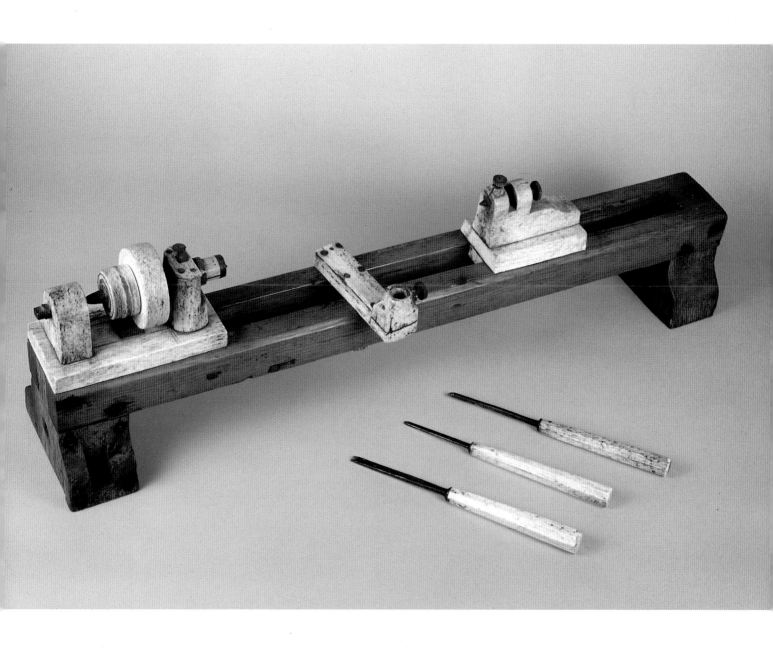

LATHE,
Josiah Robinson, c. 1867, bone, wood, steel,
H. 8¾", W. 5⅝", L. 28¹³/₁₆". (Mystic Seaport Museum)

Massachusetts-born Josiah Robinson worked on whalers from 1865 to 1878. One voyage on the bark *Cape Horn Pigeon* lasted from 1869 to 1872. It is thought that he was either the ship's carpenter or cooper. He had this table-sized wood and bone lathe with him while aboard the *Pigeon*. In addition to this tool, Robinson is credited with scrimshandering, for himself and his wife Lucy, two rolling pins, a mallet, a cooper's croze, and a frame saw, all of which might have been done on this lathe.

Lathes were not ordinarily used by scrimshanders because most turning was done by hand using saws, files, and chisels. The lathe held the work tightly as it revolved, allowing hand-turning tools to shape rounded sections. And because these chisel-shaped hand tools actually did the work the end product is still considered handmade as opposed to machine-made.

BOX,
John Ropes, 1820–1840, bone, wood, metal, coloring,
H. 4¼", W. 5¾", L. 7¾". (Peabody Essex Museum)

This richly decorated oval panbone box was created by John Ropes for his Aunt Rebecca sometime between 1820 and 1840, and she must have been thrilled to receive it. Subsequently it descended through the family, which later gave it to the museum. Like most oval boxes, the top and bottom are wooden. The carved rim of the vine-engraved lid is most unusual. The circumference of the box is richly embellished with flowering vines, an eagle with flags, a vase of flowers, and two American ships at the entrance of a harbor. The carved cornucopias that fasten the panbone of the box and lid are especially noteworthy.

Scholars believe that this scrimshander was the same John Ropes who was the captain of the clipper *John Gilpin* in 1857. It is recorded that Ropes hit an iceberg when sailing back to New Bedford and consequently abandoned the *John Gilpin* as it was on fire and sinking. The ship's carpenter and three seamen accused Ropes of acting in haste in a situation where they felt the vessel could have been saved. Ropes, however, was exonerated of these charges.

ROLLING PIN,
Abraham T. Sanford, c. 1857, ivory, mahogany, baleen,
L. 16", Diam. 2¼". (New Bedford Whaling Museum)

Two extant letters provide us with the history of the Abraham Sanford rolling pin. One was written by the daughter of the first owner, and the other, dated 1945, came from the owner's niece. Sanford had been erroneously identified as a captain by one writer, when in fact he was a cooper, who had in one known voyage shipped out of New Bedford on the bark *Le Baron*. Constructed of mahogany from the coast of Peru, the pin's sperm-whale ivory handles have five inlaid baleen circles at each end. Sanford gave this rolling pin to Louise Burlingame, who rented a room to him in New Bedford. She in turn presented it to her niece Grace Rogers Saterlee some years later. For a Christmas gift in 1945 Miss Saterlee turned over the rolling pin to her niece Martha Rogers Alexander, who donated it to the New Bedford Whaling Museum.

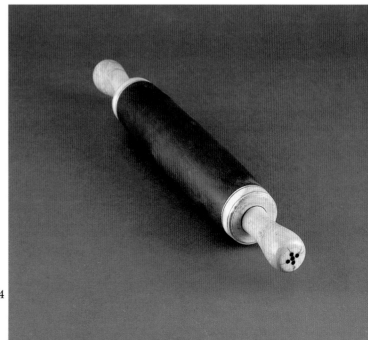

BOX OF DOMINOES,
Jonathan P. Saunders, c. 1837, ivory, baleen, wood, mother-of-pearl, ink,
H. 1½", W. 3", L. 4½". (Peabody Essex Museum)

The only known whaling voyage taken by Jonathan P. Saunders was aboard the ship *Elizabeth* out of Salem in the 1836–1840 period. While on this expedition, Saunders scrimshawed two boxes, one oval and one rectangular, a scarf slide, perhaps a tooth, and this handsome box of dominoes. A label on the box states that the dominoes were made by Saunders on a whaling trip about 1837. It is quite possible that this label was not written by Saunders, but was attached later for identification purposes. Inasmuch as this scrimshaw was donated to the museum between 1905 and 1913 by a descendant of Saunders, we can assume the information is correct. Each of the thin, small oblong pieces of bone is marked in two halves with a strip of baleen and each half is blank or has inlaid baleen dots numbering from one to six. The twenty-eight dominoes are stored in a wooden box with a sliding lid that is decorated with inlaid bone.

BUSK,
attributed to John Stratton, c. 1835–1849, walrus ivory, red, green, blue, black coloring,
H. ⅛", W. 1⁷⁄₁₆", L. 14⁷⁄₁₆". (The Kendall Whaling Museum)

BUSK,
attributed to John Stratton, c. 1835–1849, whale skeletal bone, black ink,
H. ⅛", W. 1⅝", L. 13³⁄₁₆". (The Kendall Whaling Museum)

John Stratton, born in Philadelphia about 1814, was known to have been a whaleman from about 1835 to 1849, sailing first as crew on the *William Rotch* and then as the ship's carpenter on the bark *Russell*. Because of the similarities in style to his signed scrimshaw these two busks are attributed to him on the basis that both signed and unsigned depictions of human figures whether alone or in pairs suggest the hand of the same artist. A close inspection of the busks shows that Stratton was quite an accomplished artist with a particular interest in depicting men and women.

SWIFT,
Charles F. Smith, c. 1850, ivory, bone, wood, brass, string, black ink,
H. 18½", W. 8", L. 8¼". (New Bedford Whaling Museum)

Charles Franklin Smith was born on June 14, 1837 and died on January 19, 1906. While much of his whaling history is unknown, we do know from his granddaughter that he scrimshawed this swift and also a lap desk. Early Dartmouth city directories support the belief that this Charles Smith probably lived his whole life in this Massachusetts seaside town. The bone slats of the swift are held together with both brass rivets and string and are attached to a turned central ivory post with a yarn cup on top. The middle section of this piece is designed to hold eight spools of thread on removable ivory posts that date the swift after 1850, while the octagonal wooden base with four ivory ball feet and four drawers with round ivory knobs makes for a handy compartmentalized box to hold sewing paraphernalia. Charles Smith produced a beautifully assembled, free-standing, and aesthetically pleasing multipurpose piece of scrimshaw.

BIRD CAGE,
attributed to Rodolphus N. Swift, 1825–1850, whale skeletal bone,
wood, tin, walrus ivory,
H. 19½", W. 14", L. 17½". (The Kendall Whaling Museum)

Seventeen years after his birth in Fairhaven, Massachusetts, Rodolphus Swift began whaling. From 1827 to 1834 he made three voyages out of New Bedford on the same vessel. Four years after becoming a captain at the age of twenty-four in 1834, he married a young lady from his hometown, who bore him five children. For sixteen years Swift captained whaling vessels until 1850, when he retired and became involved in the lumber business.

This architecturally attractive bird cage may have been created for his children. Surely it was a labor of love, for the carving of the several hundred whalebone ribs for the sides and vaulted dome must have consumed countless hours. Both utilitarian and decorative, the cage with its carved and turned ivory carrying handle and the sliding tin drawer with its ring pull for catching droppings shows that it was well planned. The bone corner posts are embellished with walrus ivory feet and finials.

DITTY BOX,
Frederick H. Smith, 1875–1878, bone, ivory, wood, baleen, horn, metal,
H. 3⅞", W. 6⅝", L, 8¹¹/₁₆". (Mystic Seaport Museum)

SCOOP,
Frederick H. Smith, 1875–1878, whalebone, wood,
H. 1⅜", W. 5½", L. 13½". (Mystic Seaport Museum)

PARALLEL RULE,
Frederick H. Smith, 1875–1878, whalebone, brass,
H. ⅛", W. 2⁹/₁₆", L. 13¾". (Mystic Seaport Museum)

Here is one scrimshander that we know quite a lot about because of his existing logs, his wife's journal, and a brief autobiographical description of himself. Born in 1840 in Dartmouth, Massachusetts, and beginning his whaling career in 1854, Smith eventually rose to

the rank of captain. In addition to recording whom he sailed for and on what vessel, he also wrote the length of the journeys, where they went, the amount of oil secured, and even the money he earned.

Sarah Smith, known as Sallie, accompanied her husband on several whaling expeditions. While on board the *Ohio*, her journal refers to her husband's scrimshaw, and suggests that she, too, may have created a few scrimshaw objects.

The double fingers on the joinings of this oval panbone ditty box are very attractive, but look at the intricate inlay work on the compass-rose design of the lid, which is an astonishing composition of bone, ivory, wood, horn, and metal. In direct contrast to this great piece is the simplicity of the ivory and wood scoop. Smith's whalebone and brass parallel rule undoubtedly helped him plot his course or find bearings on navigational charts. This prolific scrimshander also produced knitting needles, clothespins, funnels, a yardstick, and a crochet hook.

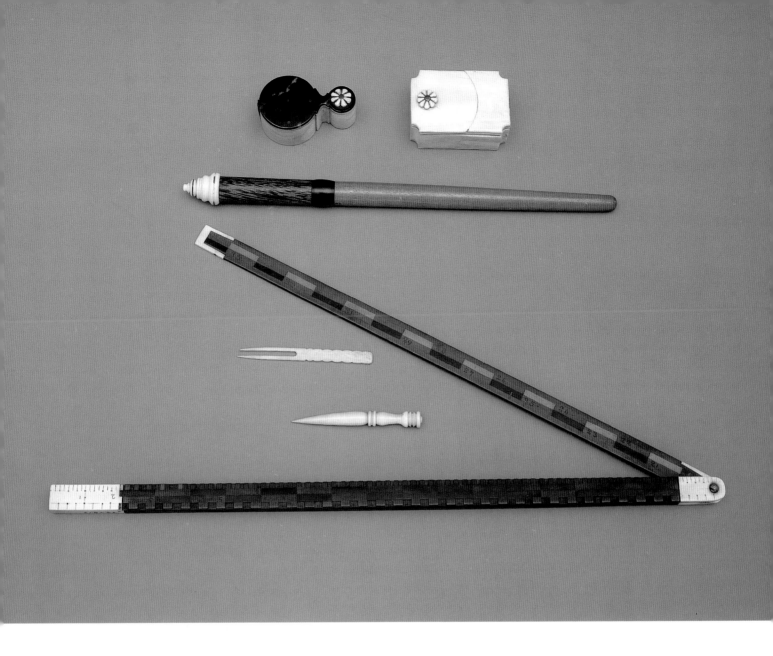

TORTOISE BOX,
Albert A. Thomas, ivory, tortoise, brass,
H. 1¼", W. 1¾", L. 3".

IVORY BOX,
Albert A. Thomas, ivory, brass,
H. 1⅜", W. 2⅛", L. 3⅛".

CURLING ROD,
Albert A. Thomas, wood, ivory, red and blue wax,
L. 13¾", Diam. 1".

TWO-PRONGED FORK,
Albert A. Thomas, bone,
H. 1/16", W. ⅜", L. 4⅛".

BODKIN,
Albert A. Thomas, ivory,
H. 3⅞", Diam. 7/16".

FOLDING YARDSTICK,
Albert A. Thomas, wood, ivory, brass, black ink,
H. 9/16", W. 11/16", L. 36⅛". (All objects are from the collection of the New Bedford Whaling Museum)

Although only six objects are pictured here, Albert A. Thomas also scrimshawed some two dozen other pieces. His skill and artistry are easily seen in these two puzzle boxes, the curling iron, and the folding yardstick. Family history comes from his granddaughter Sylvia E. Thomas, who wrote that Thomas was born in Salem, New York, on November 3, 1833, and that his whaling career consisted of five voyages out of New Bedford. He started as a carpenter with a lay of 1/150 on a voyage lasting from 1853 to 1857. This was immediately followed by a sailing that ended in a shipwreck. For this voyage he had been promoted to fourth mate and boat steerer and was to have had a 1/55 lay. He did well enough to be first mate on his next trip, before being named captain with a 1/16th lay on a voyage lasting from 1867 to 1871, when the ship was sold in New Zealand. Thomas's wife and young son accompanied him on this last assignment. Although his whaling career spanned twenty-three years up to 1876, Captain Thomas did not die until 1915.

FOOTSTOOL,
Charles Perry Worth and Mrs. John Marble, c. 1854–1860,
mahogany, pine, wood, needlepoint, horsehair, metal,
H. 17", W. 15½", L. 15¼". (The Kendall Whaling Museum)

FOOTSTOOL,
Charles Perry Worth and Mrs. John Marble, 1854, wood, needle-
point, horsehair, metal,
H. 16½", W. 14½", L. 14½". (The Kendall Whaling Museum)

Charles Perry Worth came from a seafaring Nantucket family and
married a Nantucket girl, but he captained four whalers out of New
Bedford. One of the four, the *Edward*, was sunk by the Confederate
navy during the Civil War. Another, the bark *Drago*, went on two
expeditions to the South Seas from 1854 to 1862. It was on the
Drago that these two footstools were made. As can be seen, the stool
on the left has the date 1854 inlaid in the frame. Although nearly the
same size, each has its own distinctive shape, with the dated example having the more delicate inlays. Captain Worth gave these footstools to John Marble, captain of the *Kathleen*, also of New Bedford
and his wife, when the two vessels met in the South Seas. Mrs.
Marble completed the needlepoint covers while still on the
Kathleen, and then handed them over to her husband who did the
upholstering.

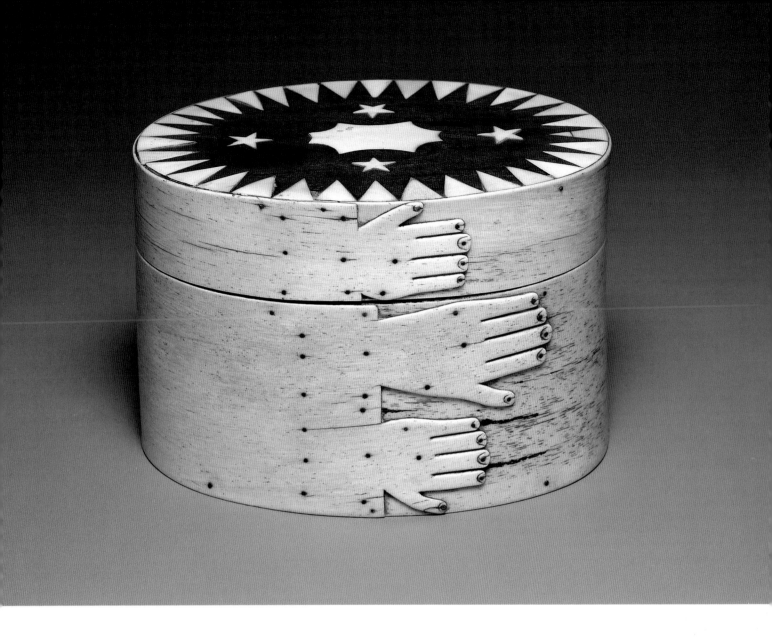

BOX,
Horace Young, c. 1850, sperm-whale bone, baleen, wood, ivory, brass,
H. 6⅝", W. 10", L. 14⁹/₁₆". (New Bedford Whaling Museum)

Horace Young rose from the rank of seaman to captain, even though his whaling career only encompassed four voyages, two out of New Bedford and one each out of Fairhaven and Westport. Finding himself unhappy, Young left whaling and settled on the coast of Chile. His wife's and baby daughter's journey from Nantucket to Chile took so long that he had given them up for lost. Shortly after they were all finally reunited Horace Young was drowned in a typhoon, so his wife and daughter returned to Nantucket. Among the things they took with them was this handsome box that contained coffee and was always located on the second shelf in the kitchen closet.

The top of this fascinating box has a border of ivory triangles surrounding four stars and a scalloped name plate. The bone sides of the box and its top are joined with carved hands showing crisply detailed fingernails—a right hand secures the side of the top, and large and small left hands fasten the bottom. Captain Young may not have enjoyed whaling, but he was certainly an accomplished and imaginative scrimshander.

111

CHAPTER SIX

Ornamentation

Patterns and designs, and symbols and motifs have decorated objects for centuries. When examining ornamentation, those who study it seriously consider its historical origin, which often is found in a remote locale. Also, the types of decoration are examined, together with the roles of folk art, symbolism, and the function of objects in everyday life. Because of war, commerce, and travel, designs go through transitional stages resulting in modification and change.

Decoration, whether it is an element of a utilitarian object or is decorative for its own sake, has a basis in taste and knowledge. The former, an aesthetic factor, relies on a conceived beauty, while the latter utilizes meaning as portrayed in symbolism. Any form of ornamentation needs to be attached to something. It does not stand by itself; it always enhances something. Even the material of the object being decorated has an influence on what the decor will be.

Why is a particular pattern or motif chosen? Well, there are many influences. Because we are dealing with scrimshaw, let us consider four major forces that helped direct these choices in America from 1830 to 1870: the impact of the water and steam power of the Industrial Revolution, the expansion westward, the rise of the common people, and all the factors leading up to the Civil War. Americans were being inventive, creative, and energetic. The feeling of a national identity was strong. The horn of plenty signified the abundance to be found in America; the oak tree its strength; and the tobacco leaf its economic importance.

Each artist applied decoration in his own fashion, and folk artists often developed the most unusual techniques for doing so. Artistic ability obviously varied among scrimshanders, but whatever the degree of talent this art form was an important means of pictorial expression for the whalers. For the most part their themes, patterns, and colors were of a conservative nature. Whether this ornamentation was done freehand, or in the case of some images on whale's teeth by transfer, it was a slow process. Some cut out while others added on. There was

pierced work, and countersinking for inlay. Although it is often referred to as engraving, the ivory, baleen, or wood was actually incised or scratched. The many examples of extraordinary turning are all the more amazing when one realizes that most turned objects were created without the aid of a lathe. It was the work of the chisel, saw, and file. Color, which was hand-rubbed into the incised lines in order to highlight them, might be supplied by red sealing wax, black or blue ink, tar or soot from the try works, or even a hue borrowed from the tattoo artist. Exotic dyes found in foreign ports were occasionally put to use. Generally, however, it was black ink that gave color to a piece, some of which has turned brown with age. Handsome or unusual ornamentation was often the result of using baleen, mother-of-pearl, common or exotic woods, and an assortment of metals. The scrimshander obviously felt that all of this added to the success of his work.

There were innumerable choices of themes, patterns, and designs. Those taken from whittling experience and other folk arts were often simplified. The obvious sources were the whalers' home life and their life on board the whaleships. Nineteenth-century customs associated with their home regions also proved a valuable resource for their imaginations. Ethnic background, church affiliation, visual idioms popular at the time, and just a keen sense of observation led to other choices of decoration. Earlier, things English had significant impact but this was because so many Americans at the time were of British derivation.

Classical literature and Greek mythology might also have served as inspiration. After all, it was Homer who referred to the ocean as the whale's road. Perseus, the son of Jupiter, was considered the first whaler because it was he who harpooned the whale that was about to carry off Andromeda. Poseidon, the god of the sea, must not be forgotten, either.

The abundance and love of nature in America made it another font to be drawn from. Many associated the earth's bountifulness with young America. Flowers, leaves, and fruit

112

were popular in all types of decoration, including scrimshaw. The importance of nature patterns is understandable when one remembers that America was still primarily rural at this time.

After Jean-François Champollion deciphered the Rosetta Stone in the 1820s there developed a craze for things Egyptian. Cats and crocodiles appeared in decoration, and even the architecture of the Old Whaler's Church in Sag Harbor, New York, was inspired by an Egyptian Revival style. The Empire Style and the Greek Revival or Neoclassical Style introduced other new motifs that the scrimshander might choose to put to use. Victorian designs emphasizing romance and sentiment, such as the heart remained strong.

Although some whalemen may have developed original designs, their work was more likely to be a repetition or an interpretation of pieces by other men on board. Tools made for use by the whaler had no standard of decoration. This was left to the individual pride of the owner. On the other hand, the objects intended for gifts usually relied heavily on ornamentation. The sea was the oldest design source for mariners, with whaling being a prime one for scrimshaw artists. Their obvious familiarity with ships and navigation inspired designs drawn from rigging, knots, rope, constellations in the sky involving Cetus the whale and Delphinus the dolphin, existing shipboard carvings such as figureheads and sternboards, marine animals, birds, and parts of the ship like the anchor or wheel. New ports, previously unseen scenery, icebergs, islands, mermaids, drinking sailors, and naval books and insignia also supplied ideas.

Patriotism in the form of flags and battles were popular motifs, as were presidents and other political and historical figures. A universal source for the scrimshander was the multitude of geometric figures that were often seen in multiples and in combinations. Crosshatching was just one simple, popular pattern; others were the ubiquitous dot and circle. This type of ornamentation often involved central symmetry. The easy-to-use compass also provided handsome designs.

Pictorial images to be found in newspapers, magazines, and books appeared about 1825 and in abundance. Their use as decorative motifs on scrimshaw can actually be documented. Tombstones, the female form, stenciled furniture, coverlets, and quilts also supplied potential designs. The popular quilt pattern called Mariner's Compass was an obvious choice. Trade signs and weathervanes were also borrowed from. The decorative borders found on busks, boxes, baskets, and whale's teeth could be quite fancy, but they too came from other sources. Borders seen on commercial products were often repeated.

Symbolism must not be overlooked as it was an important decorative source. A symbol is something that can stand by itself, but at the same time stands for, suggests, or means something else by means of relationships, association, convention, or even accident. Symbols are outward signs for other things. These signs, marks, or tokens do not aim to be reproductions, but are a way of reading without words. The interpretation of symbols may prove more difficult than one might suppose for several reasons. First, different symbols may have the same meaning or they may have contradictory meanings, all of which depends on the context in which they are depicted. Symbols can also change in meaning from one ethnic background to another. The significance of this change can be drastic, sometimes to the point of losing all meaning. At the point of losing a meaning, the symbol then becomes pure ornament. Sometimes an artist will apply his own meaning to a symbol, thus giving it yet another definition or significance. Such an alteration could well be lost on others. This complicated role of symbolism is made more difficult because its use today is not nearly as popular as it was in the nineteenth century. Part of the reason for this is that people today are considerably more literate.

Attributes and emblems were yet another source of inspiration for ornamentation. Attributes are objects closely associated with or belonging to a specific person, office, or event. An example would be the scales held by the figure of justice. Emblems are just a sign, such as a star being recognized as the emblem of a sheriff.

Add to all this the practice of writing names, initials, and dates on scrimshaw to complement the existing ornamentation. This was a means of personalizing the item and most often held a place of importance or prominence. Initials presupposed knowing the accompanying name. A monogram on a work was understood by both the maker and the receiver, but a researcher can find it very difficult if not impossible to discover the person behind the monogram.

Over one hundred kinds of decorative patterns were examined on scrimshaw objects by the author in the preparation of this book. The most popular forms included the hand, the fist, ball-in-cage, flowers, initials, geometric shapes, and turning. Are all of these designs of importance? Yes, indeed, because they help us have an understanding of the customs and lives of the whalers, thus making it possible for us to see nineteenth-century America through the whaling industry.

KNIFE,
sperm-whale ivory, baleen, ebony, steel, mother-of-pearl, black ink, H. ⅝", W. 1⅞", L. 9¾". (The Kendall Whaling Museum)

This handsome, manly ebony-handled knife in a baleen sheath has whale ivory at its top, midsection, and bottom. Although a primitive bird is scratched in the ivory just above the hilt and mother-of-pearl was used as inlay on the handle it is the skull-and-crossbones finial to the handle that is of most interest. This design appears on both sides of the knife. On the high seas a skull and crossbones were displayed on the flags of pirate ships, but whalers would have been familiar with this design from the mainland, for it was a common motif on seventeenth- and eighteenth-century tombstones in New England. In cemeteries the skull and crossbones reflected death and melancholy, but it was really an emblem of man's mortality.

THIMBLE,
bone,
H. ¾", W. 2⅞", L. 4⅛". (Mystic Seaport Museum)

Of all symbolic designs used in the folk arts, the heart is probably the most popular. Because the heart is considered the source of one's emotions, it has come to be the symbol of affection—be it love, joy, devotion, or sympathy. The heart can be both sacred and secular, and it is found in quilts, hooked rugs, fraktur, redware, stenciling, toleware, painted furniture, and even on early tombstones. Here the heart is carved into a bone thimble, but it is not the kind used in sewing. Made for use in rigging, the thimble is grooved along the entire outer edge so as to hold a rope or line tightly.

114

GREASE HORN,
sperm-whale tooth,
L. 4³/₄". (The Kendall Whaling Museum)

TUMBLER,
c. 1850, horn, antler, black ink,
H. 3⁷/₈", Diam. 3¹/₁₆". (The Kendall Whaling Museum)

The decoration of these two pieces is certainly not surprising. The utilitarian grease horn carved from a whale's tooth is ornamented in the most nautical way: a jaunty sailor. Dressed in a uniform that was perhaps more typical of sailors in the navy than on whalers, this figure nevertheless represented the average man at sea. While the relief-carved sailor might symbolize a wanderer, the pictures engraved on the horn and antler tumbler certainly reflect the desire for solid roots. It is a folk-art tradition to portray the farms, villages, and houses that inspire fond memories of the homelife left behind, and which have been touchingly depicted on this tumbler by the scrimshandering whaler longing for the friends, family, and familiar sights of his hometown.

SEAM RUBBER,
Thomas Freeman, bone, black ink,
H. 1¹/₁₆", W. 1³/₄", L. 6". (New Bedford Whaling Museum)

Most inscriptions appearing on scrimshaw tend to be sentimental, with references to the home, everlasting love, and requests to wait. The words on this piece are surprising to say the least. One side has "Thomas Freeman his rubber," but the verso warns, "Drop it you bugger." This raises the question of homosexuality on whalers, for the term *bugger* is usually defined as a sodomite, although a very secondary meaning is that of a contemptible person. In writings about whaling homosexuality is seldom mentioned, and it is the rare log book that makes note of it. It is possible that Victorian authors and families censored such references. When homosexuality was cited, it was often with veiled remarks, or that such a person was flogged or discharged from his duties.

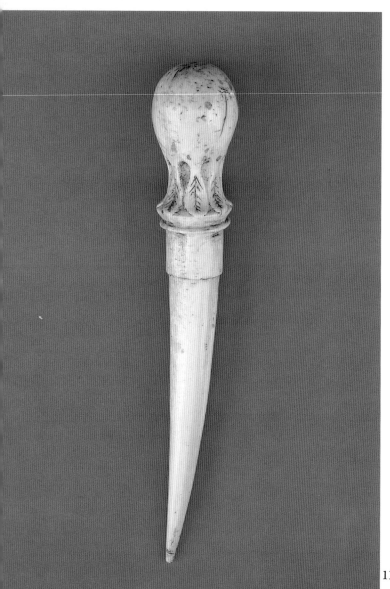

FID,
walrus ivory,
H. 1¹⁵/₁₆", W. 1¹⁵/₁₆", L. 7¹⁵/₁₆". (The Kendall Whaling Museum)

In contrast to the solidity of this walrus-ivory fid, the decorative leaves carved on the base of the handle are small and delicate as if to indicate new spring growth, for decorative leaves often symbolize revived hope. Leaves also exemplify a transitory life. It is quite possible that the leaves on this fid were meant to be tobacco leaves that, in America, were commonly used decoratively. This would not be surprising because of the major role of tobacco on board, where it was one of the few pleasures on which whalers could always rely.

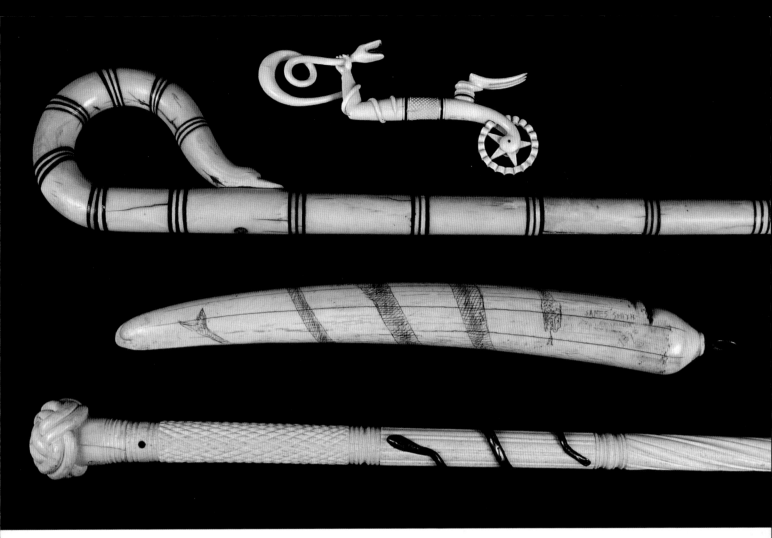

CRIMPER,
ivory, baleen, metal,
L. 7³/₄", Diam. 1⁵/₈".

CANE,
ivory, bone, metal, baleen,
L. 34", Diam. 1¹/₈".

FID,
James Smith, 1836, walrus ivory, coloring,
L. 15", Diam. 1³/₄".

CANE,
bone, ivory, baleen, sterling silver,
L. 34", Diam. 1". (All pieces are from the collection of Mystic Seaport Museum)

The two canes, the fid, and the crimper show some of the variations available to scrimshanders who carved snakes. It should be remembered that the snake played an historical role in the history of the United States, for it preceded the eagle as the symbol of the unity of the Colonies. Today, however, the serpent is usually thought of as a symbol of evil and Satan. Other possible symbolic meanings include fertility, night, secrecy, and temptation. In the folk arts where it was most used, the snake was not much used symbolically. It was more an object of curiosity. A hand clasping a snake, as seen in the crimper, was probably the most common use of the snake motif. More exotic examples are the snake that has been drawn to wind around the length of the ivory fid, and the sterling-silver snake that circles the midsection of the lower cane.

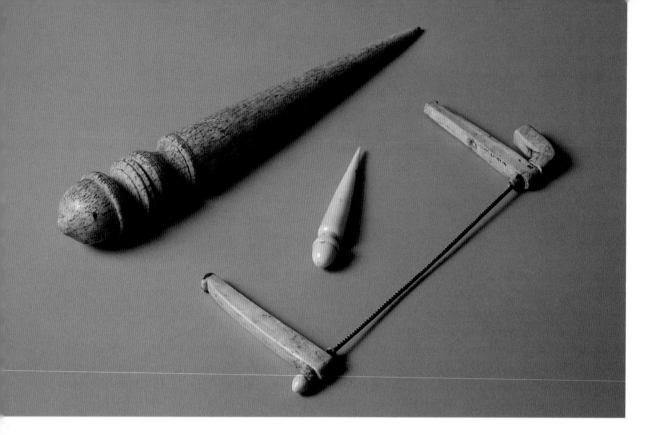

FID,
bone,
L. 12", Diam. 1⁵⁄₈". (Mystic Seaport Museum)

BODKIN,
ivory,
L. 4¹⁄₈", Diam. ⁵⁄₈". (Mystic Seaport Musuem)

JIGSAW,
bone, ivory, steel,
H. ¹⁄₂", W. 3⁵⁄₈", L. 9⁷⁄₈". (Mystic Seaport Museum)

The acorns that decorate these pieces of scrimshaw indicate the ubiquity of this popular symbol. The large fid would have been used on shipboard, while the smaller bodkin would have been found in a sewing basket. The jigsaw could well have been employed in the scrimshandering of the other two objects. The acorn as a symbol dates back as far as the late sixteenth century. Nordic peoples regarded it as a sign of life and immortality; for others it represented fertility. In America it was associated with the strength and vitality of oak.

CANE,
ivory, wood, metal,
H. 2", W. 2¹⁄₄", L. 34¹⁄₄".

CANE,
ivory, wood, bone, metal,
H. 1¹⁄₂", W. 1³⁄₄", L. 34¹⁄₂".

CANE,
ivory, wood, metal,
H. 1¹⁄₄", W. 1¹⁄₂", L. 32¹⁄₂".

CANE,
ivory, wood, metal,
H. 2", W. 2¹⁄₄", L. 34¹⁄₄".

CANE,
ivory, ebony, ink, metal,
H. 1", W. 1¹⁄₄", L. 33¹⁄₄". (All pieces are from the collection of the New Bedford Whaling Museum)

This fist, especially when labeled "clenched," has often been said to represent the anger or rage of the carver; another interpretation was that it indicated a weapon. Both of these theories seem very misleading for sporty walking canes. Others have said that the clenched fist shows one how to grasp the cane, but a closed fist can hardly grasp something. A much better explanation is to be found in *The Yankee Scrimshander* by Fredericka Burrows, who believes that the closed fist usually seen with a cuff at the wrist symbolizes the Friendship Hand. Such a hand conveys friendliness and good will. The cane head was joined to the staff by being slipped over the top and attached with rivets, as seen in three of the examples illustrated, or by being screwed on top of the staff. Various woods and even solid bone were used for the staffs as seen in the illustration. The various lengths, however, show that each cane was custom made to fit the height of its owner.

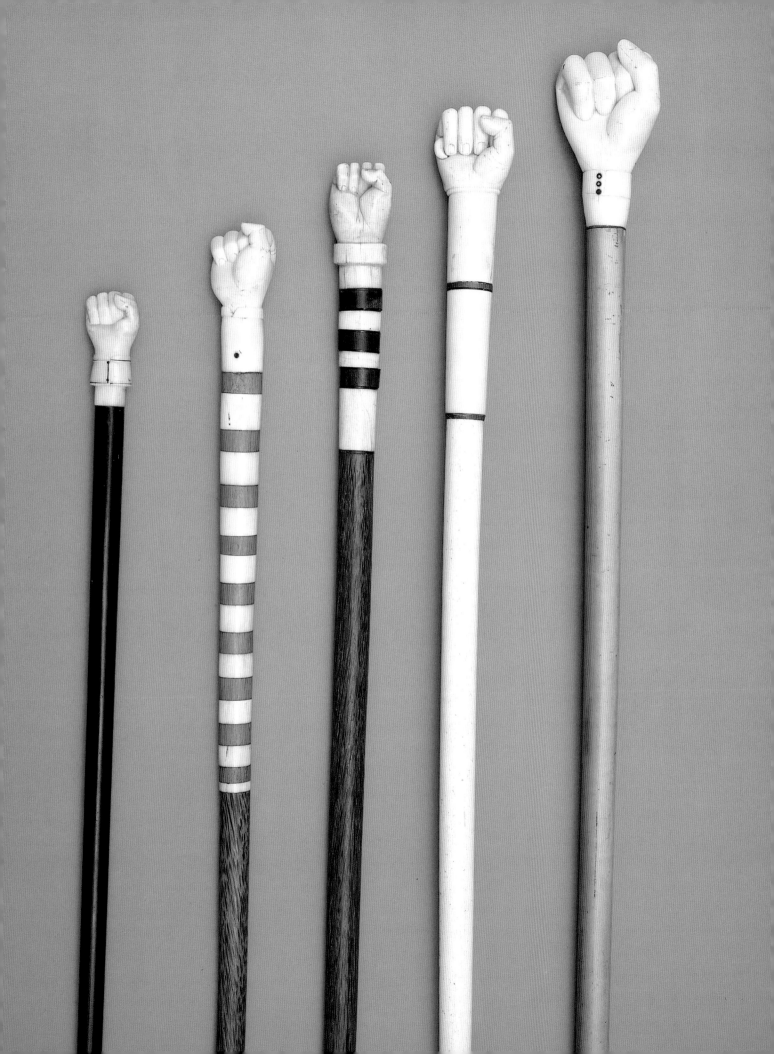

PIPE BOX,
1794, wood, ivory,
H. 21⅛", W. 5⅜", L. 5½". (Mystic Seaport Museum)

The 1794 date on this pipe box inlaid with ivory tells us that it is a very early example of scrimshaw, so early that it predates the existence of the word *scrimshaw*. Only a small amount of this folk art was done previous to 1800, and those pieces generally are made with more wood than ivory or bone. Sperm whales, such as the one displayed on the box and which supplied the carvers with ivory teeth, were not discovered by Yankee whalers off the Nantucket coast until the first quarter of the eighteenth century. It was not until after 1795 that scrimshaw assumed greater importance, for it was at this time the long Pacific voyages began. By 1825, the art form was established. This early pipe box well represents the scrimshaw of the period, for it is mostly wood with carving on the wood itself and with ivory inlay. The wood rosettes and the diamond, heart, and star inlays are popular patterns of the period. The sperm whale was then and continued to be a favorite design of the scrimshander.

CANE,
bone,
H. 1¼", W. 1¼", L. 34¼". (Peabody Essex Museum)

The turkshead knot, in addition to being very decorative, was also practical if so large a knot was needed. In its tubular form the knot was placed around a cylindrical object, frequently on the up-and-down spoke of a ship's steering wheel, so that at a glance one could see if the helm was amidship. When worked with a logline the knot will form a turban, thus the name turkshead. In this form the practical uses included footholds on footropes, handholds on manropes, bell ropes, a gathering hoop on ditty bags, old chest beckets, neckerchiefs, and even small buttons. But being so obviously decorative, the turkshead knot was also duplicated by bone, ivory, wood and stone cutters. This panbone cane shows the turbanhead at the top and the cylindrical form of the turkshead just below it. The endless knot with no seams or visible beginning or end was likened to love, and so the turkshead knot became a symbol of interdependence and of a union. The spiral shaft of this cane was carved to resemble the tusk of the narwhal.

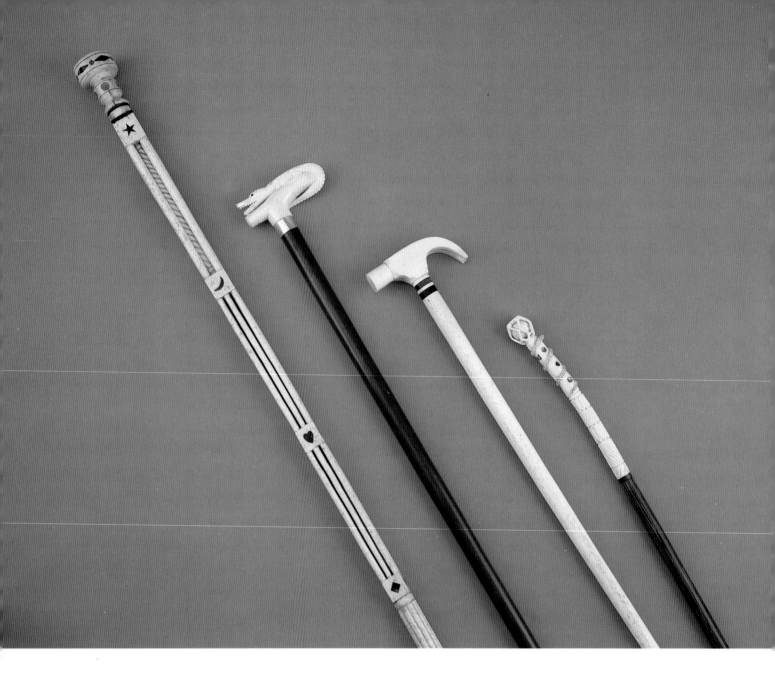

CANE,
*1850–1875, whale skeletal ivory, walrus ivory, tortoiseshell, baleen,
abalone shell, red sealing wax, black ink,
L. 39¹/₂", Diam. 1¹³/₁₆".*

CANE,
*wood, walrus ivory, silver, metal,
L. 33³/₄²", Diam. ⁷/₈".*

CANE,
*sperm-whale ivory, wood, whale skeletal bone, brass,
H. ³/₄", W. 4¹/₄", L. 34¹/₂".*

CANE,
*walrus ivory, wood, baleen, abalone shell, black ink,
L. 34¹/₂", Diam. 1".* (All pieces are from the collection of The Kendall
Whaling Museum)

These custom-made canes were never used on board a whaleship,
but they were a quite popular item for scrimshanders, perhaps
because they were initially fairly easy to carve. These exceptional
examples show that most time was spent on the fancy handles. The
ivory hand knob and its geometric designs inlaid with abalone shell,
tortoiseshell, and red sealing wax complement the bone shaft with its
baleen inlays, assorted turnings, and fancy carving. The crocodile,
the only animal without a tongue, is the subject of the next ivory handle. For some the crocodile was a deity and therefore did not need
to talk—therefore no tongue. Whalers, knowing that their prey had
very small tongues, drew a parallel between the two animals. In a
way the whale was considered the god of the whaling industry, and
like the crocodile it was thought to be fecund and powerful. The
common claw hammer was used in the next piece as symbolic of
manual labor and the power of the carpenter, who undoubtedly produced this elegant walking stick. The walrus-ivory ball in a cage top
fascinates us in the last cane, for carving a free-rolling floating ball in
a cage was a way for skilled scrimshanders to show off. This cage, an
open polyhedron, was even more complicated than usual, thus
demonstrating the extraordinary patience and the unlimited available hours needed to accomplish this feat.

CANE,
bone, wood, brass,
H. 1", W. 3¼", L. 35¼". (New Bedford Whaling Museum)

Fraternal organizations were very popular during the nineteenth century. Perhaps the best known were the Freemasons, but there were also the groups called the Knights of the Golden Eagle and the Order of Mules. The design carved on the handle of this cane is the insignia of the Independent Order of Odd Fellows, a fraternal and benevolent secret society that was founded in England during the eighteenth century. Often the purpose of these societies was to maintain the separation of church and state and to encourage states' rights. The Odd Fellows were quite active in Connecticut in the 1850s, which might account for their emblem being on this cane. Many fraternal groups had specific regalia that was used in their ceremonies, but canes were not part of such regalia.

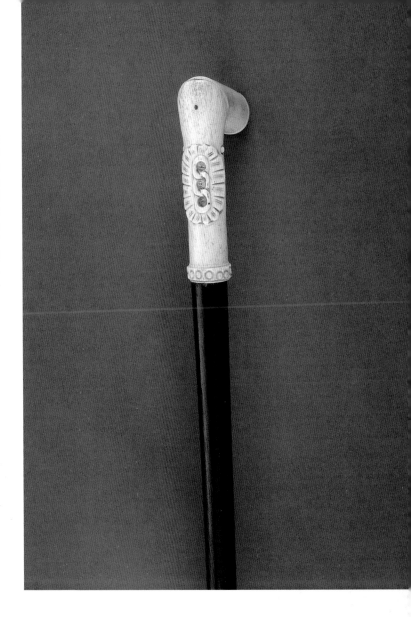

JAGGING WHEEL,
ivory, wood, metal,
L. 5¾", Diam. ⅞". (Mystic Seaport Museum)

Nationalism ran strong in the United States through the first half of the nineteenth century, and patriotic symbols strengthened this spirit by evoking strong emotional responses. The combination of an eagle and "E Pluribus Unum" engraved freehand on this whale-shaped crimper made of ivory and wood is a fine example of a scrimshander's patriotism. Of all nationalistic emblems the eagle was the most common, having been adopted for the Great Seal of the United States in 1782. This majestic bird had been a symbol of independence, freedom, and strength since ancient Greece and Rome.

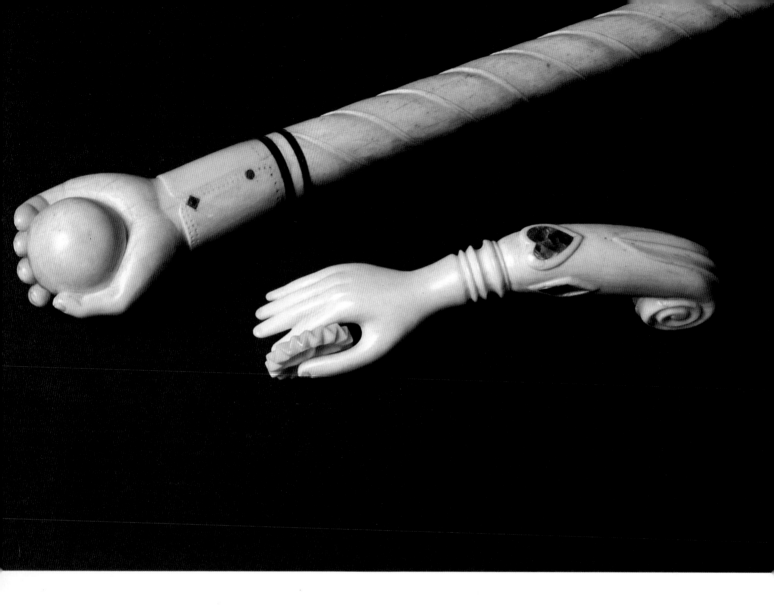

CANE,
ivory, abalone, baleen,
L. 36¼", Diam. 1". (Mystic Seaport Museum)

JAGGING WHEEL,
ivory, abalone,
L. 5⅜", Diam. 1". (Mystic Seaport Museum)

This cane and jagging wheel or crimper show variations of the hand pattern that are not to be confused with the clenched fist. The hand symbolized protection, justice, and power. If it was an open hand, like the one shown that grasps a ball, the meaning could well be beneficence and generosity, while an extended hand like that of the jagging wheel indicated either an invitation or protection. Just how large a role was played by symbolism in scrimshaw objects would only be known to the anonymous creators. Symbolism did play a much more active role in everyday life in the nineteenth century than it does in contemporary life.

DITTY BOX,
bone, baleen, coloring, wood,
H. 4⅝", W. 7¹⁵/₁₆", L. 10¼". (Mystic Seaport Museum)

JAGGING WHEEL,
ivory, paint,
L. 8", Diam. 1½". (Mystic Seaport Museum)

The vine and grapes carved on the ivory jagging wheel speak not only of Bacchus, the god of wine, but also of fertility, abundance, and charity. Grapes were also considered a good-luck gift. Another interesting aspect of this crimper is the fact that the cutting wheel and spacer rings have been painted on the ivory; there is no baleen or wood in this piece. It is all ivory.

Ditty boxes were also gifts, gifts that were chiefly intended for the womenfolk. Although ivy signified longevity, laurel inspiration and fame, acanthus admiration for the arts, and a vine luck and strength, of greater importance was the fact that these patterns reflected the feeling that Nature was considered the best source of inspiration in the nineteenth century. Books about ornamental foliage, like that painted on this oval ditty box, illustrated how such designs could make edgings and space dividers. Floral and foliage patterns were a fundamental form of decoration that began in this country as far back as the earliest gravestones and continued to have an important role in all aspects of American folk art.

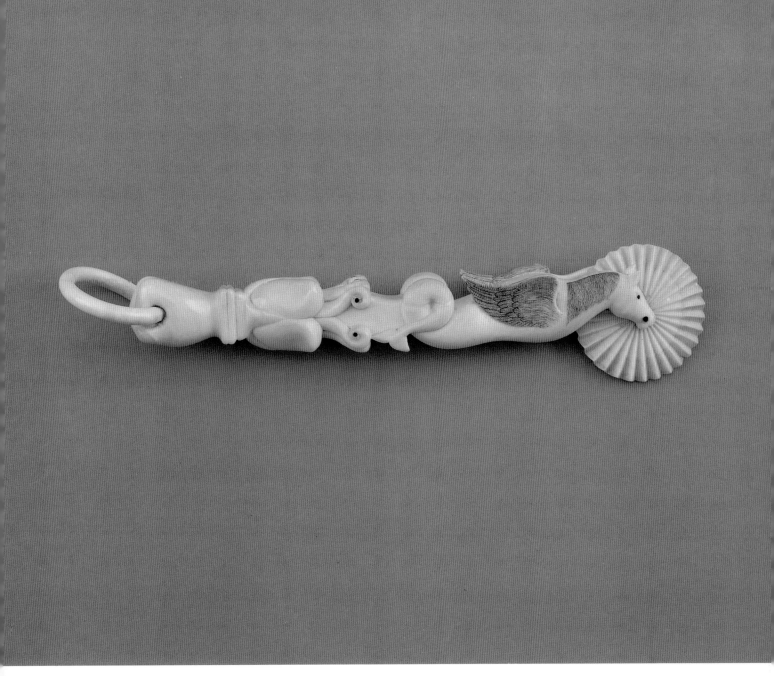

JAGGING WHEEL,
walrus ivory, black ink, copper,
H. 1⁵/₁₆", W. 1¹/₂", L. 7⁵/₁₆". (The Kendall Whaling Museum)

It is the intricate and imaginative carving that catches the eye and makes many jagging wheels so totally fascinating. Our attention is held here by the beautifully carved fluted wheel, the fist holding the hanging ring, the fern-like growth emanating from pods, and especially by the elegant winged horse with a curled fish tail, which may well have been inspired by Pegasus, the famous winged horse of Greek mythology that came to symbolize imagination, poetry, and fame.

JAGGING WHEEL,
walrus ivory, copper,
H. 2¹/₈", W. 2³/₈", L. 13³/₈". (The Kendall Whaling Museum)

This jagging wheel is a rare example of a scrimshander carving a totally nude woman. The absence of women and their companionship for the length of a whaling voyage was understandably responsible for this piece of sculpture. Many strict Christian captains would be dismayed by such licentious objects and have them thrown overboard. Scrimshanders often did this themselves before arriving in home port, rather than offend their womenfolk. The carvers did produce female figures, but they were usually clothed. Acceptable nudity was granted in the depiction of mermaids that were considered less offensive because they were objects of fantasy.

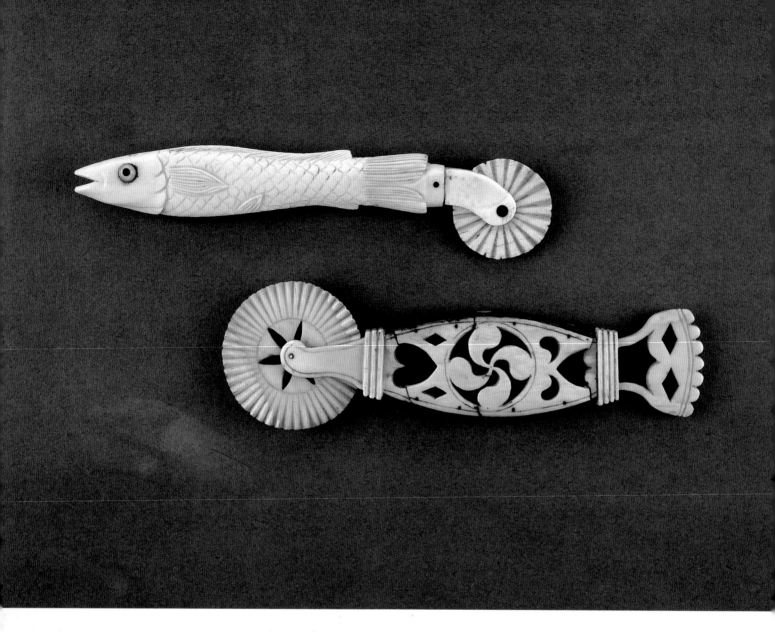

JAGGING WHEEL,
ivory, baleen, glass,
H. ½", W. 1¼", L. 6". (New Bedford Whaling Museum)

JAGGING WHEEL,
ivory, baleen, metal,
H. ½", W. 1¾", L. 6⅛". (New Bedford Whaling Museum)

Jagging wheels have for a long time been made from a wide assortment of materials. An early wooden example with an English coin of the reign of George I dates from 1753. Other examples were made from steel. This ivory fish with carved scales and fins has glass eyes and baleen rivets that hold the fluted cutting wheel. The fish is a major symbol of Christianity, but a Yankee whaler probably chose this design because fish filled the ocean around him or because the codfish was central to New England's prosperity.

The second ivory crimper that has baleen borders on the central section has a fylfot as its central design along with the ubiquitous heart, four diamonds, a star, and a bird's head where the wheel connects to the handle. All these designs are executed in cut-out work. The fylfot is actually a variation on the swastika, a symbol of good luck and prosperity, and is found in many forms of American folk art.

JAGGING WHEEL,
ivory, metal, black ink,
H. ½", W. 2¼", L. 7⅛". (New Bedford Whaling Museum)

JAGGING WHEEL,
ivory, metal,
H. ⅝", W. 1⅝", L. 6". (New Bedford Whaling Museum)

Scrimshanders chose both familiar and unfamiliar motifs for their carvings. Nature, of course, was one of the richest sources of inspiration, for at that time there was the popular belief that God was the Supreme Designer. The eagle connecting the handle to the fluted wheel on this crimper is a good example. Although the eagle was the ancient symbol of power and vitality, its head, portrayed alone as shown here, was thought to represent the center of the universe. The codfish of the lower jagging wheel had been a mainstay of the economy of New England from the beginnings of our nation, and it was the symbol of the fishing trade.

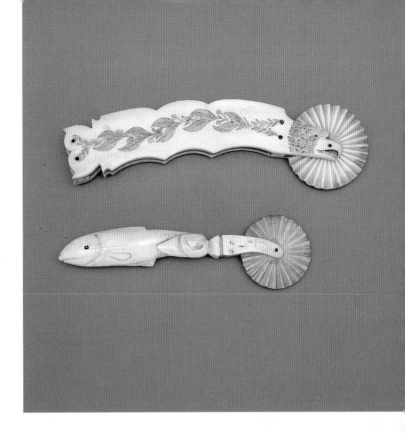

JAGGING WHEEL,
ivory, baleen, metal,
H. 1¼", W. 1¾", L. 6⅞".

JAGGING WHEEL,
ivory, baleen,
H. ¹⁵⁄₁₆", W. 2⅛", L. 9⅛".

JAGGING WHEEL,
ivory, baleen, brass,
H. ¾", W. 2⅞", L. 10¼".

JAGGING WHEEL,
ivory, metal,
H. ½", W. 1⅞", L. 6¾". (All pieces are from the collection of the New Bedford Whaling Museum)

These four jagging wheels are excellent examples of the highly individual character to be found in these implements. The feminine hand with its two extended fingers might well be demonstrating how the baker should hold the jagging wheel, and it may also represent the generosity of the giver. Whether the scrimshander knew it or not, the dog seen on the next crimper symbolized fidelity and watchfulness, or as the whaler may have intended: I will be faithful and care for you. The eagle head on the third jagging wheel probably was not meant to be patriotic. Full-figured eagles tended to fulfill that role. Because even old eagles renew their feathers, this important bird was symbolic of eternal life, or, in the case of the sailor, eternal love. The open work of the last jagging wheel boasts sixteen hearts, making it clear how deeply the scrimshander thought of the recipient. Note also the spiral column carved in the center of this fine piece. The spiral design is thought to have been inspired by a snail's form.

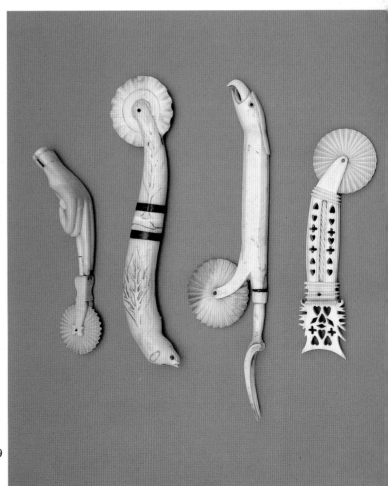

129

(A) JAGGING WHEEL—OPEN
WORK,
ivory, metal,
H. ⁷⁄₁₆", W. 2¹⁄₂", L. 9¹⁄₂".

(B) JAGGING WHEEL,
ivory, wood, metal,
H. ⁷⁄₈", W. 3³⁄₈", L. 8".

(C) JAGGING WHEEL,
ivory, wood, metal,
H. ³⁄₄", W. 2¹⁄₄", L. 9¹⁄₄".

(D) JAGGING WHEEL,
ivory, tortoiseshell, metal,
H. ¹⁄₂", W. 2³⁄₄", L. 6¹⁄₂".

(E) JAGGING WHEEL,
ivory, tortoiseshell, baleen,
H. 1", W. 2⁷⁄₈", L. 8⁵⁄₈".

(F) JAGGING WHEEL,
ivory, wood, metal, red and blue wax,
*H. ¹⁄₂", W. 2⁵⁄₈", L. 7³⁄₄". (All pieces are from
the collection of the New Bedford
Whaling Museum)*

Six more jagging wheels continue to
demonstrate the range of patterns and
their variations as portrayed in the art of
scrimshaw. Open work, seen in example
(A) was also known as fretwork, pierced
work, or cutouts. The various designs here
were patterns easily copied from objects
in the home or a variety of books and magazines. It is probable that the carver of the
ivory-toothed crocodile eating some
unidentified animal (B) meant it to be a
symbol of his hunger for good food. The
horse (C) in an infinite variety of poses is
the animal most commonly found in jagging sculptures. This is not surprising, for
in the nineteenth century the horse was
still the automobile of its day. Additionally,
the horse was a symbol of lust and longing.
In example (D) the snake may have been
used to exemplify healing because a snake
sheds its skin and then grows a new one.
The handle inlaid with tortoiseshell in
example (E) is a variation on a classical
column, which is emphasized by the
baleen inlay on the base and capital. The
two birds in example (F) refer to the
winged soul or the sailor who is at sea, but
who has loving thoughts for the recipient.
Because these jagging wheels were one
of the most popular forms of scrimshaw,
they are also one of the most important
sources of symbolism used in this form of
American folk art.

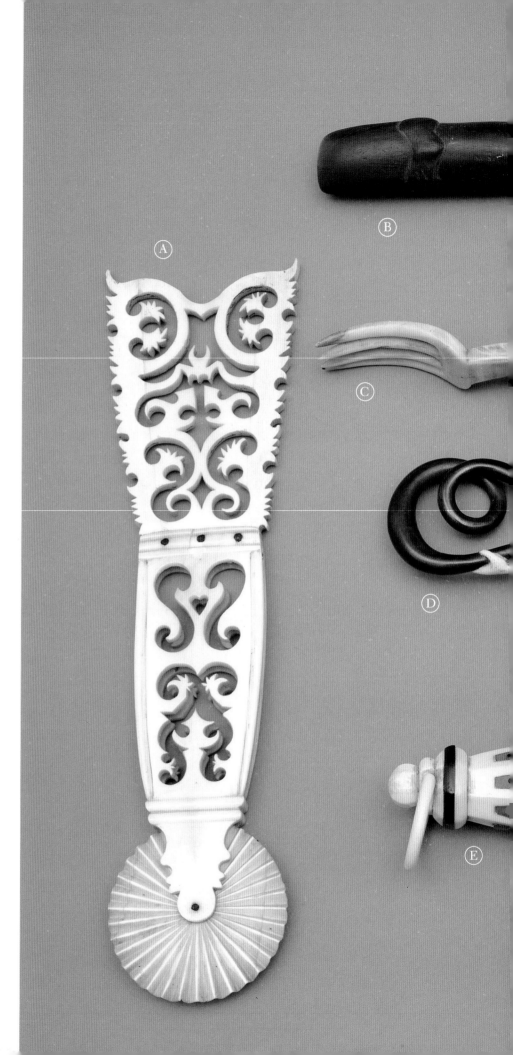

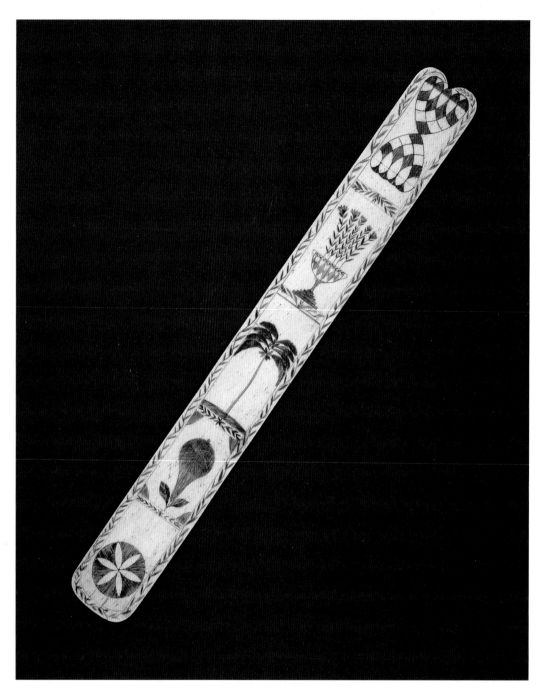

BUSK,
bone, coloring,
H. ¼", W. 1½", L. 13¼". (Peabody Essex Museum)

Busks were popular scrimshaw items because they provided a surface that could be easily engraved. A flat, even slab of panbone
invited pictorial treatment. Patriotism, nostalgia, love, and sentimen-
tality were all popular themes, but love was the most popular because
the busk was worn next to the lady's heart. The polychromed hearts
placed end to end that decorate the top of the busk convey a clear
endearment. The vase offers a floral tribute to the scrimshander's
lady. The palm tree is a reminder of the whaler's travels to exotic
lands, while the hot-air balloon reflects the excitement caused by this
popular nineteenth-century pastime. The rosette at the bottom of
the busk is an example of the carver's dexterity with a compass.

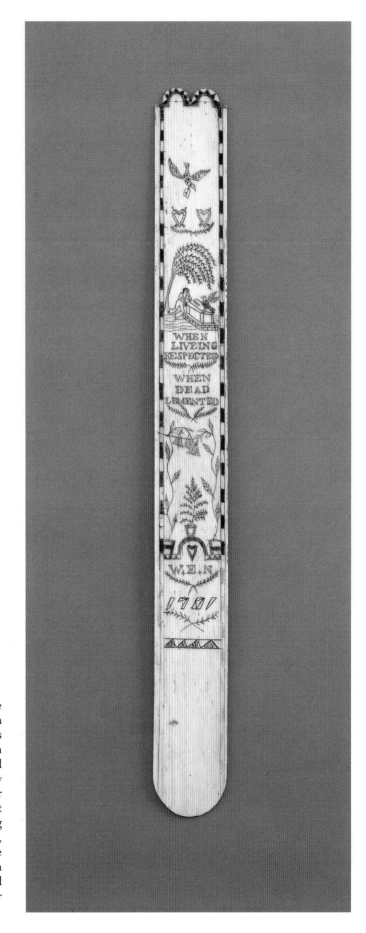

BUSK,
c. 1850, whale skeletal bone, black ink,
H. ⅛", W. 1½", L. 13¹⁵/₁₆". (The Kendall Whaling Museum)

The engraved images on this busk were clearly familiar to the scrimshander, who would have seen them in mourning pictures, a popular schoolgirl art form popular at that time. Mourning pictures started in the United States with the death of George Washington in December 1799. Their popularity peaked in the 1820s and ended about 1840 when women's education became more serious. They were considered a historical record and a decorative item rather than a true symbol of grief. The carrier pigeon symbolizes the flight to heaven of one of the pair represented by the hearts; the weeping willow signifies loneliness and mourning as does the weeping man, indicating the loss of a wife or mother. The inscription could have just as easily been carved on a tombstone. The vine and evergreen symbolize life after death. Mourning pieces were often completed many years after a person's death, and this is the probable reason for the 1701 date being so deep in the past.

BUSK,
whalebone, black coloring,
H. ³/₃₂", W. 1⅝", L. 13". (New Bedford Whaling Museum)

BUSK,
whalebone, black coloring,
H. ³/₃₂", W. 1⅝", L. 13¼". (New Bedford Whaling Museum)

Few whalers were devout Christians, even though the majority of them strongly requested extra rest time on the Sabbath. The fact remains that religion played a very minor role on board except for burials at sea. The portrayal of Christ Crucified at the top of the busk on the left with its devout inscription was probably carved by a Portuguese whaler because these Catholic men tended to be more religious than their American counterparts.

By the end of the eighteenth century, the common drawing compass was a standard tool used in geometrical ornamentation. The busk on the right is a prime example of the handsome decoration achieved by a scrimshander whose geometrical designs were limited only by his imagination. Patterns like these were favorites of those handy with a compass. The precision of the designs was enhanced by using black coloring to highlight the engraving. The four-armed fylfot interspersed with vine decoration was a symbol of good luck, while the two groups of arrows symbolize the maker's affection.

BUSK,
whalebone,
H. ³⁄₃₂", W. 1³⁄₄", L. 13³⁄₄". (New Bedford Whaling Museum)

BUSK,
whalebone, black ink,
H. ³⁄₃₂", W. 1⁵⁄₈", L. 13¹⁄₄". (New Bedford Whaling Museum)

Both these busks have double-arched tops, rounded bottoms, and unadorned edges. There the similarity ends. The busk at the left has fine open work. Florets at the top were created in a positive image, while those at the bottom are negative. A graceful fylfot has paired diamonds above it and paired hearts below. A large heart centers the busk, and a crisp five-pointed star sits just below small paired stars. Filigree work of this caliber was obviously accomplished by a master scrimshander.

The crudely inscribed words on the second busk are just one version of a much used verse:

"This bone once in a sperm whale's jaw did rest
Now tis intended for a woman's breast
This my love I do intend
For you to wear and not to lend."

Note that one of the engraved ships is under full sail, while the other has furled sails.

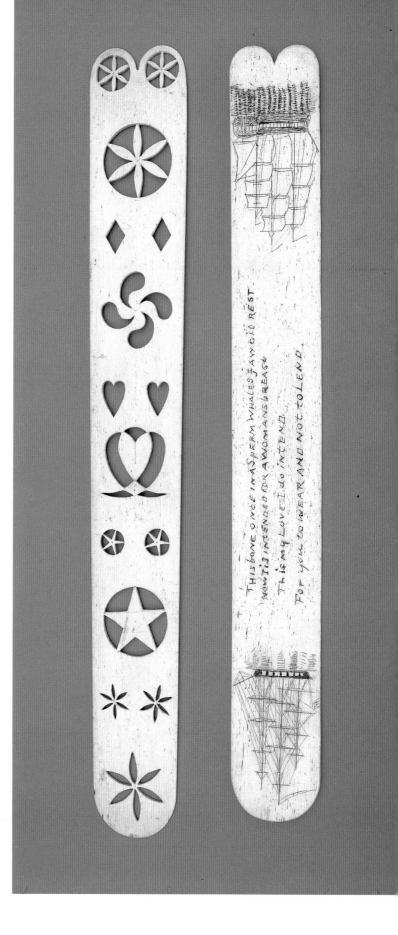

135

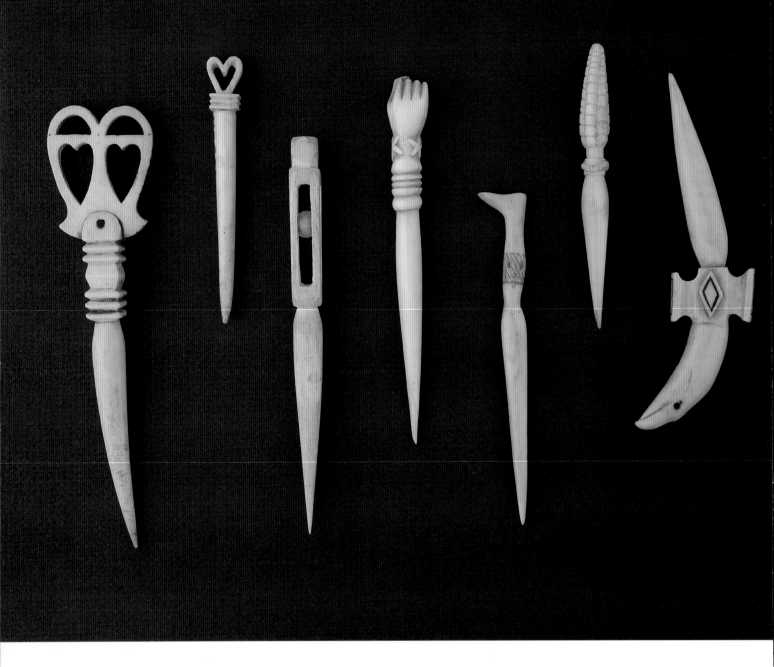

BODKIN,
ivory,
H. ½", W. 2", L. 5½".

BODKIN,
bone,
H. ½", W. ½", L. 3½".

BODKIN,
bone,
H. ½", W. ½", L. 5".

BODKIN,
ivory,
H. 1½", W. ½", L. 4½".

BODKIN,
ivory,
H. ¾", W. ¼", L. 4½".

BODKIN,
ivory,
H. ½", W. ½", L. 3½".

BODKIN,
ivory,
H. ½", W. 1", L. 4½".

(All pieces are from
the collection of the
Peabody Essex Museum)

Scrimshawed bodkins, that sewing implement used by so many needlewomen, abound in symbolic and traditional patterns. Hearts have been a primary folk-art symbol since the mid-seventeenth century in Europe, and because they are obviously a symbol of love they are to be found on many gifts of love. The two hearts paired within a larger one exemplifies the love of two people in a single partnership. The free-moving sphere held within a carved open-work cage was inspired by the lengthy wooden chains with ball-in-cage links made by ambitious whittlers. The Friendship Hand, which is a clenched fist with a cuff at the wrist, signifies good will and friendliness, and the stars on the cuff indicate vigilance. The "for men only" carved woman's leg and foot has sexual overtones in addition to symbolizing humility and servitude. The ear of corn pays homage to Ceres, the goddess of agriculture, and denotes abundance. The seventh bodkin is graced with the carved head of an eagle, in honor of the young nation.

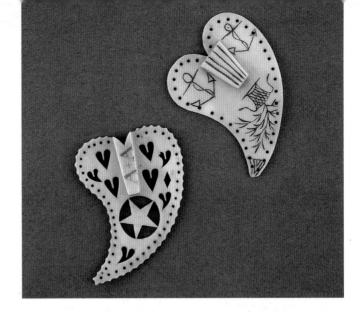

KNITTING-NEEDLE SHEATH,
ivory, black ink,
H. ¼", W. 1½", L. 2". (New Bedford Whaling Museum)

KNITTING-NEEDLE SHEATH,
ivory, black ink,
H. ³⁄₁₆", W. 1½", L. 2". (New Bedford Whaling Museum)

Like a great many knitting-needle sheaths, these two examples have the form of an asymmetrical heart. Some believe that this specific shape has its roots in Roman Catholicism, more specifically in the Sacred Heart of Jesus. The Sacred Heart, however, was not always portrayed in this shape; most Yankee whalers were Protestant; and Roman Catholicism was a relatively minor religion in the United States until the first wave of Irish immigration in the mid-nineteenth century. In addition, the heart motif first appeared on knitting-needle sheaths at the turn of the eighteenth century. Because so many sheaths were made in this shape it is quite possible that scrimshanders used this asymmetrical shape because they thought it was the best shape for a knitting-needle sheath.

PAPER KNIFE,
bone, metal, coloring,
H. ½", W. 1", L. 8¾". (Peabody Essex Museum)

This bone paper knife or letter opener combines a maritime theme with the name of the woman for whom it was made. The blade, which is almost shaped like a scimitar, combines beautifully shaded lettering of the name Lizzie with the tendrils of a vine and a small bird in flight. The symbolism on the carved handle is of particular interest. The anchor was an early Christian emblem for hope, steadfastness, and salvation. Also, in the nineteenth century an anchor tattoo showed that a sailor had done service in the Atlantic Ocean. The cross, of course, underscores the Christian meaning of the anchor.

DIPPER,
bone, coconut, wood, metal, ivory,
H. 3½", W. 3½", L. 14½". (Peabody Essex Museum)

Scrimshanders who voyaged into the South Seas often chose to make objects from coconuts because they were easy to carve. Even though the shells were cut when fresh and green, they were still fragile. Breakage often occurred when handles were attached to dippers and scoops, which were the primary objects made from this fruit. This coconut dipper with its wooden handle and bone heart-shaped ferrule is particularly interesting because of the carved head of a woman wearing an unusual type of Liberty Cap that forms the finial of the handle. Before the Statue of Liberty came into being, three female figures were national symbols for young America: Lady Liberty, Columbia, and Justice. Both Liberty and Columbia wore the Liberty Cap as an accessory, and they became interchangeable figures between 1815 and 1860. The Liberty Cap is generally seen combined with a flag, an eagle, the Stars and Stripes, E Pluribus Unum, or even George Washington; so this is a rare instance of its appearing by itself. The Liberty Cap dates as far back as 750 B.C., when the freed slaves of Troy wore them to demonstrate their free status. It was also a powerful symbol during the French Revolution.

137

CHAPTER SEVEN

Not What It Seems

Most scrimshanders felt that some sort of ornamentation enhanced their work. At the same time, the whalers knew that they should not minimize the utilitarian value of the objects by overdecorating. The unwritten rule was firm: the purpose of an object should dictate its form, and decoration should be secondary. Design and finish were important, but should never be overpowering.

Ornamentation was, therefore, basically an addition to, and not a replacement of, function. It should never obstruct the proper operation that was the purpose of the object. Even though ornamentation cannot stand on its own, it might well cause the piece to become purely decorative by muting its utilitarian value. Too much ornamentation could even be the cause of breakage, for the excessive carving of a piece could result in fragility.

It is interesting to note that when these men were scrimshanding tools for their own use, they never overdecorated. The original purpose of the tool was always kept in mind. Sometimes, however, when making things for others they simply got carried away with the creation of adornments. This is most evident in the case of jagging wheels, and over half of the scrimshaw objects illustrated in this chapter are of that type. These small, hand-held, fancy kitchen implements seem to lend themselves to impractical flights of fancy, for one often sees so many extra wheels, forks, and other enhancements that the object bewilders and sometimes seems ridiculous. A possible reason for this may be that the whaler had

never actually used such a tool himself. After all, it was a rare man in the nineteenth century that baked a pie.

On the other hand, it seems probable that many examples of elaborately ornamented scrimshaw were created for the sheer joy of such elaboration and as a testament to the creator's skill. Perhaps objects like the coconut tea caddy, sugar bowl, cream pitcher, and waste bowl illustrated here were from the first intended to be decorative parlor pieces that were meant to be seen rather than used.

Other scrimshaw objects were made to be formal presentation pieces like the two inscribed canes in this section, where the inscriptions on the canes assumed greater importance than the canes themselves.

Of course, much elaborate scrimshaw may never have been intended for use. Such objects were made just for the fun of it and happened to be in the form of a useful object. Both the scissors and the straight razor, which are illustrated, fit this category. As mentioned above, some overly decorated scrimshaw pieces were made just to show off the carver's skills. However, without any specific documentation we will never know what was made useless on purpose or became useless through error. Today, however, examples of elaborate scrimshaw hold our fascination not for their utilitarian qualities but for their decorative ones. We accept them for what they are: splendid examples of scrimshaw carving that can be set side by side, and appreciated and studied, with equally fine examples of engraved whale's teeth.

DOUBLE-SHEAVE BLOCK,
ivory, rope, leather, metal,
H. 1", W. 1¹⁵/₁₆", L. of block 2³/₄", L. overall 4¹/₂". (Mystic Seaport Museum)

Here is a splendid miniature in ivory—a perfectly proportioned double-sheave block that is properly fitted out with rope seizing and a leather-covered hanging hook. But the ivory block is only 2³/₄ inches long so it probably was made as a keepsake symbol of the ship's utilitarian life.

HAMMER,
walrus ivory, coloring,
H. ¹/₂", W. 3", L. 6⁵/₈". (Mystic Seaport Museum)

Made of walrus ivory and engraved with the portrait of a walrus, this little hammer is utterly useless, yet a delight to have made. It is quite possible that this piece was made by a cooper, for its design resembles that of a cooper's hammer, which has a straight-edged peen and a straight-edged unbeveled face.

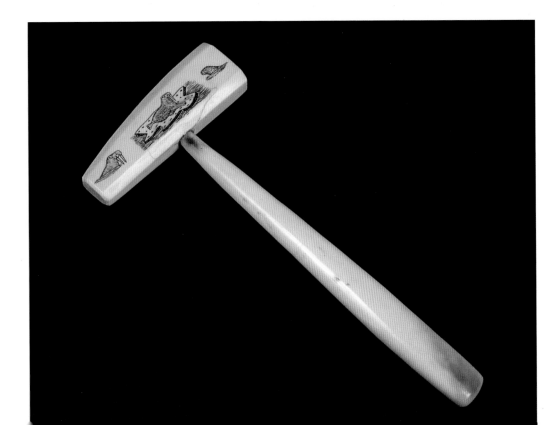

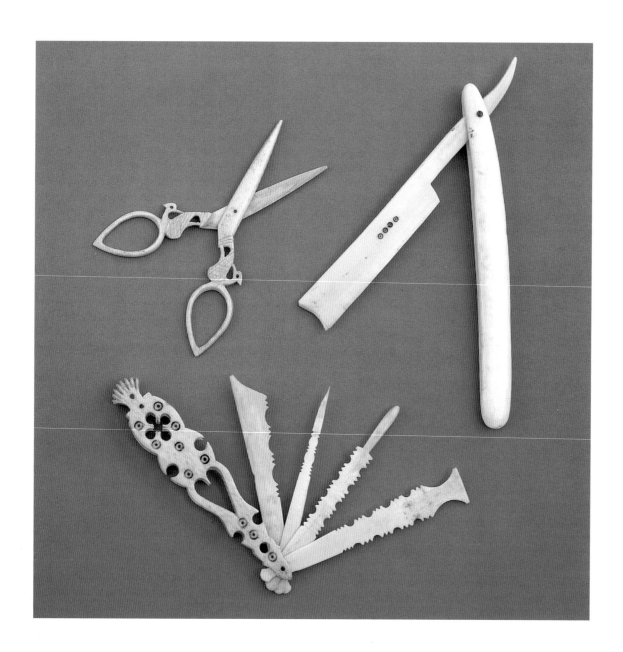

SCISSORS,
c. 1850, whale skeletal bone, brass,
H. ¼", W. 2½", L. 4". (The Kendall Whaling Museum)

STRAIGHT RAZOR,
walrus ivory, copper,
H. ½", W. 3", L. 6⁹⁄₁₆". (The Kendall Whaling Museum)

TOOTHPICK, EAR SPOON, BACK SCRATCHER,
LETTER OPENER,
1800–1825, bone, red coloring, brass,
H. ⁷⁄₁₆", W. 3³⁄₈", L. 6⁵⁄₁₆". (The Kendall Whaling Museum)

Here again are handsome examples of scrimshaw that have familiar forms but lack true function. The ivory straight razor is good-looking but obviously useless, and the scissors with the handles carved with birds is delightful and equally nonfunctional. It is worth noting that the ivory razor cannot be called "Neptune's razor" because it is much too small to wipe off the tar and slush used in the Neptune ceremony when a whale ship crossed the equator. At the bottom is an impressive set of bone tools—a letter opener that would have shred an envelope, a toothpick, an ear spoon that could scratch the ear, and a too-short back scratcher. All are very pretty indeed, and deserve much admiration for the artist's skill at carving, but their utility is negligible.

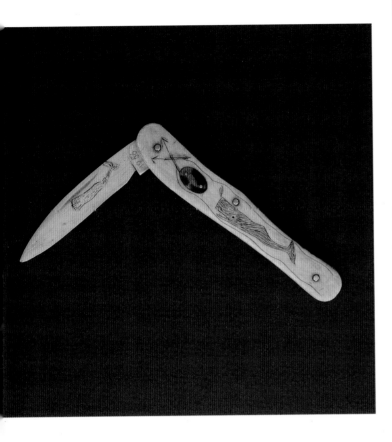

JACKKNIFE,
1856, bone, shell, metal, coloring,
H. ¹/₄", W. ¹/₂", L. 5¹/₂". (Peabody Essex Museum)

It looks like a jackknife, and it has certainly been made attractive by the addition of the engravings of whales, harpoons, the initials "J.O.H.," and the date 1856. But this is a scrimshawed gift or keepsake made entirely of bone and with no possibility of being useful as a knife.

CANE,
c. 1853, ivory, bone, brass, baleen,
H. 1¹/₄", W. 1¹/₄", L. 34¹/₂". (New Bedford Whaling Museum)

This many-sided cane was apparently created as a presentation piece, yet the inscription on it is puzzling indeed. It reads, "Carved from a whale's tusk/And presented about 1853 by/Captain James Lincoln to Lemuel Perry." The mention of a whale's tusk is very odd because only a narwhal could be considered to have a tusk. The inscriber must have been unfamiliar with whales. The date of "about 1853" implies that this bit of information may have been put on the cane at a later date, because the exact date was unknown. Perhaps the cane was used by Perry, and a descendant labeled it later to preserve its history.

141

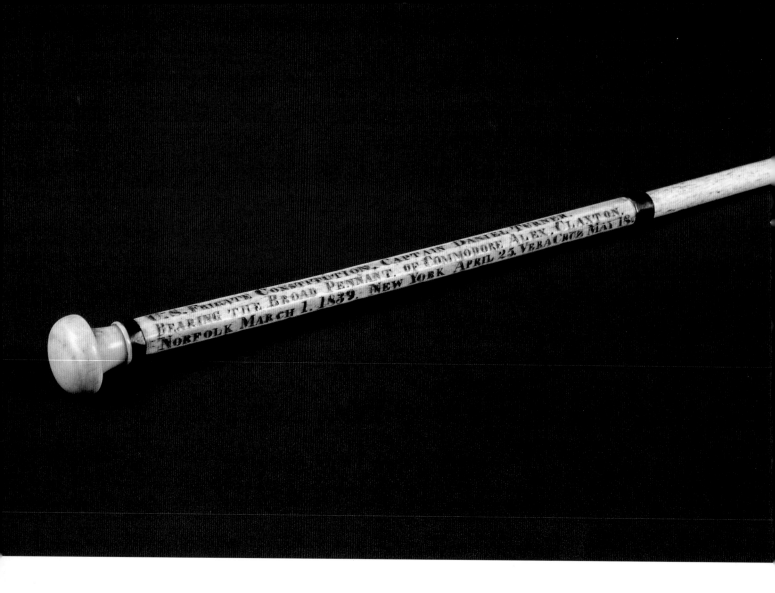

PRESENTATION CANE,
William S. Somerby, 1841, bone, ivory, metal,
L. 36¹/₈", Diam. ⁵/₈". (Mystic Seaport Museum)

This scrimshawed walking stick was obviously meant to be a keepsake or presentation piece, not a functional cane. Such items bore information marking a specific time or special occasion. The scrimshander William S. Somerby was the sailmaker aboard the frigate *Constitution*, which served as the flagship of the South Pacific squadron. Beneath the ivory cap there is a polyhedral section on which Somerby inscribed the following information that is framed with silver bands.

US Constitution Captain Daniel Turner
Bearing the broad pennant of Commodore Alex Claxton
Norfolk March 1, 1839, New York April 25, Veracruz May 18
Havanna July 4, Rio Janiero Sept 1, Valparaiso Nov 2
Callao Jan. 1 1840, Talcuhuana March 15, Payta May 11.
Puna Sept 20 Juan Fernandez. July 24, 1841.
William S. Somerby.

MORTAR AND PESTLE,
ivory; mortar: H. ⅝", Diam. ⁹/₁₆"; pestle L. ¹³/₁₆", Diam. ³/₁₆". (Mystic Seaport Museum)

Compared to the toylike double-sheave block and hammer previously illustrated, this infinitesimal example of scrimshaw is best labeled a miniature miniature. Only a mite over half an inch in height, one wonders how the scrimshander had enough purchase on the piece to create the turnings. Obviously, the artist was determined to make a small wonder, and so he did.

ROLLING PIN,
hardwood, ivory, L. 16¾", Diam. 2¼". (Mystic Seaport Museum)

Almost everything is right about this rolling pin. Like most others made by scrimshanders, it was made of hardwood and has ivory handles. But the scrimshander also wanted to make his rolling pin pretty, so he added ivory polka-dot inlays. The result is good-looking but frustrating for the person trying to use the rolling pin, for the inlays would cause the dough to snag and stick on it.

143

CREAM PITCHER,
Stephen Morgan, c. 1831, coconut, ivory, metal,
H. 4½", Base diam. 2⁷⁄₁₆".

SUGAR BOWL,
Stephen Morgan, c. 1831, coconut, ivory, metal, H. 3¾", Base
diam. 2".

TEA CADDY,
Stephen Morgan, c. 1831, coconut, ivory, copper, metal,
H. 5⅜", Base diam. 2⅞".

WASTE BOWL,
Stephen Morgan, c. 1831, coconut, metal,
H. 2⅜", Diam. 4⅝". (All pieces are from the collection of Mystic
Seaport Museum)

The Connecticut whaling master Stephen Morgan obviously traveled to some tropical waters where he was able to accumulate the coconuts with which to make this cream pitcher, sugar bowl, tea caddy, and waste bowl. The initials "SM" and the date "AD/1831/X" on the caddy lead us to believe that he made this set. The pieces are small and simply formed, and three of them have been fitted with elegant ivory handles and finials. Coconuts were not ideal for holding liquids, nor were they suitable for storing loose tea. Inasmuch as the pieces show no signs of wear, it seems probable that they were just used decoratively in a parlor.

It has already been noted in the introduction to this chapter that too much ornamentation often muted or negated the purpose of a scrimshaw object. The following gallery of ten jagging wheels or crimpers amply proves that statement, but at the same time it provides much beauty and fascination. There can be little doubt that the jagging wheels—although many were quite useless in the family kitchen—were favorite objects with the scrimshanders, for these quite astonishing examples of bone and ivory sculpture allowed the whalers with too much time on their hands to indulge their skill and imagination in creating what often developed into wild flights of fancy—a giddy mélange of wheels and forks and knives fashioned with no thought as to their manageability, their fragility, or the problem of keeping them clean—and yet all so expertly and lovingly carved. Because so many examples have come through the years in good condition, it seems obvious that the artists' womenfolk treasured these gifts, kept them out of harm's way, and used more mundane tools for their baking.

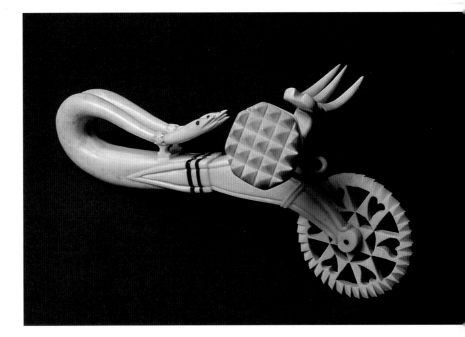

JAGGING WHEEL,
ivory, baleen, metal,
L. 8½", W. 3¾", Diam. 2½". (Mystic Seaport Museum)

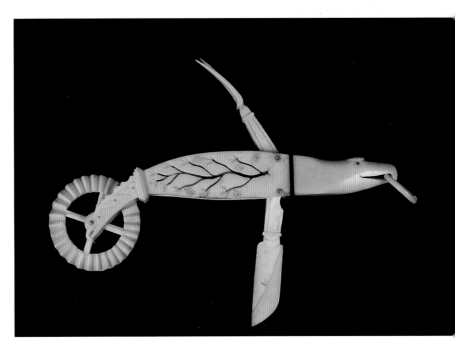

JAGGING WHEEL,
ivory, baleen, steel,
L. 6⅝", Diam. 1¾". (Mystic Seaport Museum)

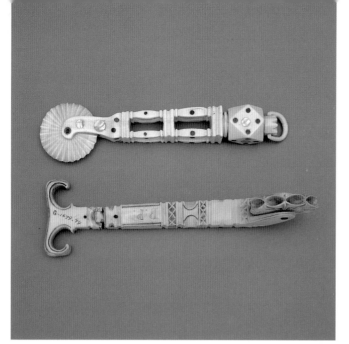

JAGGING WHEEL,
ivory, metal,
H. 2", W. 2", L. 7¼". (New Bedford Whaling Museum)

JAGGING WHEEL,
ivory, tortoiseshell, metal,
H. ¹⁵/₁₆", W. 1⁵/₈", L. 7¼". (New Bedford Whaling Museum)

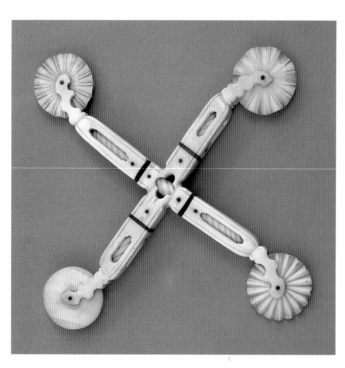

JAGGING WHEEL,
walrus ivory, baleen, copper,
H. ¹¹/₁₆", W. 10", L. 9¹¹/₁₆". (The Kendall Whaling Museum)

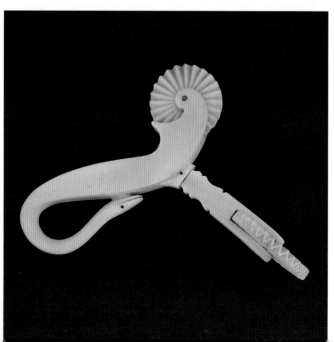

JAGGING WHEEL,
bone, metal,
H. 2", W. 5¾", L. 6½". (Peabody Essex Museum)

JAGGING WHEEL,
ivory, wood, metal,
H. 1½", W. 3½", L. 6¼". (New Bedford Whaling Museum)

JAGGING WHEEL,
ivory, metal,
H. ½", W. 3", L. 8¾". (New Bedford Whaling Museum)

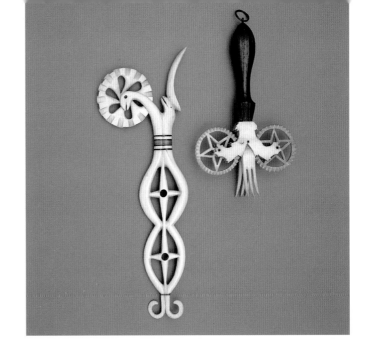

JAGGING WHEEL,
walrus ivory, baleen, brass,
H. 1¹⁄₁₆", W. 5⅜", L. 7⁷⁄₁₆". (The Kendall Whaling Museum)

JAGGING WHEEL,
walrus ivory,
H. 1⅛", W. 7⅝", L. 9⅜". (The Kendall Whaling Museum)

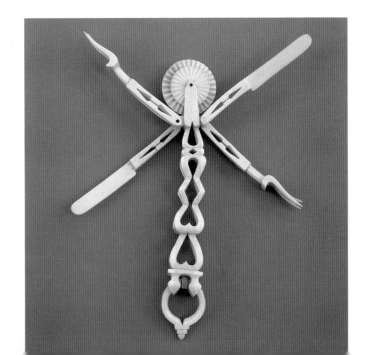

Bibliography

(No author). *A Book of Tools*, Charles Strelinger and Co., Detroit, 1895.

(No author). *A Short Dictionary of Furniture*, Allen, London, 1962.

Ackerman, Diane. "Whales," *The New Yorker*, February 26, 1990, pp. 51–86.

Arbor, Marilyn. *Tools and Trades of America's Past: The Mercer Collection*, The Bucks County Historical Society, Doylestown, Pa., 1981.

Ashley, Clifford W. *The Ashley Book of Knots*, Doubleday & Co., Garden City, N.Y., 1953.

———. *The Yankee Whaler*, Halcyon House, Garden City, N.Y., 1942.

Banks, Steven. *The Handicrafts of the Sailor*, Arco Publishing Company, New York, 1974.

Barbeau, Marius. "All Hands Aboard Scrimshawing," *American Neptune*, Vol. 12, No. 2, April 1952, pp. 99–122.

———. "Seafaring Folk Art," *Antiques*, Vol. 66, July 1954, pp. 47–49.

Barnes, Clare and Bowen, Crosewell. "The Scrimshaw Collector," *American Heritage*, Vol. 15, No. 6, October 1964, pp. 8–13.

Basseches, Joshua, and Frank, Stuart M. *Edward Burdett, 1805–1833, America's First Master Scrimshaw Artist*, The Kendall Whaling Museum, Sharon, Mass., 1991.

Bayley, Harold. *The Lost Language of Symbolism*, Benn, London, 1912.

Beaber, Alex. *The Tools That Built America*, Barre Publications, Barre, Mass., 1976.

Burrows, Fredricka Alexander. *The Yankee Scrimshanders*, William S. Sullwood Publishing, Taunton, Mass., 1973.

Busch, Briton Cooper. *Whaling Will Never Do for Me*, The University Press of Kentucky, Lexington, 1994.

Carpenter, Charles Jr. "Early Dated Scrimshaw," *Antiques*, Vol. 102, September 1972, pp. 414–19.

Caulfield, Sophia. *The Dictionary of Needlework*, London, facsimile of 1882 edition.

Chapman, Charles F. *Piloting, Seamanship and Small Boat Handling*, American Book–Stratford Press, New York, 1972.

Clabburn, Pamela. *The Needleworker's Dictionary*, William Morrow & Co. New York, 1976.

Clark, Stephen. *The Complete Illustrated Tool Book*, Galahad, New York, 1974.

Creighton, Margaret S. *Dogwatch & Liberty Days*, The Peabody Museum of Salem, Salem, 1982.

Crosby, Everett. *Susan's Teeth and Much About Scrimshaw*, Nantucket, 1955.

Daland, Edward L. "Engraved Types of Scrimshaw," *Antiques*, Vol. 28, October 1935, pp. 153–55.

D'Alviella, Count. *The Migration of Symbols*, Franklin, New York, 1972.

D.L.G., *Godey's Lady's Book and Magazine*, Vol. 76, January 1868, p. 100.

Davidson, Marshall B. *Three Centuries of American Antiques*, American Heritage Publishing Co., New York, 1967–69.

———. *Early American Tools*, Olivetti, 1975.

Diagram Group. *Handtools of Arts and Crafts*, St. Martin's Press, New York, 1981.

Dow, George Francis. *Whale Ships and Whaling*, Argosy Antiquarian Ltd., New York, 1967.

Durant, Stuart. *Ornament*, Overlook, New York, 1986.

Earle, Walter K. *Scrimshaw Folk Art of the Whalers*, Whaling Museum Society, Cold Spring Harbor, N.Y., 1957.

Ellis, Richard. *Men and Whales*, Knopf, New York, 1991.

Falconer, William, *Falconer's Marine Dictionary (1780)*, Augustus M. Kelley, Publishers, New York, 1970.

Ferguson, George. *Signs and Symbols in Christian Art*, Oxford University Press, New York, 1954.

Flayderman, E. Norman. *Scrimshaw and Scrimshanders*, N. Flayderman & Co., New Milford, Conn., 1972.

Fleming, E. McClung. *Seeing Snakes in the American Arts*, The Delaware Antique Show Catalogue, 1969.

(No author). Flyer from Wilkie Foundation.

Frank, Stuart M. *Biographical Dictionary of Scrimshaw Artists in The Kendall Whaling Museum*, Kendall Whaling Museum Monograph Series No. 4, The Kendall Whaling Museum, Sharon, Mass., 1989.

———. *Dictionary of Scrimshaw Artists, Vol. II (Supplement)*, 1994.

Frere-Cook, Gervis, ed. *The Decorative Arts of the Mariner*, Little, Brown & Co., Boston, 1966.

Gilkerson, William. *The Scrimshander*, Troubadour Press, San Francisco, 1978.